THE VISION OF THE ANOINTED

D0839028

THE
VISION
OF THE
ANOINTED

SELF-CONGRATULATION AS A

BASIS FOR SOCIAL POLICY

THOMAS SOWELL

BASIC

BOOKS

A Member of the Perseus Books Group

Copyright © 1995 by Thomas Sowell.
Published by Basic Books, A Member of the Perseus Books Group

All rights reserved. Printed in the United States of America. No part of this book may be reproduced in any manner whatsoever without written permission except in the case of brief quotations embodied in critical articles and reviews. For information, address Basic Books, 387 Park Avenue South, New York, NY 10016-8810.

Designed by Ellen Levine

Library of Congress Cataloging-in-Publication Data
Sowell, Thomas, 1930–
    The vision of the anointed : self-congratulation as a basis for social policy / Thomas Sowell.
        p.   cm.
    Includes bibliographical references and index.
    ISBN-13 978-0-465-08995-6
    ISBN-10 0-465-08995-X
    1. Elite (Social sciences)—United States. 2. United States—Social policy. I. Title.
HN90.E4S67 1995
305.5'2'0973—dc20   95–12670
                                                                          CIP

DHSB   35   34   33   32   31   30

At most only a tiny set of policies have been studied with even moderate care.
      —George J. Stigler, Nobel Laureate in Economics

In the flaring parks, in the taverns, in the hushed academies, your murmur will applaud the wisdom of a thousand quacks. For theirs is the kingdom.
      —Kenneth Fearing, poet

CONTENTS

PREFACE

The views of political commentators or writers on social issues often range across a wide spectrum, but their positions on these issues are seldom random. If they are liberal, conservative, or radical on foreign policy, they are likely to be the same on crime, abortion, or education. There is usually a coherence to their beliefs, based on a particular set of underlying assumptions about the world—a certain vision of reality.

Visions differ of course from person to person, from society to society, and from one era to another. Visions also compete with one another, whether for the allegiance of an individual or of a whole society. But in some eras one vision so predominates over all others that it can be considered the prevailing vision of that time and place. This is the current situation among the intelligentsia of the United States and much of the Western world, however much their vision may differ from the visions of most other people. Individual variations in applying this underlying vision do not change the fundamental fact that there is a particular framework of assumptions within which most contemporary social and political discourse takes place in the media, in academia, and in politics.

The rise of the mass media, mass politics, and massive government means that the beliefs which drive a relatively small group of articulate people have great leverage in determining the course taken by a whole society.

The analysis that follows is not only an examination of the vision of this elite intelligentsia and their numerous followers in the political arena and in the courtrooms, but is also an empirical comparison between the promised benefits of policies based on that vision and the grim and often bitter consequences of those political and judicial decisions. In short, the purpose is not simply to see what kind of world exists inside the minds of a self-anointed elite, but to see how that world affects the world of reality in terms as concrete as crime, family disintegration, and other crucial social phenomena of our times.

The immediacy of the issues involved only makes it more imperative to understand the past from which they came and the future toward which they lead. Many of the intellectual and political patterns analyzed here became dominant during the 1960s and many of the assumptions underlying today's continuations of those trends were either expressed or implied during that decade. However, the historical roots of the currently prevailing vision go back much further, in some cases for centuries. Both the past and the present must be explored, in order to understand the vision of the anointed and its dangerous legacy for the future.

Thomas Sowell
Hoover Institution

CHAPTER 1

FLATTERING UNCTION

Lay not that flattering unction to your soul.

—Hamlet

Dangers to a society may be mortal without being immediate. One such danger is the prevailing social vision of our time—and the dogmatism with which the ideas, assumptions, and attitudes behind that vision are held.

It is not that these views are especially evil or especially erroneous. Human beings have been making mistakes and committing sins as long as there have been human beings. The great catastrophes of history have usually involved much more than that. Typically, there has been an additional and crucial ingredient—some method by which feedback from reality has been prevented, so that a dangerous course of action could be blindly continued to a fatal conclusion. Much of the continent of Europe was devastated in World War II because the totalitarian regime of the Nazis did not permit those who foresaw the self-destructive consequences of Hitler's policies to alter, or even to influence, those policies. In earlier eras as well, many individuals foresaw the self-destruction of their own civilizations, from the days of the Roman Empire to the eras of the Spanish, Ottoman, and other empires.[1] Yet that alone was not enough to change the course that was leading to ruin. Today, despite free speech and the mass media, the prevailing social vision is dangerously close to sealing itself off from any discordant feedback from reality.

Even when issues of public policy are discussed in the outward form of an argument, often the conclusions reached are predetermined by the assumptions and definitions inherent in a particular vision of social processes. Different visions, of course, have different assumptions, so it is not uncommon for people who follow different visions to find themselves in opposition to one another across a vast spectrum of unrelated issues, in such disparate fields as law, foreign policy, the environment, racial policy, military defense, education, and many others.[2] To a remarkable extent, however, empirical evidence is neither sought beforehand nor consulted after a policy has been instituted. Facts may be marshalled for a position already taken, but that is very different from systematically testing opposing theories by evidence. Momentous questions are dealt with essentially as conflicts of visions.

The focus here will be on one particular vision—the vision prevailing among the intellectual and political elite of our time. What is important about that vision are not only its particular assumptions and their corollaries, but also the fact that it is a *prevailing* vision— which means that its assumptions are so much taken for granted by so many people, including so-called "thinking people," that neither those assumptions nor their corollaries are generally confronted with demands for empirical evidence. Indeed, empirical evidence itself may be viewed as suspect, insofar as it is inconsistent with that vision.

Discordant evidence may be dismissed as isolated anomalies, or as something tendentiously selected by opponents, or it may be explained away ad hoc by a theory having no empirical support whatever—except that this ad hoc theory is able to sustain itself and gain acceptance because it is consistent with the overall vision. Examples of such tactics will be numerous in the chapters that follow. What must first be considered are the reasons behind such tactics, why it is so necessary to believe in a particular vision that evidence of its incorrectness is ignored, suppressed, or discredited—ultimately, why one's quest is not for reality but for a vision. What does the vision offer that reality does not offer?

What a vision may offer, and what the prevailing vision of our time emphatically *does* offer, is a special state of grace for those who believe in it. Those who accept this vision are deemed to be not merely factually correct but morally on a higher plane. Put differently, those who disagree with the prevailing vision are seen as being not merely in error, but in sin. For those who have this vision of the world, the anointed and the benighted do not argue on the same moral plane or play by the same cold rules of logic and evidence. The benighted are to be made "aware," to have their "consciousness raised," and the wistful hope is held out that they will "grow." Should the benighted prove recalcitrant, however, then their "mean-spiritedness" must be fought and the "real reasons" behind their arguments and actions exposed. While verbal fashions change, this basic picture of the differential rectitude of the anointed and the benighted has not changed fundamentally in at least two hundred years.[3]

These are not mere debating tactics. People are never more sincere than when they assume their own moral superiority. Nor are such attitudes inherent in polemics, as such. Some very strong polemicists have argued that their opponents were well-meaning and even intelligent—but dangerously mistaken on the issue at hand. Some "may do the worst of things, without being the worst of men," Edmund Burke said in the eighteenth century.[4] Similarly, when Malthus attacked a popular vision of his time, exemplified in the writings of William Godwin and Condorcet, he said:

> I cannot doubt the talents of such men as Godwin and Condorcet. I am unwilling to doubt their candor.[5]

Yet Godwin's response was quite different. He called Malthus "malignant," questioned "the humanity of the man," and said, "I profess myself at a loss to conceive of what earth the man was made."[6]

More was involved here than mere differences in personal styles of polemics. This asymmetry in arguments reflected an asymmetry in visions that has persisted for centuries. When Friedrich Hayek's *The Road to Serfdom* attacked the welfare state and socialism in 1944, he characterized his adversaries as "single-minded idealists" and "authors whose sincerity and disinterestedness are above suspicion," but his own book was treated as something immoral, which some

American publishers refused to publish, despite its already demonstrated impact in England.[7] Similarly, a 1993 book, highly critical of liberal social policies, nevertheless credited the proponents of those policies as being people who "want to help" out of "decent and generous motives,"[8] even though it concludes that the net result has been to "keep the poor in their poverty."[9] By contrast, a 1992 bestseller by a proponent of such liberal social policies declared, "conservatives don't really care whether black Americans are happy or unhappy."[10] Nor is this demonizing of opponents of the vision confined to America or to racial issues. The distinguished French writer Jean-François Revel, who has opposed many aspects of the prevailing vision, reports being treated, even in a social setting, as someone with only "residual traces of *homo sapiens*."[11]

A contemporary writer has summarized the differences between those with the vision of the anointed—the left—and others this way:

> Disagree with someone on the right and he is likely to think you obtuse, wrong, foolish, a dope. Disagree with someone on the left and he is more likely to think you selfish, a sell-out, insensitive, possibly evil.[12]

The contemporary anointed and those who follow them make much of their "compassion" for the less fortunate, their "concern" for the environment, and their being "anti-war," for example—as if these were characteristics which distinguish them from people with opposite views on public policy. The very idea that such an *opponent* of the prevailing vision as Milton Friedman, for example, has just as much compassion for the poor and the disadvantaged, that he is just as much appalled by pollution, or as horrified by the sufferings and slaughter imposed by war on millions of innocent men, women, and children—such an idea would be a very discordant note in the vision of the anointed. If such an idea were fully accepted, this would mean that opposing arguments on social policy were arguments about methods, probabilities, and empirical evidence—with compassion, caring, and the like being common features on both sides, thus cancelling out and disappearing from the debate. That clearly is *not* the vision of the anointed. One reason for the preservation and insulation of a vision is that it has become inextricably intertwined with the egos of those who believe it. Despite Hamlet's warning against self-flattery, the vision of the anointed is not simply a vision of the world and its functioning in a causal sense, but is also a vision of themselves and of their moral role in that world. *It is a vision of differential rectitude*. It is not a vision of the tragedy of the human condition: Problems exist because others are not as wise or as virtuous as the anointed.

The great ideological crusades of twentieth-century intellectuals have ranged across the most disparate fields—from the eugenics movement of the early decades of the century to the environmentalism of the later decades, not to mention the welfare state, socialism, communism, Keynesian economics, and medical, nuclear, and automotive safety. What all these highly disparate crusades have in common is their moral exaltation of the anointed above others, who are to have their very different views nullified and superseded by the views of the anointed, imposed via the power of government. Despite the great variety of issues in a series of crusading movements among the intelligentsia during the twentieth century, several key elements have been common to most of them:

1. Assertions of a great danger to the whole society, a danger to which the masses of people are oblivious.
2. An urgent need for action to avert impending catastrophe.
3. A need for government to drastically curtail the dangerous behavior of the many, in response to the prescient conclusions of the few.
4. A disdainful dismissal of arguments to the contrary as either uninformed, irresponsible, or motivated by unworthy purposes.

Specific arguments on particular issues will be dealt with in the chapters that follow, but these specific arguments need not detain us at this point. What is remarkable is how few arguments are really engaged in, and how many *substitutes* for arguments there are. These substitutes for arguments are, almost by definition, more available to adherents of the prevailing vision, whose assumptions are so widely accepted as to permit conclusions based on those assumptions to pass muster without further scrutiny.

The prevailing vision of our era is long overdue for a critical re-examination—or, for many, a first examination. This vision so permeates the media and academia, and has made such major inroads into the religious community, that many grow to adulthood unaware that there is any other way of looking at things, or that *evidence* might be relevant to checking out the sweeping assumptions of so-called "thinking people." Many of these "thinking people" could more accurately be characterized as *articulate* people, as people whose verbal nimbleness can elude both evidence and logic. This can be a fatal talent, when it supplies the crucial insulation from reality behind many historic catastrophes.

Despite the power of the prevailing vision, some have escaped its gravitational pull. Indeed, most of the leading contemporary opponents of the prevailing vision were themselves formerly within its orbit. Milton Friedman, Friedrich Hayek, Karl Popper, Edward Banfield, Irving Kristol, Norman Podhoretz—the list goes on and on—once shared many of the assumptions of those with whom they came ultimately to differ so fundamentally. Even in the realm of practical politics, the most prominent and most successful opponent of the prevailing vision, Ronald Reagan, was once so much a part of it that he belonged to the liberal organization Americans for Democratic Action.

In short, few have spent their entire lives outside the vision of the anointed, and virtually no one has been unaffected by it. Understanding that vision, its current impact and its future dangers, is the purpose of this book.

CHAPTER 2

THE PATTERN

*They went to work with unsurpassable efficiency.
Full employment, a maximum of resulting output,
and general well-being ought to have been the consequence. It is true that instead we find misery, shame
and, at the end of it all, a stream of blood. But that
was a chance coincidence.*

—Joseph A. Schumpeter[1]

What is intellectually interesting about visions are their assumptions and their reasoning, but what is socially crucial is the extent to which they are resistant to evidence. All social theories being imperfect, the harm done by their imperfections depends not only on how far they differ from reality, but also on how readily they adjust to evidence, to come back into line with the facts. One theory may be more plausible, or even more sound, than another, but if it is also more dogmatic, then that can make it far more dangerous than a theory that is not initially as close to the truth but which is more capable of adjusting to feedback from the real world. The prevailing vision of our time—the vision of the anointed—has shown an extraordinary ability to defy evidence.

Characteristic patterns have developed among the anointed for dealing with the repeated failures of policies based on their vision. Other patterns have developed for seizing upon statistics in such a way as to buttress the assumptions of the vision, even when the same set of statistics contains numbers that contradict the vision. Finally, there is the phenomenon of honored prophets among the anointed, who continue to be honored as their predictions fail by vast margins, time and again. The first of these phenomena will be explored in this chapter, the others in the chapters that follow.

PATTERNS OF FAILURE

A very distinct pattern has emerged repeatedly when policies favored by the anointed turn out to fail. This pattern typically has four stages:

STAGE 1. THE "CRISIS": Some situation exists, whose negative aspects the anointed propose to eliminate. Such a situation is routinely characterized as a "crisis," even though all human situations have negative aspects, and even though evidence is seldom asked or given to show how the situation at hand is either uniquely bad or threatening to get worse. Sometimes the situation described as a "crisis" has in fact already been getting better for years.

STAGE 2. THE "SOLUTION": Policies to end the "crisis" are advocated by the anointed, who say that these policies will lead to beneficial result A. Critics say that these policies will lead to detrimental result Z. The anointed dismiss these latter claims as absurd and "simplistic," if not dishonest.

STAGE 3. THE RESULTS: The policies are instituted and lead to detrimental result Z.

STAGE 4. THE RESPONSE: Those who attribute detrimental result Z to the policies instituted are dismissed as "simplistic" for ignoring the "complexities" involved, as "many factors" went into determining the outcome. The burden of proof is put on the critics to demonstrate to a certainty that these policies alone were the only possible cause of the worsening that occurred. No burden of proof whatever is put on those who had so confidently predicted improvement. Indeed, it is often asserted that things would have been even worse, were it not for the wonderful programs that mitigated the inevitable damage from other factors.

Examples of this pattern are all too abundant. Three will be considered here. The first and most general involves the set of social welfare policies called the "war on poverty" during the administration of President Lyndon B. Johnson, but continuing under other labels since then. Next is the policy of introducing "sex education" into the public schools, as a means of reducing teenage pregnancy and venereal diseases. The third example will be policies designed to reduce crime by adopting a less punitive approach, being more concerned with preventive social policies beforehand and rehabilitation afterward, as well as showing more concern for the legal rights of defendants in criminal cases.

The "War on Poverty"

Governmental policies designed to alleviate the privations of the poor go back much further than President Johnson's "war on poverty," and of course reach far beyond the boundaries of the United States. What was different about this particular set of social programs, first proposed to Congress during the Kennedy administration and later enacted into law during the Johnson administration, was that its stated purpose was a reduction of *dependency*, not simply the provision of more material goods to the poor. This was the recurring theme of the "war on poverty," from the time President Kennedy introduced this legislation in 1962 until President Johnson saw it passed and signed it into law in 1964.

John F. Kennedy stated the purpose of the "war on poverty" to be "to help our less fortunate citizens to help themselves."[2] He said: "We must find ways of returning far more of our dependent people to independence."[3] The whole point of currently increased federal spending on this effort was "to strengthen and broaden the rehabilitative and preventive services" offered to "persons who are dependent or who would otherwise become dependent," so that long-run savings in government spending were expected from a subsequent decline in dependency. As President Kennedy put it:

Public welfare, in short, must be more than a salvage operation, picking up the debris from the wreckage of human lives. Its emphasis must be directed increasingly toward prevention and rehabilitation—on reducing not only the long-range cost in budgetary terms but the long-range cost in human terms as well.[4]

The same theme of increased short-run spending for long-run savings, as a result of reduced dependency, was a theme repeated in a *New York Times* editorial:

President Kennedy's welfare message to Congress yesterday stems from a recognition that no lasting solution to the problem can be bought with a relief check. Financial help to the needy must be supplemented by a vastly expanded range of professional and community services. Their aim: to keep men, women and children from having to rely on public assistance by making them useful, creative citizens. The President does not pretend it will be cheap to provide the needed build-up in staff, facilities and rehabilitation allowances. The initial cost will actually be greater than the mere continuation of handouts. The dividends will come in the restoration of individual dignity and in the long-run reduction of the need for government help.[5]

The *Congressional Quarterly* of the same date (February 2, 1962) likewise reported: "The President stressed that the welfare program should be directed toward the prevention of dependence and the rehabilitation of current relief recipients."[6]

The same theme carried over into the Johnson administration, where the anti-poverty program was sold as a way to "break the cycle of poverty" and to make "taxpayers out of taxeaters."[7] "Give a hand, not a handout" was the slogan of the "war on poverty." In keeping with that theme, President Johnson said in August 1964, when the legislation was finally passed: "The days of the dole in our country are numbered."[8] This initial thrust of the "war on poverty" programs must be clearly recognized at the outset, for one of many responses to the failures of government programs has been to redefine their goals after the fact, to make the programs look "successful."

A subsidiary theme of the "war on poverty" was that social programs were a way of heading off urban violence. Lyndon Johnson spoke of "conditions that breed despair and violence." He said:

All of us know what those conditions are: ignorance, discrimination, slums, poverty, disease, not enough jobs.[9]

The same theme was echoed in the celebrated 1968 Kerner Commission report on ghetto riots, which proclaimed that pervasive discrimination and segregation were "the source of the deepest bitterness and lie at the center of the problem of racial disorder."[10] The riots of 1967 were attributed to "the failure of all levels of government—Federal and state as well as local—to come to grips with the problems of our cities." In keeping with this theme that bad social conditions and official neglect lead to despair, which in turn leads to violence, civil rights leaders and other minority spokesmen began regularly predicting "a long hot summer" of violence if their demands for more government programs were not met.[11] Such predictions became a staple of political discourse and have remained so over the years. Government agencies seeking to expand their budgets and extend their powers likewise encouraged the belief that social programs reduced the incidence of riots and other violence, while a reduction of such programs would escalate civil disorder.[12]

A diametrically opposite set of beliefs and predictions came from critics of the "war on poverty" proposals. Senator Barry Goldwater predicted that these programs would "encourage poverty" by encouraging "more and more people to move into the ranks of those being taken care of by the government."[13] Nor did he expect expanded social programs to lead to a more harmonious society, for he saw their underlying philosophy as an "attempt to divide Americans" along class lines, to "pigeon-hole people and make hyphenated Americans."[14] As these programs got under way, the mayors of Los Angeles, San Francisco, and Detroit blamed the "war on poverty" for "fostering class struggle" through its support of community activists, radical intellectuals, and others with a vested interest in disaffection and turmoil.[15] The assumption that initial increases in government spending on social programs would lead to reduced spending in later years, as dependency declined, was likewise disputed by opponents like columnist Henry Hazlitt, who said, "we can expect the price tag to increase geometrically as the years go on."[16]

From an analytical standpoint, the issues were virtually ideal for testing: Two conflicting sets of belief led logically to opposite conclusions, stated in terms that could be tested empirically. Almost never, however, were such empirical tests made. The views expressed in the vision of the anointed became axiomatic. A reexamination of that vision, as it applied to the "war on poverty," shows that it went through the four stages already described:

STAGE 1. THE "CRISIS": Given that the purpose of the "war on poverty" was to reduce dependency, the question is: How much dependency was there at the time and was it increasing or decreasing before the new policies were instituted? In short, what was the "crisis" for which the anointed were proposing a "solution"?

As of the time the "war on poverty" programs began, the number of people who lived below the official poverty line had been declining continuously since 1960, and was only about half of what it had been in 1950.[17] On the more fundamental issue of *dependency*, the situation was even more clearly improving. The proportion of people whose earnings put them below the poverty level *without counting government benefits* declined by about one-third from 1950 to 1965.[18] In short, dependency on government transfers as a means of warding off poverty was declining when the "war on poverty" began.

STAGE 2. THE "SOLUTION": The Economic Opportunity Act was passed in 1964, creating the Office of Economic Opportunity, the "war on poverty" agency. As an historian of poverty programs put it, "Congress was quick to buy a program that might help welfare wither away."[19] The Council of Economic Advisers declared, "conquest of poverty is well within our power."

STAGE 3. THE RESULTS: The percentage of people dependent upon the federal government to keep above the poverty line *increased*. Although the number of such dependent people had been declining for more than a decade before the "war on poverty" programs began, this downward trend now reversed itself and began rising within a few years after that program got under way.[20]

Official poverty continued its decline for some time, as massive federal outlays lifted many people above the official poverty line, but not out of dependency—the original goal. Eventually, however, even official poverty began to rise, so that a larger number of people were in poverty in 1992 than were in poverty in 1964, when the "war on poverty" began.[21] Although the Office of Economic Opportunity itself was modestly funded, by government standards, it was a spearhead, a catalyst, and to some extent a coordinator of anti-poverty programs in other agencies as well. The massive expansion of anti-poverty social programs continued even after the Office of Economic Opportunity was disbanded in 1974 and its programs were reassigned to other agencies. Overall federal spending on programs for the poor escalated as eligibility rules for welfare and Social Security were loosened, the size of benefits was increased, and unemployment insurance was made more available to more people, and for longer periods of time.[22]

Despite initial claims that various government services would lead to reduced federal outlays on welfare programs as more people became self-sufficient, the very opposite happened. The number of people receiving public assistance more than doubled from 1960 to 1977.[23] The dollar value of public housing rose nearly five-fold in a decade and the amount spent on food stamps rose more than tenfold. All government-provided in-kind benefits increased about eight-fold from 1965 to 1969 and more than twenty-fold by 1974.[24] Federal spending on such social welfare programs not only rose in dollar terms and in real terms, but also a percentage of the nation's gross national product, going from 8 percent of GNP in 1960 to 16 percent by 1974.[25]

As for urban ghetto riots, they raged across the country during this era.[26] Later, they declined sharply after the beginning of the Nixon administration, which opposed the whole "war on poverty" approach and eventually abolished the Office of Economic Opportunity, which had been the spearhead of this program. Still later, during the eight years of the Reagan presidency—supposedly the nadir of neglect— major urban riots became virtually extinct. The fact that the actual course of events followed a pattern diametrically the opposite of what was assumed and proclaimed by those with the vision of the anointed made not the slightest dent in the policies they advocated or in the assumptions behind those policies. In this respect as in others, the vision of the anointed had achieved a sacrosanct status, hermetically sealed off from the contaminating influence of facts.

STAGE 4. THE RESPONSE: The failure of the "war on poverty" to achieve its goal of reducing dependency—and in fact an *increasing* dependency as these policies went into effect—brought no acknowledgment of failure. In the many retrospective evaluations of these programs in later years and decades, most of their political and media proponents resolutely ignored the original goal of reducing dependency. The goal was instead redefined as reducing poverty by transferring resources. As former Johnson White House aide Hodding Carter III put it, "millions of people were lifted out of poverty during the period, or had their plight considerably alleviated, by government programs and public expenditures."[27] A member of President Johnson's Cabinet suggested yet another criterion of success: "Ask the 11 million students who have received loans for their college education whether the Higher Education Act failed." Similar questions were suggested for those who used a wide range of other government programs.[28] In short, the test for whether a program was good for the country as a whole was whether those who personally benefitted from it found it beneficial. Yet a third line of defense of failed policies has been to claim moral merit for their good intentions. Hodding Carter III was only one of many to use this defense when he wrote of the "war on poverty" as "a clear, steady trend away from the majority's long and shameful disregard of the other, hidden America of hard-core hopelessness."[29]

Related to the moral redemption of the uncaring masses was the excitement and inspiration of the elite. At a twentieth anniversary commemoration of the Johnson administration's social programs, another former aide to President Johnson referred to "the vision that excited and inspired the nation."[30] Mrs. Johnson spoke of the "sense of caring" and the "exhilaration" of her husband's efforts.[31] Finally, it was asserted that things would have been even worse, were it not for these programs. "The question is not what the bottom line is today—with poverty up—but where would we be if we didn't have these programs in place?" asked Professor Sheldon Danziger, director of the University of Wisconsin's Institute for Research on Poverty. "I think we'd have poverty rates over 25 percent."[32] Even though poverty and dependency were going down for years before the "war on poverty" began, Professor Danziger chose to assert that poverty rates would have gone up. There is no possible reply to these heads-I-win-and-tails-you-lose assertions, except to note that they would justify any policy on any subject anywhere, regardless of its empirically observed consequences.

In short, no matter what happens, the vision of the anointed always succeeds, if not by the original criteria, then by criteria extemporized later—and if not by empirical criteria, then by criteria sufficiently subjective to escape even the possibility of refutation. Evidence becomes irrelevant.

Sex Education

Among the many crusades which gathered new steam during the 1960s was the crusade to spread sex education into the public schools and through other channels. Among the first acts of the Office of Economic Opportunity in 1964 was making a grant to a Planned Parenthood unit in Texas. From a total expenditure of less than half a million dollars in fiscal year 1965, OEO expanded its financing of sex education more than five-fold by fiscal year 1966.[33]

Not only did the federal government begin in the late 1960s to greatly expand its own expenditures on sex education—often known as "family planning" or by other euphemisms—but it also began to mandate that states promote such programs as well. The number of patients served by "family planning" clinics increased approximately five-fold between 1968 and 1978.[34] As early as 1968, the National Education Association in its *NEA Journal* was saying that a federally funded project in a Washington school "demonstrated the need for sex education as an integral part of school curriculum beginning in the early grades." Some of the pregnant girls counseled "reported feeling that if they had studied human sexuality with understanding teachers during elementary school, they would not have become pregnant."[35] Sex education and "family planning" clinics—so called despite their being established to prevent having babies—not only grew rapidly but also changed in the clientele they served. As a study of this era put it:

Family planning services grew phenomenally from the mid-60s to the mid-70s. In 1964, the federal government made its first family planning grant, which served only married women. By 1970, Congress had passed the first national family planning and population legislation. Federal expenditures grew from $16 million to close to $200 million. In 1969, there were less than a quarter of a million teenagers using family planning clinics; by 1976 this had swollen to 1.2 million.[36]

According to the Alan Guttmacher Institute, a leading research and advocacy organization promoting sex education, the federal government's support of "family planning services" rose from less than $14 million in 1968 to $279 million a decade later[37]—nearly a twenty-fold increase. By the early 1980s, nearly two-thirds of the money received by "family planning" agencies came from the federal government.[38] What was the purpose of all this activity? "Sex education is considered one of the primary tools to help adolescents avoid unwanted pregnancy," according to a typical comment of the period.[39] Once more, we have the four-stage pattern:

STAGE 1. THE "CRISIS": In 1968, it was claimed that "contraception education and counseling is now urgently needed to help prevent pregnancy and illegitimacy in high school girls."[40] The head
of Planned Parenthood testified before a congressional subcommittee in 1966 as to the need for sex education "to assist our
young people in reducing the incidence of out-of-wedlock births
and early marriage necessitated by pregnancy."[41] The incidence of
venereal disease among young people was cited by the head of the
New York City Board of Education as showing the need for "a
crash educational program." An article in the *American School
Board Journal* in 1969 depicted sex education as a way of combat-
ting "illegitimacy and venereal disease."[42] *PTA Magazine* likewise
urged sex education to combat "the spiraling rate of venereal diseases, the pregnancies before marriage, the emotionally disastrous
results of irresponsible sexual behavior."[43]

Similar statements abounded from a variety of sources. But what
was in fact the situation when this kind of "crisis" mentality was
being used to push for more sex education in the schools? Fertility
rates among teenage girls had been *declining* for more than a decade
since 1957.[44] Venereal disease was also *declining*. The rate of infection for gonorrhea, for example, declined every year from 1950
through 1959, and the rate of syphilis infection was, by 1960, less
than half of what it had been in 1950.[45] This was the "crisis" which
federal aid was to solve.

STAGE 2. THE "SOLUTION": Massive federal aid to sex education
programs in the schools, and to "family planning" clinics, was
advocated to combat teenage pregnancy and venereal disease.
After sex education, according to a "Professor of Family Life," a
boy "will find decreased need for casual, irresponsible and self-
centered experimentation with sex."[46] Critics opposed such
actions on various grounds, including a belief that sex education
would lead to more sexual activity, rather than less, and to more
teenage pregnancy as well. Such views were dismissed in the
media and in politics, as well as by the advocates of sex educa-

tion. The *New York Times* editorially rejected "emotions and un-examined tradition" in this area[47] and its education editor declared: "To fear that sex education will become synonymous with greater sexual permissiveness is to misunderstand the fundamental purpose of the entire enterprise."[48] As in many other cases, *intentions* were the touchstone of the vision of the anointed.

STAGE 3. THE RESULTS: As early as 1968, nearly half of all schools in the country—public and private, religious and secular—had sex education, and it was rapidly growing.[49] As sex education programs spread widely through the American educational system during the 1970s, the pregnancy rate among 15- to 19-year-old females rose from approximately 68 per thousand in 1970 to approximately 96 per thousand by 1980.[50] Among unmarried girls in the 15- to 17-year-old bracket, birth rates rose 29 percent between 1970 and 1984,[51] despite a massive increase in abortions, which more than doubled during the same period. Among girls under 15, the number of abortions surpassed the number of live births by 1974.[52] The reason was not hard to find: According to the Alan Guttmacher Institute, the percentage of unmarried teenage girls who had engaged in sex was higher at every age from 15 through 19 by 1976 than it was just five years earlier.[53] The rate of teenage gonorrhea tripled between 1956 and 1975.[54] Sargent Shriver, former head of the Office of Economic Opportunity, which led the early charge for more sex education and "family planning" clinics, testified candidly to a congressional committee in 1978: "Just as venereal disease has skyrocketed 350% in the last 15 years when we have had more clinics, more pills, and more sex education than ever in history, teen-age pregnancy has risen."[55] Such candor was, however, the exception rather than the rule among those who had pushed for sex education and birth control ("family planning") clinics.

STAGE 4. THE RESPONSE: Sex education advocates continue to treat as axiomatic the need for more sex education to combat teenage pregnancy and venereal disease. As late as 1980, and in spite of mounting evidence, the Alan Guttmacher Institute proclaimed: "Teenage pregnancy can, through better education and preventive services, be, if not altogether avoided, at least reduced, and through better maternity, abortion and social services, be reduced in its personal impact on the teenager who does get pregnant." Opposition to sex education continued to be dismissed as a "simplistic view" in the *American Biology Teacher* journal.[56] Congressman James H. Scheuer of New York found that the alarming statistics on rising teenage pregnancy only "highlights the need for strong leadership by the Federal Government in solving this problem."[57] The very possibility that "strong" federal "leadership" might have worsened the situation was not even mentioned. To the Alan Guttmacher Institute as well, an "almost quadrupling" of venereal disease between 1960 and 1972[58] only showed that more "broadly based national programs channeled through the public school system are needed and are long overdue."[59] Opposition to sex education has been depicted as "a threat to a democratic society."[60] When confronted with the evidence that pregnancy and abortions increased during the 1970s, sex education advocates often deny that sex education was widespread during that decade, by restricting the term "sex education" to *compulsory* sex education, which tended to be mandated later.

Although sex education programs have been sold to the public, to Congress, and to education officials as ways of reducing such tangible social ills as teenage pregnancy and venereal disease, many of the leaders of this movement have long had a more expansive agenda. As a congressional committee report noted gingerly:

> The primary objective of Federal efforts in family life and sex education has been to reduce unwanted pregnancy rates among teenagers, while the primary goal of most sex educators appears to be encouragement of healthy attitudes about sex and sexuality.[61]

In short, however politically useful public concern about teenage pregnancy and venereal disease might be in obtaining government money and access to a captive audience in the public schools, the

real goal was to change students' *attitudes*—put bluntly, to brainwash them with the vision of the anointed, in order to supplant the
values they had been taught at home. In the words of an article in the
Journal of School Health, sex education presents "an exciting opportunity to develop new norms."[62] Only in the light of this agenda does
it make sense that so-called "sex education" should be advocated to
take place throughout the school years—from kindergarten to college—when it could not possibly take that much time to teach basic
biological or medical information about sex. What takes that long is
a constant indoctrination in new attitudes.[63] An example of such
indoctrination may be useful:

> A popular sex instructional program for junior high school students,
> aged 13 and 14, shows film strips of four naked couples, two homo-
> sexual and two heterosexual, performing a variety of sexually explicit
> acts, and teachers are warned with a cautionary note from the sex
> educators not to show the material to parents or friends: "Many of the
> materials of this program shown to people outside the context of the
> program itself can evoke misunderstanding and difficulties."[64]

Parents who learned of this program and protested were quickly
labeled "fundamentalists" and "right-wing extremists," even though
they were in fact affluent Episcopalians in Connecticut.[65] Here is an
almost textbook example of the vision of the anointed, preempting
the decisions of parents as to when and how their own children shall
be introduced to sex—and dismissing out of hand those with different views. Nor was this episode peculiar to this particular school.
Similar things have happened all over the country.[66] Parents are den-
igrated both in discussions of public policy and in the materials
given to students in the schools.[67] A typical comment from "experts"
is that "sex and sexuality have become far too complex and technical
to leave to the typical parent, who is either uninformed or too bashful
to share useful sexual information with his child."[68]

This utter certainty of being right, even to the point of circumventing parents, is completely consistent with the vision, however inconsistent it is with decades of empirical evidence on the actual conse-

quences of "healthy attitudes toward sex" as promoted by "experts." The key point about the sex education crusade, from the standpoint of understanding the vision of the anointed, is that evidence proved to be as irrelevant here as on other issues.

Criminal Justice

Like so many negative social trends, soaring crime rates began in the 1960s, amid glowing optimism about how much better things could be if the traditional beliefs of the many were replaced by the special new insights of the few. In the case of criminal justice, however, the policy changes did not originate so much in legislation as in judicial and administrative rulings and policies. But the *zeitgeist* alone did not initiate the changing policies, which depended on specific people doing specific things. Among the key people whose words and actions set the tone for the changes in the criminal justice system in the 1960s were the chief justice of the U.S. Supreme Court, the attorney general of the United States, and the chief judge of the Circuit Court of Appeals for the District of Columbia, then as now regarded as de facto the second highest court in the land. By name they were, respectively, Earl Warren, Ramsey Clark, and David L. Bazelon. What was the problem or "crisis" they were attempting to "solve"?

STAGE 1. THE "CRISIS": Although Chief Judge Bazelon said in 1960 that "we desperately need all the help we can get from modern behavioral scientists"[69] in dealing with the criminal law, the cold facts suggest no such desperation or crisis. Since the most reliable long-term data are on murder, what was the murder rate at that point? The number of murders committed in the United States in 1960 was less than in 1950, 1940, or 1930—even though the population was growing over those decades and murders in the two new states of Hawaii and Alaska were counted in the national statistics for the first time in 1960.[70] The murder *rate*, in proportion to population, was in 1960 just under half of what it had been in 1934.[71]

As Judge Bazelon saw the criminal justice system in 1960, the problem was not with "the so-called criminal population"[72] but with society, whose "need to punish" was a "primitive urge" that was "highly irrational"[73]—indeed, a "deep childish fear that with any reduction of punishment, multitudes would run amuck."[74] It was this "vindictiveness," this "irrationality" of "notions and practices regarding punishment"[75] that had to be corrected. The criminal "is like us, only somewhat weaker," according to Judge Bazelon, and "needs help if he is going to bring out the good in himself and restrain the bad."[76] Society is indeed guilty of "creating this special class of human beings," by its "social failure" for which "the criminal serves as a scapegoat."[77] Punishment is itself a "dehumanizing process" and a "social branding" which only promotes more crime.[78] Since criminals "have a special problem and need special help," Judge Bazelon argued for "psychiatric treatment" with "new, more sophisticated techniques," and asked:

> Would it really be the end of the world if all jails were turned into hospitals or rehabilitation centers?[79]

Chief Judge Bazelon's views were not the isolated opinions of one man but expressed a widespread vision among the anointed, many of whom lionized him for such statements.[80] The same therapeutic vision was still apparent more than a quarter of a century later, when Supreme Court Justice William J. Brennan referred to "the etiology of crime," for which he called upon "psychiatrists and psychologists," as well as "experts in the behavioral sciences," for help.[81] Brennan's long-time colleague on the Supreme Court, Justice William O. Douglas, likewise took the therapeutic approach:

> Rehabilitation of criminals has seldom been attempted. Killing them or locking them up is the tried-and-true ancient method. Why not turn our faces toward rehabilitation?[82]

The therapeutic vision also permeated the writings and speeches of President Lyndon Johnson's attorney general, Ramsey Clark:

Rehabilitation must be the goal of modern corrections. Every other consideration must be subordinated to it. To rehabilitate is to give health, freedom from drugs and alcohol, to provide education, voca-tional training, understanding and the ability to contribute to society.

Rehabilitation means the purpose of law is justice—and that as a generous people we wish to give every individual his chance for ful-fillment. The theory of rehabilitation is based on the belief that healthy, rational people will not injure others, that they will under-stand that the individual and his society are best served by conduct that does not inflict injury, and that a just society has the ability to provide health and purpose and opportunity for all its citizens. Reha-bilitated, an individual will not have the capacity—cannot bring him-self—to injure another or take or destroy property.[83]

With Attorney General Clark, as with Chief Judge Bazelon and others, the problem was with the benighted public and its outdated attitudes. Society imposes long prison sentences "because we are angry," according to Clark, but "this will not reduce crime." He said: "If it is the public safety we are concerned about, the question is how persons convicted of crimes can be rehabilitated, not how long they should be locked up."[84] Again, it is necessary to emphasize that these were not the isolated opinions of one man. Ramsey Clark's book, *Crime in America,* was widely praised among the opin-ion elites. *New York Times* columnist Tom Wicker, for example, called Clark "an awesomely knowledgeable professional" and praised his "generosity and understanding" as well as his "courage and persistence and eloquence."[85] The *Saturday Review* called *Crime in America* one of "the best books written on violence in America."[86] Similar praise appeared in *Time* magazine and in the *New Republic.*[87] As far away as London, the *Times Literary Supple-ment* said in its review of *Crime in America* that no one has "done more to state the problem and light the way to improvement than Ramsey Clark."[88] More importantly, the attorney general, Chief Judge Bazelon, and justices of the Supreme Court were not simply people whose words received a large and favorable public notice from opinion-making elites. They were people in a position to act.

STAGE 2. THE "SOLUTION": A series of landmark Supreme Court decisions in the 1960s changed the course of criminal justice in the United States. *Mapp v. Ohio* (1961), *Escobido v. Illinois* (1964), and *Miranda v. Arizona* (1966) successively expanded the rights of criminals in the custody of the police by making their convictions invalid if the procedures specified by the courts were not followed in detail by the police. *Gideon v. Wainwright* (1963) required states to provide free attorneys to criminal defendants, subject to the threat that their convictions would be overturned, even if guilt was unquestioned, when such attorneys were not provided. In California, even when state-appointed attorneys were supplied, if these attorneys' defense strategies were second-guessed by appellate judges and considered inadequate, convictions could be overturned on grounds of denial of the constitutional right to counsel.[89]

Although the U.S. Supreme Court began this judicial revolution in criminal law in the 1960s, even earlier Chief Judge Bazelon had expanded the scope of the "insanity" defense in the landmark case of *Durham v. United States* (1954) and he continued to lead the D.C. Circuit Court of Appeals toward more expansive views of criminals' rights. In addition, courts across the land involved themselves more and more in the administration of prisons, prescribing better living conditions and imposing on the prison system a duty to provide prisoners with access to law books, in order to prepare appeals of their convictions. Moreover, sentences were less often imposed and tended to be of shorter duration.[90]

In short, the vision of the anointed triumphed in the criminal justice system. The assumptions underlying its actions were the same as elsewhere. Sweeping presumptions about the irrationality and mean-spiritedness of the public were made without either evidence or a sense of need for evidence. Conversely, the validity and applicability of the beliefs of "experts" were taken as axiomatic. Judge Bazelon, for example, referred to the insanity defense as "merely one way of welcoming the psychiatrist into the courtroom."[91] Whatever the merits or demerits of this approach, it fulfilled the essential requirements for the vision of the anointed: It established that the anointed and the benighted were on vastly different moral and intellectual planes and it justified taking decisions out of the hands of those who passed the existing laws, in response to the voting public, and put these decisions in the hands of judges responsive to those with "expertise." Moreover, it put the burden of proof on others. As Judge Bazelon put it, "in the absence of decisive empirical data,"[92] he was prepared to experiment. There was no suggestion of what empirical data should be used to test the success of that experiment, either absolutely or relative to the approach discarded with such disdain. Although judges took the lead in this revolution in criminal justice, they were seconded by those in politics and in the media who shared the prevailing vision. President Lyndon Johnson saw social programs as the real way to fight crime. As quoted in the *New York Times:*

> "I don't know why some people sit idly by and are willing to take the more expensive route—the delinquency route, the jail route, the penitentiary route," he asserted.
> "It takes more of our money to take care of a convict in a penitentiary than it does to prepare a boy to be a good, taxpaying citizen who can read and write," he said. . . .[93]

Similar views were expressed by 1968 Democratic vice-presidential candidate Edmund Muskie. Responding to the law and order issues raised by his opponents in the election campaign, Senator Muskie said:

> But you can't have law and order based on ignorance. . . . You've got to build it by education, enlightenment and opportunity. That's the way to make a society safe.[94]

These views did not pass unchallenged, though the legal changes became "the law of the land," largely by judicial rather than legislative process. On the Supreme Court itself, there were bitter dissents from the continued expansions—or creations—of criminals' "rights."

The *Miranda* decision of 1966, which climaxed the judicial revolution in criminal law, led to this scene in the Supreme Court:

> Justice Harlan, his face flushed and his voice occasionally faltering with emotion, denounced the decision as "dangerous experimentation" at a time of a "high crime rate that is a matter of growing concern."
>
> He said it was a "new doctrine" without substantial precedent, reflecting a balance in favor of the accused.
>
> Justice White said:
>
> "In some unknown number of cases the Court's rule will return a killer, a rapist or other criminal to the streets and to the environment which produced him, to repeat his crime whenever it pleases him.
>
> "As a consequence, there will not be a gain, but a loss, in human dignity."[95]

Such dissents were brushed aside and outcries from the public and from law enforcement officials were dismissed. At a 1965 judicial conference, where a former police commissioner of New York City complained about the trend of the Supreme Court's decisions on criminal law, his concerns were immediately met with sarcastic ridicule by a law professor who asked, "I wonder what rights we'd have left if we always yielded to the police hysteria." According to the *New York Times* account, Justice William J. Brennan and Chief Justice Earl Warren sat "stony-faced" during the police commissioner's statements, but then "frequently roared with laughter" as the law professor poured scorn and derision on those statements, which were characterized as "simplistic, narrow-minded and politically expedient."[96] The benighted were simply not to be taken seriously by the anointed.

Had anyone been seriously interested in testing the opposing theories of crime empirically, those theories were ideally suited for such testing, since each theory led to conclusions which were not only logically consistent with its own premises but which were virtually inescapable, given their respective premises. Moreover, these conclusions were clearly distinguishable empirically and data were readily available.

In the prevailing vision of the anointed, emphasis on punishment was mistaken when what was needed were therapeutic alternatives to punishment, social programs to get at the "root causes" of crime, and more rights for those accused and convicted of crimes, so as to establish that the law was fair and worthy of respect, which respect would then be an ingredient in more law-abiding behavior by those otherwise alienated from society. By contrast, the traditional view would lead one to expect a rising crime rate after the changes of the 1960s. If punishment deters, as the traditionalists believed, then the reduction in imprisonment that occurred in the 1960s would tend to produce more crime. But if imprisonment itself exacerbated the crime problem, as Judge Bazelon, Ramsey Clark, and numerous others with the vision of the anointed claimed, then this reduction in imprisonment would tend to reduce crime. Similarly, if social programs for the poor, for minorities, and for the mentally disturbed were needed to get at the "root causes" of crime, as the anointed claimed, then the vast and unprecedented expansion of such programs during the 1960s should have reduced the crime rate. The logical implications of each vision were quite clear. All that was needed was empirical evidence.

STAGE 3. THE RESULTS: Crime rates skyrocketed. Murder rates suddenly shot up until the murder rate in 1974 was more than twice as high as in 1961.[97] Between 1960 and 1976, a citizen's chances of becoming a victim of a major violent crime tripled.[98] The number of policemen killed also tripled during the decade of the 1960s.[99] Young criminals, who had been especially favored by the new solicitude, became especially violent. The arrest rate of juveniles for murder more than tripled between 1965 and 1990, even allowing for changes in population size.[100]

As in other areas, such evidence has made little or no difference in the vision of the anointed, except to spur them on to new feats of ingenuity in interpretation.

STAGE 4. THE RESPONSE: Since neither criminal law changes nor any other social changes are likely to produce truly instantaneous effects, there was a brief period during which no change in the crime rate was discernible—and this momentary lull provided occasions for expressions of much disdain toward those who had predicted that the new criminal justice practices would lead to higher crime rates. Just two months after the *Miranda* decision in 1966, the *New York Times* declared that "the gloomy predictions of its critics have been happily unrealized."[101] However, once the crime rates had clearly begun to rise in the wake of this and many other judicial changes designed to reduce them, the tactics of the proponents of those innovations shifted. Among the early responses to soaring crime rates, in the wake of policies designed to reduce them, were denials that crimes were in fact more frequent. Increased reporting of crime or better collection of data was held responsible for the upsurge in the official statistics.[102] However, as James Q. Wilson put it, "by 1970, enough members of the liberal audience had had their typewriters stolen to make it difficult to deny the existence of a crime wave."[103] Moreover, even in the absence of accumulating personal experience, it was difficult to believe that soaring murder statistics reflected simply better record keeping, since it had always been hard to ignore a dead body.

An alternative to denying rising crime rates was to make it socially unacceptable to talk about it, by equating discussions of "law and order" with racism, since it was well known that crime rates were higher among blacks. "Law and order" was "an inflammatory statement," according to the well-known psychiatrist Karl Menninger. "What it really means, I'm afraid, is that we should all go out and find the niggers and beat them up."[104] This was only one of many expressions of the prevailing vision by Dr. Menninger, whose book *The Crime of Punishment* was widely hailed as it blamed "society" for crime, treated criminals as more wronged than wronging, and urged a substitution of psychiatric treatment for punishment. Another remarkable attempt to evade the bitter implications of the data on the reversal of the crime rate decline after the criminal justice system was transformed in the 1960s was made in another highly touted book,

Criminal Violence, Criminal Justice, by Charles E. Silberman, who wrote:

> For all the talk about the decline in punishment and the hobbling effect of the Warren Court, moreover, what data are available indicate that contemporary criminal courts prosecute, convict, and incarcerate a larger proportion of those arrested for a felony today than did the courts of the 1920s.[105]

What was not explained was why the 1920s were selected as a base period for determining the effect of the Warren Court, which began in 1953 and whose landmark criminal law decisions were made in the 1960s. If this desperate expedient of choosing an irrelevant base period suggests that Silberman's conclusions could not have been supported if his before-and-after comparison had been based on the actual dates of the actual decisions, or even on the date of the beginning of the Warren Court, a look at a few readily available facts confirms that suspicion. First of all, the likelihood that someone who committed a serious crime would be arrested fell until it was only one-fifth as high by 1979 as it had been in 1962.[106] As for going to prison, an earlier trend toward rising imprisonment rates was ended in the late 1950s and early 1960s, and imprisonment rates remained low as crime rates rose during the 1960s.[107]

In short, contrary to what Silberman suggests, criminals were no longer being apprehended, convicted, and incarcerated as they were before the Warren Court remade the criminal law. Moreover, the consequences were precisely what anyone without the vision of the anointed would have expected: When Earl Warren became chief justice in 1953, the homicide rate in the United States was 4.8 per 100,000 population—lower than it had been in four decades.[108] But a sharp rise in homicides began in the 1960s, more than doubling from 1963 to 1973,[109] and by 1991 the rate for murder and deliberate manslaughter alone was 9.8 per 100,000[110]—even omitting other forms of homicide which had been counted in earlier statistics. Whatever the weight of before-and-after statistics, insofar as they are cited at all, the "before" year selected can change the conclusion completely. Silberman's selection of the 1920s as his base of comparison suggests a desperate evasion of the obvious. Once again, it must be noted that Charles E. Silberman's views were not simply the opinions of one man, as the widespread praise of his book in the elite media demonstrated.[111]

The general public and law enforcement officials who did not share the elite vision continued to complain, but while their concerns found some response in the political arena, the anointed were unmoved. Chief Justice Earl Warren brushed aside those whose "self-righteous indignation" about rising crime rates was based on "oversimplification." According to the chief justice, "all of us must assume a share of the responsibility," for he attributed the rising crime rates to the fact that "for decades we have swept under the rug" the slum conditions which breed crime.[112] He ignored the fact that crime rates had been *declining* during all those decades when they should have been rising, according to his theory. Nor is there any reason to believe that Warren ever reconsidered that theory as crime rates continued to soar, for he said in his memoirs:

> A sizable proportion of the American people, too, groping for a reason for so much criminal activity in our disturbed society but overlooking the root causes of crime—such as the degradation of slum life in the ghetto, ignorance, poverty, the drug traffic, unemployment, and organized crime (often made possible by the corruption of law enforcement officials)—joined in placing the blame on the courts and particularly on the Supreme Court.[113]

No attempt was made to show how any of these other factors had worsened so dramatically during the 1960s as to explain the complete turnaround in the historically declining murder rate, for example, or why none of the supposed benefits of the new criminal justice reforms materialized. The relationship between theory and evidence was simply not discussed. The vision was axiomatic.

CHAPTER 3

BY THE NUMBERS

We knew a lot of things we could hardly understand.

—Kenneth Fearing[1]

Anyone who looks through enough statistics will eventually find numbers that seem to confirm a given vision. Often, the same set of statistics contains other numbers that seem to confirm diametrically opposite conclusions. The same is true of anecdotal "facts." That is why *evidence* is different from mere data, whether numerical or verbal.

Scientific evidence, for example, comes from systematically determining—in advance—what particular empirical observations would be seen if one theory were correct, compared to what would be seen if an alternative theory were correct. Only after this careful and painstaking analysis has been completed can the search begin for facts that will differentiate between the competing theories. Seldom is this approach used by those who believe in the vision of the anointed. More typically, they look through statistics until they find some numbers that fit their preconceptions, and then cry, "Aha!" Others with different views can, of course, do the same thing. But only those with the prevailing views are likely to be taken seriously when using such shaky reasoning. This is only one of many misuses of statistics that goes unchallenged as long as the conclusions are consonant with the vision of the anointed.

"AHA!" STATISTICS

Perhaps the purest examples of the problems of the "Aha!" approach
are sets of statistics which themselves contain numbers completely
at odds with the conclusions drawn from other numbers in the same
set. This is not as rare as might be expected.

Infant Mortality and Prenatal Care

A widely reported study from the National Center for Health Statistics showed that (1) black pregnant women in the United States
received prenatal care less often than white pregnant women and
that (2) infant mortality rates among blacks were substantially higher
than among whites.[2] "Aha!" reactions in the media were immediate,
vehement, and widespread. It was automatically assumed that the
first fact was the cause of the second, that this showed American
society's "neglect" of its minorities, if not outright racism, and that
what was needed was more government spending on prenatal care.
According to a New York Times editorial, one-fourth of the infant
deaths in the United States were "easily preventable" and were "primarily attributable to their mothers' lack of prenatal care." What was
needed was "an increase in Federal spending on prenatal care."[3]
The Washington Post likewise urged legislation to "provide vital
assistance to pregnant women who cannot afford normal medical
care."[4]

In the very same report that showed racial disparities in infant
mortality—indeed, on the very same page—statistics showed that (1)
Mexican Americans received even less prenatal care than blacks,
and that (2) infant mortality rates among Mexican Americans were no
higher than among whites.[5] Had anyone been seriously interested in
testing an hypothesis, the conclusion would have been that something other than prenatal care must have been responsible for intergroup differences in infant mortality. That conclusion would have
been further buttressed by data on infant mortality rates for Americans of Chinese, Japanese, and Filipino ancestry—all of whom
received less prenatal care than whites and yet had lower infant mor-

tality rates than whites.[6] But, of course, no one with the vision of the anointed was looking for any such data, so there was no "Aha!"

In a reprise of the pattern of justification for government spending on the "war on poverty," it has been claimed that money invested in prenatal care will prevent costly health problems, thereby saving money in the long run. Various numbers have been thrown around, claiming that for every dollar spent on prenatal care, there is a saving of $1.70, $2.57, or $3.38, depending on which study you believe. Marian Wright Edelman of the Children's Defense Fund, for example, used the $3.38 figure.[7] However, a careful analysis of these studies in the *New England Journal of Medicine* found such claims unsubstantiated.[8] What is even more striking was the response to these damaging findings:

> Dr. Marie McCormick, chairman of the department of maternal and fetal health at the Harvard School of Public Health, said it was true that "justification of these services on a cost-benefit analysis is a weak reed," but added that "people were reduced to this sort of effort" by politicians reluctant to spend money on services for the poor.[9]

In other words, if they told the truth, they wouldn't get the money. Invalid statistics serve the purpose of allowing the anointed to preempt the decision by telling the public only what will gain political support.

Intergroup Disparities

Media and academic preoccupation with black-white comparisons permits many conclusions to be reached in consonance with the prevailing vision, but whose lack of validity would immediately become apparent if just one or two other groups were included in the comparison. For example, the fact that black applicants for mortgage loans are turned down at a higher rate than white applicants has been widely cited as proof of racism among lending institutions. The *Washington Post*, for example, reported that a "racially biased system of home lending exists"[10] and Jesse Jackson called it "criminal activity" that banks "routinely and systematically discriminate against African-Americans and Latinos in making mortgage loans."[11] But the very same data also showed that whites were turned down at a higher rate than Asian Americans.[12] Was that proof of racism against whites, and in favor of Asians?

Similarly, a statistical analysis of the racial impact of layoffs during the recession of 1990–91 turned up the fact that blacks were laid off at a higher rate than whites or others. Although this was a "news" story, as distinguished from an editorial, the story was sufficiently larded with quotations alleging racism that it was clear what conclusion the reader was supposed to draw. However, here again, Asian American workers fared better than white workers. Nor could this be attributed to high-tech skills among Asian Americans. Even among laborers, Asian Americans increased their employment at a time when white, black, and Hispanic laborers were all losing jobs.[13] Yet no one claimed that this showed discrimination against whites and in favor of Asians.

Such Asian-white statistical disparities cause no "Aha!" because their implications are not part of the prevailing vision. In short, numbers are accepted as evidence when they agree with preconceptions, but not when they don't.

In many cases, academic and media comparisons limited to blacks and whites—even when data on other groups are available in the same reports or from the same sources—may reflect nothing more than indolence. However, in other cases, there is a positive effort made to put other kinds of comparisons off-limits by lumping all nonwhites together—as "people of color" in the United States, "visible minorities" in Canada, or generic "blacks" in Britain, where the term encompasses Chinese, Pakistanis, and others. Whatever the rationale for this lumping together of highly disparate groups, its net effect is to suppress evidence that would undermine conclusions based on "Aha!" statistics, and with it undermine the prevailing vision of the anointed.

Perhaps the best-known use of the "Aha!" approach is to "prove" discrimination by statistics showing intergroup disparities. Once again, these inferences are drawn only where they are consonant with the prevailing vision. No one regards the gross disparity in "representation" between blacks and whites in professional basketball as proving discrimination against whites in that sport. Nor does anyone regard the gross "overrepresentation" of blacks among the highest-paid players in baseball as showing discrimination.

The point here is not that whites are being discriminated against, but that a procedure which leads logically to this absurd conclusion is being taken in deadly seriousness when the conclusion fits the vision of the anointed. In short, what is claimed by the anointed to be evidence is clearly recognized by them as not being evidence when its conclusions do not fit the prevailing vision.

Implicit in the equating of statistical disparity with discrimination is the assumption that gross disparities would not exist in the absence of unequal treatment. However, international studies have repeatedly shown gross intergroup disparities to be commonplace all over the world, whether in alcohol consumption,[14] fertility rates,[15] educational performance,[16] or innumerable other variables. A reasonably comprehensive listing of such disparities would be at least as large as a dictionary. However, a manageably selective list can be made of disparities in which it is virtually impossible to claim that the statistical differences in question are due to discrimination:

1. American men are struck by lightning six times as often as American women.[17]
2. During the days of the Soviet Union, per capita consumption of cognac in Estonia was more than seven times what it was in Uzbekistan.[18]
3. For the entire decade of the 1960s, members of the Chinese minority in Malaysia received more university degrees than did members of the Malay majority—including more than 400 degrees in engineering, compared to 4 for the Malays.[19]
4. In the days of the Ottoman Empire, when non-Moslems were explicitly second-class under the law, there were whole industries and sectors of the economy predominantly owned and operated by Christian minorities, notably Greeks and Armenians.[20]

5. When Nigeria became an independent nation in 1960, most of its riflemen came from the northern regions while most of its officers came from southern regions. As late as 1965, half the officers were members of the Ibo tribe[21]—a southern group historically disadvantaged.

6. In Bombay, capital of India's state of Maharashtra, most of the business executives are non-Maharashtrian, and in the state of Assam, most of the businessmen, construction workers, artisans, and members of various professions are non-Assamese.[22]

7. Within the white community of South Africa, as late as 1946, the Afrikaners earned less than half the income of the British,[23] even though the Afrikaners were politically predominant.

8. As of 1921, members of the Tamil minority in Ceylon outnumbered members of the Sinhalese majority in both the medical and the legal professions.[24]

9. A 1985 study in the United States showed that the proportion of Asian American students who scored over 700 on the mathematics portion of the Scholastic Aptitude Test (SAT) was more than double the proportion among whites.[25]

10. In Fiji, people whose ancestors immigrated from India—usually to become plantation laborers—received several times as many university degrees as the indigenous Fijians,[26] who still own most of the land.

11. Although Germans were only about one percent of the population of czarist Russia, they were about 40 percent of the Russian army's high command, more than half of all the officials in the foreign ministry, and a large majority of the members of the St. Petersburg Academy of Sciences.[27]

12. In Brazil's state of São Paulo, more than two-thirds of the potatoes and more than 90 percent of the tomatoes have been grown by people of Japanese ancestry.[28]

13. As early as 1887, more than twice as many Italian immigrants as Argentines had bank accounts in the *Banco de Buenos Aires*,[29] even though most Italians arrived destitute in Argentina and began work in the lowest, hardest, and most "menial" jobs.

14. In mid-nineteenth-century Melbourne, more than half the clothing stores were owned by Jews,[30] who have never been as much as one percent of Australia's population.

15. Even after the middle of the twentieth century in Chile, most of the industrial enterprises in Santiago were controlled by either immigrants or the children of immigrants.[31]

Although these examples were deliberately selected to exclude cases where discrimination might plausibly have been regarded as the reason for the disparities, this in no way excludes the possibility that discrimination may be behind other disparities. The point here is that inferences cannot be made *either way* from the bare fact of statistical differences. Nor does it necessarily help to "control" statistically for other variables. Most social phenomena are sufficiently complex—with data on many variables being either unavailable or inherently unquantifiable—that often such control is itself illusory. That illusion will be analyzed as a special phenomenon which can be called the residual fallacy.

THE RESIDUAL FALLACY

A common procedure in trying to prove discrimination with statistics is to (1) establish that there are statistical disparities between two or more groups, (2) demonstrate that the odds that these particular disparities are a result of random chance are very small, and (3) show that, even holding constant various nondiscriminatory factors which might influence the outcomes, that still leaves a substantial residual difference between the groups, which must be presumed to be due to discrimination. Since essentially the same intellectual procedure has been used to "prove" genetic inferiority, the choice of what to attribute the residual to is inherently arbitrary. But there is yet another major objection to this procedure. Not uncommonly, as the gross statistics are broken down by holding various characteristics constant, it turns out that the groups involved differ in these characteristics on every level of aggregation—and differ in different proportions from one level to another.

The residual fallacy is one of the grand non sequiturs of our time, as common in the highest courts of the land as on the political platform or in the media or academe. At the heart of the fallacy is the notion that you really can hold variables constant—"controlling" the variables, as statisticians say—in practice as well as in theory.

"Controlling" for Education

A commonly made claim is that discrimination is so pervasive and so severe that even people with the same educational qualifications are paid very differently according to whether they are male or female, black or white, etc. Holding years of education constant is often illusory, however, since groups with different quantities of education often have qualitative differences in their education as well. Thus, when group A has significantly more years of education than group B, very often group A also has a higher quality of education, whether quality is measured by their own academic performance at a given educational level, by the qualitative rankings of the institutions attended, or by the difficulty and remuneration of the fields of study in which the group is concentrated. At the college or university level, for example, group A may be more heavily concentrated in mathematics, science, medicine, or engineering, while group B is concentrated in sociology, education, or various ethnic studies. In this context, claims that members of group B are paid less than members of group A with the "same" education (measured quantitatively) are clearly fallacious. Qualitative differences in education between groups have been common around the world, whether comparing Asian Americans with Hispanic Americans in the United States, Ashkenazic Jews with Sephardic Jews in Israel, Tamils with Sinhalese in Sri Lanka, Chinese with Malays in Malaysia, or Protestants with Catholics in Northern Ireland.[32]

Male-female differences in income are often likewise said to prove discrimination because men and women with the "same" education receive different pay. Suppose, for example, that we try to hold education constant by examining income statistics just for those women and men who have graduated from college. There is still a sex difference in income at this level of aggregation, and if we are content to stop here—the choice of stopping point being inherently arbitrary—then we may choose to call the residual differences in income evidence of sex discrimination. However, if we recognize that college graduates include people who go on to postgraduate study, and that postgraduate education also influences income, we may wish to go on to the next level of aggregation and compare women and men who did postgraduate study. Now we will find that the proportion of women and men with postgraduate degrees differs from the proportions with college degrees—women slightly outnumbering men at the bachelor's degree level, but being outnumbered by men by more than two-to-one at the master's degree level, and by 59 percent at the Ph.D. level.[33] Clearly, when we compare college-educated women and men, which includes those who went on to postgraduate work, we are still comparing apples and oranges because their total education is not the same.

Suppose, then, that we press on to the next level of aggregation in search of comparability, and look only at women and men who went all the way to the Ph.D. Once more, we will discover not only disparities but changing ratios of disparities. Although women receive 37 percent of all Ph.D.s, the fields in which they receive them differ radically from the fields in which men receive their Ph.D.s—with the men being more heavily concentrated in the more mathematical, scientific, *and remunerative* fields. While women receive nearly half the Ph.D.s in the social sciences and more than half in education, men receive more than 80 percent of the Ph.D.s in the natural sciences and more than 90 percent of the Ph.D.s in engineering.[34] We are still comparing apples and oranges.

Some specialized studies have permitted even finer breakdowns, but sex disparities in education continue in these finer breakdowns as well. For example, if we examine only those women and men who received Ph.D.s in the social sciences, it turns out that the women were more likely to be in sociology and the men in economics—the latter being the more remunerative field. Moreover, even within economics, there have been very large male-female differences as to what proportion of the economics Ph.D.s were specifically in econometrics—a difference in a proportion of ten men to one woman.[35] In short, we have still not held constant the education we set out to hold constant *and which we could have said that we had held constant by simply stopping the disaggregation at any point along the way.*

While the disaggregation process must stop at some point, whether because the statistics are not broken down any further or because time is not limitless, the fatal fallacy is to assume that all factors left unexamined must be equal, so that all remaining differences in outcome can be attributed to discrimination. In other words, having found causal disparities at every level of aggregation—and often changing ratios of such disparities, as well—it is arbitrarily assumed that the causal disparities end where our disaggregation ends, so that all remaining differences in reward must be due to discrimination.

Innumerable historical and cultural differences, found among many groups in countries around the world—as the numbered examples listed above suggest—make statistical disparities fall far short of proof of discrimination. Such data may be accepted as evidence or proof in courts of law but, logically speaking, such data prove nothing. They are "Aha!" statistics.

Mortgage "Discrimination" Statistics

In the studies of black and other minority mortgage loan applicants who were turned down at higher rates than whites, some attempt was made to control for nonracial variables that might have affected these decisions, by comparing minorities and whites in the same income brackets. However, anyone who has ever applied for a mortgage loan knows that numerous factors besides income are considered, one of the most obvious being the net worth of the applicants. Other data, from the U.S. Census, show that blacks average lower net worth than whites in the same income brackets. Indeed, even blacks in the highest income bracket do not have as much net worth as whites in the second-highest bracket.[36] Controlling for income gives only the illusion of comparability. That illusion has been further undermined by the fact that a widely cited Federal Reserve study on racial disparities in mortgage loan approval rates did not control for net worth or take into account the loan applicants' credit histories or their existing debts.[37] Nor was "the adequacy of collateral" included.[38]

When a more detailed follow-up study was done for the Boston area by the Federal Reserve Bank of Boston, it was discovered that in fact black and Hispanic applicants for mortgage loans had greater debt burdens, poorer credit histories, sought loans covering a higher percentage of the value of the properties in question, and were also more likely to seek to finance multiple-dwelling units rather than single-family homes.[39] Loan applications for multiple-dwelling units were turned down more often among both white and minority applicants, but obviously affect the rejection rate moreso among the latter, since they applied more often for loans for such units.[40] Even among those applicants whose loans were approved—and the majority of both minority and white applicants had their loans approved— minority borrowers had incomes only about three-quarters as high as whites and assets worth less than half the value of the assets of the white borrowers.[41] Nevertheless, when all these variables were "controlled" statistically, there was still "a statistically significant gap" between the loan approval rate for minority loan applicants and white loan applicants, though substantially less than in the original study.

Whereas 72 percent of the minority loan applications were approved, compared to 89 percent for whites, when other characteristics were held constant 83 percent of the minority loan applications were approved.[42] The remaining differential can be expressed either by saying that there was a residual difference of 6 percentage points in loan approval rates or that minority applicants were turned down 60 percent more often than white applicants with the same characteristics—since a 17 percent rejection rate is 60 percent higher than an 11 percent rejection rate. The Boston Federal Reserve Bank report chose the latter way of expressing the same facts.[43]

Was the residual difference of 6 percentage points due to racial discrimination? After finding minority and white loan applicants different on all the relevant variables examined, can we assume that they must be the same on all remaining variables for which data are lacking? One test might be to examine the logic of the discrimination hypothesis and to test its conclusions against other empirical data. For example, if there were racial discrimination in lending, and yet most applicants in all racial or ethnic groups were successful in obtaining loans, the implication would be that minority loan applicants had to be more credit-worthy than white applicants to be approved. And if that were so, then the subsequent default rates among minority borrowers would be lower than among white borrowers. In reality, however, census data suggest no racial difference in default rates among the approved borrowers.[44]

When the principal author of the Boston Federal Reserve Bank study, Alicia Munnell, was contacted by a writer for *Forbes* magazine and this clear implication was presented to her, she called it "a sophisticated point." When pressed, she agreed with the point made by the *Forbes* writer, that "discrimination against blacks should show up in lower, not equal default rates—discrimination would mean that good black applicants are being unfairly rejected."[45] The following discussion ensued:

> *FORBES:* Did you ever ask the question that if defaults appear to be more or less the same among blacks and whites, that points to mortgage lenders making rational decisions?
> *Munnell:* No.
>   Munnell does not want to repudiate her study. She tells FORBES, on reflection, that the census data are not good enough and could be "massaged" further: "I do believe that discrimination occurs."
> *FORBES:* You have no evidence?
> *Munnell:* I do not have evidence. . . . No one has evidence.[46]

This lack of evidence, however, has not prevented a widespread orgy of moral outrage in the media.

CHANGING ASSORTMENTS

One common source of needless alarm about statistics is a failure to understand that a given series of numbers may represent a changing assortment of people. A joke has it that, upon being told that a pedestrian is hit by a car every 20 minutes in New York, the listener responded: "He must get awfully tired of that!" Exactly the same reasoning—or lack of reasoning—appears in statistics that are intended to be taken seriously.

Claims that major industries throughout the American economy are dominated by a few monopolistic corporations are often based on statistics showing that four or five companies produce three-quarters, four-fifths, or some other similar proportion of the industry's output—and that this condition has persisted for decades, suggesting tight control by this in-group. What is often overlooked is that the particular companies constituting this "monopolistic" group are changing.[47] In short, there is competition—and particular businesses are winning and losing in this competition at different times, creating turnover. This simple fact, so damaging to the monopoly hypothesis, is evaded by statistical definition. Those with the alarmist view of a monopolistic economy define the percentage of sales by given businesses as the share of the market they "control." Thus, they are able to say that the top four or five companies "control" most of the business in the industry—turning an *ex post* statistic into an *ex ante* condition. But of course the fact that there is turnover among these companies indicates that no such control exists. Otherwise, monopolistic firms would not allow themselves to be displaced by new competitors.

Perhaps the clearest example of how illusory the "control" of a market can be was a federal case involving a Las Vegas movie-house chain which showed 100 percent of all the first-run movies in that city. The chain was prosecuted under the Sherman Antitrust Act for "monopolization" of its market. However, by the time the case reached the Circuit Court of Appeals, one of the second-run movie chains had begun to show more first-run movies than the statistically defined "monopolist."[48] Obviously, if even 100 percent "control" by statistical definition is not effective, lesser percentages are likely to be even less so.

Much the same implicit assumption of unchanging constituents underlies many discussions of "the rich" and "the poor." Yet studies that follow particular individuals over time have shown that most Americans do not remain in one income bracket for life, or even for as long as a decade.[49] Both the top 20 percent who are often called "the rich" and the bottom 20 percent who are called "the poor" represent a constantly changing set of individuals. A study of income tax returns showed that more than four-fifths of the individuals in the bottom 20 percent of those who filed income tax returns in 1979 were no longer there by 1988. Slightly more had reached the top bracket by 1988 than remained at the bottom.[50] For one thing, individuals are nine years older at the end of nine years, and may well have accumulated experience, skills, seniority, or promotions during that time. Other studies show similar patterns of mobility, though the data and the percentages differ somewhat.

A University of Michigan study, for example, found that less than half of the families followed from 1971 to 1978 remained in the same quintile of the income distribution throughout those years.[51] This turnover of individuals within each bracket may well explain some strange data on those people labeled "the poor." Nearly half of the statistically defined "poor" have air conditioning, more than half own cars, and more than 20,000 "poor" households have their own heated swimming pool or Jacuzzi. Perhaps most revealing, the statistically defined "poor" spend an average of $1.94 for every dollar of income they receive.[52] Clearly, something strange is going on.

Just as people from lower income brackets move up, so people from higher income brackets move down, at least temporarily. Someone in business or the professions who is having an off year financially may receive an income for that year that falls in the lowest bracket. That does not make these individuals poor—except by statistical definition. Such people are unlikely to divest themselves of all the things that go with a middle-class lifestyle, which they will continue to lead as their incomes rebound in subsequent years. Yet the vision of the anointed is cast in such terms as "the poor" and "the rich"—and any statistics which seem to fit the prevailing vision of such categories will be seized upon for that purpose.

In keeping with this vision, the media made much of Congressional Budget Office data that seemed to suggest that the rich were getting richer and the poor were getting poorer during the years of the Reagan administration. This was clearly an "Aha!" statistic, in keeping with what the anointed believed or wanted to believe. Even putting aside the very large question of whether the particular individuals in each of these categories were the same throughout the eight Reagan years, the statistical definitions used systematically understated the economic level of those in the lower income brackets and overstated the economic level of those in the higher brackets. For example, well over $150 billion in government benefits to lower-income people go uncounted in these statistics—more than $11,000 per poor household.[53] At the other end of the income scale, the official data count capital gains in a way virtually guaranteed to show a gain, even when there is a loss, and to exaggerate whatever gains occur.

For example, if someone invests $10,000 and the price level doubles during the years while this investment is being held, then if it is sold for anything less than $20,000 at the higher price level, it is in fact a loss in real terms. Yet if the original investment remains the same in real value by doubling in money value as the price level doubles, the official statistics will show it as a "gain" of $10,000— and will correct for inflation by dividing this by 2 to get a $5,000 gain in real income. With such definitions as these, it is no wonder that the rich are getting richer and the poor are getting poorer, at least on paper. A will always exceed B, if you leave out enough of B and exaggerate A.

One of the offshoots of the preoccupation with "rich" and "poor" has been another definitional catastrophe—"hunger in America." Here many advocacy groups put out many kinds of statistics, designed to get media attention and spread enough alarm to produce public policy favoring whatever they are advocating. The definitions behind their statistics seldom get much scrutiny. One hunger activist, for example, determined how many people were hungry by determining how many were officially eligible for food stamps and then subtracting those who in fact received food stamps. Everyone else was "hungry," by definition. Using this method, he estimated that millions of Americans were hungry and produced documents showing the 150 "hungriest" counties in the United States.

Of these "hungry" counties, the hungriest county of all turned out to be a ranching and farming community where most farmers and ranchers grew their own food, where farm and ranch hands were boarded by their employers, and where only two people in the entire county were on food stamps.[54] Because some people in this county had low money incomes in some years, they were eligible for food stamps, but because they were eating their own food, they did not apply for food stamps—thereby becoming statistically "hungry." Again, studies of actual flesh-and-blood human beings have yielded radically different results from those produced by broad-brush statistical definitions. When the U.S. Department of Agriculture and the Centers for Disease Control examined people from a variety of income levels, they found no evidence of malnutrition among people with poverty-level incomes, nor even any significant difference in the intake of vitamins, minerals, and other nutrients from one income level to another. The only exception was that lower-income women were slightly more likely to be obese.[55]

Such facts have had remarkably little effect on the media's desire to believe that the rich are getter richer, while the poor are getting poorer, and that hunger stalks the less fortunate. A CBS *Evening News* broadcast on March 27, 1991, proclaimed:

> A startling number of American children are in danger of starving . . . one out of eight American children is going hungry tonight.[56]

Dan Rather was not alone in making such proclamations. *Newsweek,* the Associated Press, and the *Boston Globe* were among those who echoed the one-in-eight statistic.[57] Alarming claims that one out of every eight children in America goes to bed hungry each night are like catnip to the media. A professional statistician who looked at the definitions and methods used to generate such numbers might burst out laughing. But it is no laughing matter to the activists and politicians pushing their agenda, and it should be no laughing matter to a society being played for suckers.

One of the common methods of getting alarming statistics is to list a whole string of adverse things, with the strong stuff up front to grab attention and the weak stuff at the end to supply the numbers. A hypothetical model of this kind of reasoning might run as follows: Did you know that 13 million American wives have suffered murder, torture, demoralization, or discomfort at the hands of left-handed husbands? It may be as rare among left-handers as among right-handers for a husband to murder or torture his wife, but if the marriages of southpaws are not pure, unbroken bliss, then their wives must have been at least momentarily discomforted by the usual marital misunderstandings. The number may be even larger than 13 million. Yet one could demonize a whole category of men with statistics showing definitional catastrophes. While this particular example is hypothetical, the pattern is all too real. Whether it is sexual harassment, child abuse, or innumerable other social ills, activists are able to generate alarming statistics by the simple process of listing attention-getting horrors at the beginning of a string of phenomena and listing last those marginal things which in fact supply the bulk of their statistics. A Louis Harris poll, for example, showed that 37 percent of married women are "emotionally abused" and 4 million "physically abused." Both of these include some very serious things—but they also include among "emotional abuse" a husband's stomping out of the room and among "physical abuse" his grabbing his wife.[58] Yet such statistics provide a backdrop against which people like *New York Times* columnist Anna Quindlen can speak of wives' "risk of being beaten bloody" by their husbands.[59] Studies of truly serious violence find numbers less than one-tenth of those being thrown around in the media, in politics, and among radical feminists in academia.[60]

Sometimes definitions are reasonable enough in themselves, but the ever-changing aggregations of individuals who fall within the defined categories play havoc with the conclusions reached from statistics. For example the ever-changing aggregations of individuals

who constitute "the rich" and "the poor"—and all the income brackets in between—raise serious questions about the whole concept of
"class," as it is applied in academia and in the media. Third-party
observers can of course classify anybody in any way they choose,
thereby creating a "class," but if their analysis pretends to have any
relevance to the functioning of the real world, then those "classes"
must bear some resemblance to the actual flesh-and-blood people in
the society.

What sense would it make to classify a man as handicapped
because he is in a wheelchair today, if he is expected to be walking
again in a month, and competing in track meets before the year is
out? Yet Americans are given "class" labels on the basis of their
transient location in the income stream. If most Americans do not
stay in the same broad income bracket for even a decade, their
repeatedly changing "class" makes class itself a nebulous concept.
Yet the intelligentsia are habituated, if not addicted, to seeing the
world in class terms, just as they constantly speak of the deliberate
actions of a personified "society" when trying to explain the results
of systemic interactions among millions of individuals.

Some people do indeed remain permanently at a particular
income level and in a particular social milieu, just as some people
remain in wheelchairs for life. But broad-brush statistics which
count the transient and the permanent the same—as all too many
social statistics do, given the much higher cost of following specific
individuals over time—are potentially very misleading. Moreover,
those on the lookout for "Aha!" statistics often seize upon these
dubious numbers when such statistics seem to confirm the vision of
the anointed.

The simple fact that everyone is getting older all the time means
that many statistics necessarily reflect an ever-changing aggregation of people. Nowhere is this more true than in statistics on
"income distribution" and the "concentration" of wealth. Younger
adults usually earn less than middle-aged people. This fact can
hardly be considered startling, much less sinister. Yet this simple
reality is often ignored by those who automatically treat statistics
on income and wealth differences as differences between classes of

people, rather than differences between age brackets. But it has long been a common pattern that the median incomes of younger individuals have been lower and that people reach their peak earnings years in their mid-forties to mid-fifties. As of 1991, for example, people in the 45- to 54-year-old bracket earned 47 percent more than those in the 25- to 34-year-old bracket. The only age bracket in which one-fifth or more of the people consistently earned more than double the national average income in 1964, 1969, 1974, 1979, 1984, and 1989 was the age bracket from 45 to 54 years old. As of 1989, 28 percent of the people in that age bracket earned more than double the national average income, compared to only 13 percent of people aged 25 to 44.[61] Looked at another way, just over 60 percent of the people in the top 5 percent of income-earners in 1992 were 45 years old or older.[62] This is an age phenomenon which the anointed insist on talking about as if it were a class phenomenon.

In accumulated wealth, the disparity is even greater—again, hardly surprising, given that older people have been accumulating longer. As of 1988, the net worth of households headed by someone in the 55- to 64-year-old bracket averaged more than ten times that for households headed by someone in the under 35 bracket.[63] Despite the enormous influence of age on income and wealth, statistical disparities are often equated with moral inequities when discussing economic differences. Yet the fact that a son in his twenties earns less than his father in his forties is hardly an "inequity" to be "corrected" by the anointed—especially since the son is likely to earn at least as much as his father when he reaches his forties, given the general rise of incomes over time in the American economy. Only by ignoring the age factor can income and wealth statistics be automatically translated into differences between classes.

Also ignored in most discussions of *family* or *household* income statistics—both favorites of those proclaiming vast inequities—is the simple fact that upper-income families contain more people than lower-income families. There are more than half again as many people per household in households earning $75,000 and up as in households earning under $15,000.[64] That is in fact one of the reasons for their being in different brackets, since it is people who earn income, and more paychecks usually mean more income. There are more than twice as many income-earners in households earning $75,000 and up as in households earning less than $15,000.[65] Families in the top 20 percent supply 29 percent of all people who work 50 weeks per year or more, while families in the bottom 20 percent supply just 7 percent of such workers.[66]

A declining size of both families and households over time[67] means that intertemporal trends in household income can be very misleading, as are intergroup comparisons, since household size differs from group to group, as well as over time.[68] Although Americans' median household income was not appreciably higher in 1992 than in 1969,[69] income *per person* rose from $3,007 in 1969 to $15,033 in 1992—approximately a five-fold increase in money income while the price index rose less than four-fold,[70] indicating about a 40 percent increase in real income per capita. The fact that more individuals could afford to have their own households in 1992 than in 1969 was a sign of increased prosperity, not stagnation.

For blacks, whose family and household size have been declining especially sharply, comparisons of family or household incomes are particularly misleading, whether comparing their own progress over time or their income relative to that of whites. For example, the real income per black household rose only 7 percent from 1967 to 1988, but real income per black person rose 81 percent over the same span. On a household basis, blacks' average income was a lower percentage of whites' average income at the end of this period than at the beginning but, on a per person basis, blacks were earning a significantly higher percentage of what whites were earning in 1988.[71]

Needless to say, the anointed much prefer to quote family and household statistics on income, claiming "economic stagnation," the "disappearance of the middle class," and miscellaneous other rhetorical catastrophes. "For all but the top 20 percent," an op-ed column in the *New York Times* said, "income has stagnated." Moreover, this alleged fact was "widely acknowledged" by "politicians, economists and sociologists."[72] That so many such people echoed the same refrain—without bothering to check readily available census data to the contrary—says more about them than about income. Moreover, not all such use of household or family income data can be attributed to statistical naivete. *New York Times* columnist Tom Wicker knew how to use per-capita income statistics when he wished to depict success for the Johnson administration and family income statistics when he wished to depict failure for the Reagan and Bush administrations.[73]

As for the top 20 percent, so often referred to as "the rich," those using "income distribution" statistics seldom say how much hard cash is involved when they talk about "the rich" in either income or wealth terms. In income, a little over $58,000 a year was enough to put a household in the top 20 percent in 1992 and a little under $100,000 was enough to put it in the top 5 percent.[74] Since a household may contain one individual or a large family, even the latter figure may reflect multiple paychecks of only modestly prosperous people. It is a little much for media pundits with six- and seven-figure incomes to be referring to top-20-percent households earning $58,000 a year as "the rich."

Wealth statistics show equally modest sums possessed by the top 20 percent. As of 1988, a net worth of $112,000 was enough to put an individual in the top 20 percent of wealth-holders. That is not $112,000 in the bank but a total of that amount from counting such things as the value of a car and the equity in a home, as well as money in the bank. The value of the individual's own residence was in fact the largest single item in net worth, constituting 43 percent nationally. Even if we count only the top 5 percent of individuals as rich, a statistically "rich" person with a $100,000 income, two children in college, and a mortgage to pay and with federal and state governments together taking nearly half his income, might have real trouble staying financially above water. And if he lost his job, it could spell disaster. There are of course genuinely rich people, just as there are genuinely poor people—but they bear little resemblance to the statistical categories referred by their names.

Those who use existing statistics to advocate government policies designed to produce greater equality in income and wealth seldom bother to consider how much *statistical* "inequality" would exist in

even a 100 percent equal world. Even if every human being in the
whole society had absolutely identical incomes at a given age, the
statistical disparities ("inequities") in income and wealth could still
be huge.

As a simple hypothetical example, imagine that each individual at
age 20 begins his working career earning an annual income of
$10,000 and—for the sake of simplicity in following the arith-
metic—remains at that level until he reaches age 30, when he
receives a $10,000 raise, and that such raises are repeated at each
decade until his 60s, with his income going back to zero when he
retires at age 70. To maintain perfect equality at each age, let us
assume that all these individuals have identical savings patterns.
They each have the same notion as to what their basic needs for
"subsistence" are (in this case, $5,000) and that they will save 10
percent of whatever they earn above that, using the rest to improve
their current standard of living as their incomes rise over time. What
kind of statistics on income and wealth would emerge from this situation of *perfect equality* in income, wealth, and savings habits? Looking at the society as a whole, there would be a remarkable amount of
statistical inequality, as shown in the table below:

AGE	ANNUAL INCOME	"SUBSISTENCE"	ANNUAL SAVINGS	LIFETIME SAVINGS
20	$10,000	$5,000	$ 500	0
30	20,000	5,000	1,500	$ 5,000
40	30,000	5,000	2,500	20,000
50	40,000	5,000	3,500	45,000
60	50,000	5,000	4,500	80,000
70	0	5,000	0	125,000

Note: Savings are given as of the day each individual reaches the age shown
in the Age column. Therefore, the person who has just turned age 20 and
enters the labor force has zero savings, even though the rate at which he
saves out of his income will be $500 per year. Conversely, the person who
has just turned age 70 and retired will have $125,000 in savings accumu-
lated out of past earnings, even though his current income is zero.

Note what statistical disparities ("inequities") there are, even in a hypothetical world of perfect equality over every lifetime. At a given moment—which is how most statistics are collected—the top 17 percent of income earners have five times the income of the bottom 17 percent and the top 17 percent of savers have 25 times the savings of the bottom 17 percent, not even counting those who have zero in either category. If these data were aggregated and looked at in "class" terms, we would find that 17 percent of the people have 45 percent of all the accumulated savings in the whole society. Obviously, there would be ample raw material here for alarums, moral indignation, and the promulgation of "solutions" by the anointed.[75]

In the real world as well, even without ideological bias or manipulation, statistics can be grossly misleading. For example, data from the 1990 census showed that Stanford, California, had one of the highest poverty rates among more than a hundred communities in the large region known as the San Francisco Bay area. Although the community of Stanford coincides with the Stanford University campus, where many faculty members live, it had a higher poverty rate than East Palo Alto, a predominantly low-income minority community not far away.[76] Stanford is the second richest university in the country, its faculty are among the highest paid, and its top administrators have six-figure salaries. How could Stanford have more poverty than a run-down ghetto community?

The answer is that students greatly outnumber professors—and although undergraduates living in dormitories are not counted by the census, graduate students living in their own apartments are.

About half the students at Stanford are graduate students and many of them are married and have children. The cash incomes from their fellowships often come in under the official poverty level for a family. Not only is their period of "poverty" as graduate students one that will end in a few years, leading to professional occupations with professional-level salaries, even during this period of "poverty" they are likely to be far better off than the residents of East Palo Alto. Stanford graduate students live in rent-subsidized housing, located within walking distance of their work and their recreation—much of the latter provided free or at subsidized prices. People in East Palo

Alto must pay transportation costs to and from work, to and from movies, sports events or other recreation, and pay what the market charges for everything from rent to newspapers. At Stanford, three campus newspapers are available free, as are tennis courts, swimming pools, and buses. Movies, lectures, football games, and a world-class hospital are available at less than market rates. In no reasonable sense is there more poverty at Stanford than in East Palo Alto. But statistically there is. This is not a product of deception but of the inherent pitfalls of statistics, made far worse by an attitude of gullible acceptance of numbers as representing human realities.

CORRELATION VERSUS CAUSATION

One of the first things taught in introductory statistics textbooks is that correlation is not causation. It is also one of the first things forgotten. Where there is a substantial correlation between A and B, this might mean that:

1. A causes B.
2. B causes A.
3. Both A and B are results of C or some other combination of factors.
4. It is a coincidence.

Those with the vision of the anointed almost invariably choose one of the first two patterns of causation, the particular direction of causation depending on which is more consistent with that vision—not which is more consistent with empirical facts. As part of that vision, explanations which exempt the individual from personal responsibility for unhappy circumstances in his life are consistently favored over explanations in which the individual's own actions are a major ingredient in unfortunate outcomes. Thus, the correlation between lack of prenatal care and high infant mortality rates was blamed by the media on society's failure to provide enough prenatal care to poor women,[77] rather than blaming those women's failure to behave responsibly—whether in seeking prenatal care, avoiding drugs and alcohol during pregnancy, or in many other evidences of deficient parental responsibility. The fact that there is no such correlation between a lack of prenatal care and high infant mortality rates in groups which traditionally take more care of their children is simply ignored.

A study making comparisons within the black community in Washington found that there was indeed a correlation between prenatal care and low birth weight among infants—but the mothers who failed to get prenatal care were also smokers twice as often as the others and alcohol users six times as often.[78] In other words, the same attitudes and behavior which jeopardized the infants' well-being in one way also jeopardized it in others. Failure to seek prenatal care was a symptom, rather than a cause. In terms of our little scheme above, C caused both A and B. However, this study going completely against the vision of the anointed was almost completely ignored in the national media.

Similarly, the fact that crime and poverty are correlated is automatically taken to mean that poverty causes crime, not that similar attitudes or behavior patterns may contribute to both poverty and crime. For a long time it was automatically assumed among social reformers that slums were "nurseries of crime." In other words, the correlation between bad housing and high crime rates was taken to mean that the former caused the latter—not that both reflected similar attitudes and behavior patterns. But the vision of the anointed has survived even after massive programs of government-provided housing have led to these brand-new housing projects quickly degenerating into new slums and becoming centers of escalating crime. Likewise, massive increases in government spending on children during the 1960s were accompanied by falling test scores, a doubling of the teenage suicide and homicide rates, and a doubling of the share of births to unwed mothers.[79] Yet, during the 1980s, such social pathologies were attributed to cutbacks in social programs under the Reagan administration[80]—to "neglect," as Marian Wright Edelman of the Children's Defense Fund put it.[81] The fact that the same kinds of social deterioration were going on during a decade (the 1960s) when government spending on programs for children was rapidly escalating, as well as during a decade (the 1980s) when it was not, simply did not matter to those for whom "investment" in social programs was axiomatically taken to be the magic key.

In general, where a correlation goes directly counter to the vision of the anointed—drastically fewer urban riots during administrations which opposed the "war on poverty" approach—it is simply ignored by those seeking "Aha!" statistics. Likewise ignored is the continued escalation of venereal diseases, long after "sex education" has become too pervasive for ignorance to be blamed, except by those for whom the vision of the anointed is an axiom, rather than a hypothesis.

While Chapter 2 showed repeated examples of policies of the anointed being followed by dramatically worsening conditions, it is not necessary here to claim that statistics prove that these various policies—the "war on poverty," sex education, changes in criminal justice procedures—caused the disasters which followed. It would be sufficient to show that the promised benefits never materialized. A consistent record of failure is only highlighted by the additional fact that things got worse. Conceivably, other factors may have been behind these disasters. But to have to repeatedly invoke unsubstantiated claims that other factors were responsible is to raise the question whether these other factors have not become another *deus ex machina* called upon in desperation to rescue predictions that began with such utter certainty and such utter disdain for any alternative views. Moreover, those with alternative views often predicted the very disasters that materialized.

"RACIAL" DIFFERENCES

As already noted in various examples, many differences between races are often automatically attributed to race or to racism. In the past, those who believed in the genetic inferiority of some races were prone to see differential outcomes as evidences of differential natural endowments of ability. Today, the more common non sequitur is that such differences reflect biased perceptions and discriminatory treatment by others. A third possibility—that there are different proportions of people with certain attitudes and attributes in different groups—has received far less attention, though this is consistent with a substantial amount of data from countries around the world. One of the most obvious of these kinds of differences is that there are different proportions of each group in different age brackets. Moreover, income differences between age brackets are comparable to income differences between the races. This of course does not mean that age differences explain everything, but it does suggest why the automatic assumption that racism explains racial disparities cannot be uncritically accepted either.

Different racial and ethnic groups not only vary in which proportions fall into which age brackets but vary as well in which proportions fall into various marital and other social conditions—and these in turn likewise have profound effects on everything from income to infant mortality to political opinions. As far back as 1969, black males who came from homes where there were newspapers, magazines, and library cards had the same incomes as whites from similar homes and with the same number of years of schooling.[82] In the 1970s, black husband-and-wife families outside the South earned as much as white husband-and-wife families outside the South.[83] By 1981, for the country as a whole, black husband-and-wife families where both were college educated and both working earned slightly *more* than white families of the same description.[84]

With differing proportions of the black and white populations living in husband-and-wife families, and differing proportions coming from homes where library cards and the like were common, the economic equality within such subsets did not make a substantial difference in the overall racial disparities in incomes. However, such facts do have a bearing on the larger question as to how much of that income disparity is due to employer discrimination or racism.

To a racist, the fact that a particular black individual comes from a husband-and-wife family or has a library card makes no real difference, even if the racist bothers to find out such things. The equality of income achieved within these subcategories of blacks suggests that racism is less of a factor in the overall differences than has been supposed—and that cultural values or behavioral differences are more of a factor.

Other studies reinforce the conclusion that varying proportions of people with particular values and behavior from one group to another make substantial differences in economic and social outcomes. Although the poverty rate among blacks in general is higher than that among whites in general, the poverty rate among families headed by black married couples has for years been consistently lower than the poverty rate among white, female-headed families, the latter living in poverty about twice as often as black intact families.[85] With infant mortality as well, although blacks in general have about twice the infant mortality rate of whites in general, black married women with only a high school education have lower infant mortality rates than white unwed mothers with a college education.[86] In short, race makes less difference than whether or not there are two parents. The real-life Murphy Browns are worse off economically than if they were black married women with less education, and their children are more likely to die in infancy.

Even as regards attitudes on political issues, family differences are greater than racial differences, according to a 1992 poll. Black married couples with children were even more opposed to homosexual marriage and to the legalization of marijuana than white married couples were.[87] Many of the "racial" differences based on gross statistics are shown by a finer breakdown to be differences between people with different values and lifestyles, who are differing proportions of different racial populations. Where the values and lifestyles are comparable, the economic and social outcomes have tended to be comparable. But to admit this would be to destroy a whole framework of assumptions behind massive social programs—and destroy with it a whole social vision that is prevalent among political and intellectual elites. Such finer breakdowns receive very little attention in the media, in politics, or in academia, where gross statistics continue to be cited in support of the vision of the anointed.

THE "DISAPPEARANCE" OF TRADITIONAL FAMILIES

Among the many unexamined "facts" endlessly repeated throughout the media are that (1) "half of all marriages end in divorce"[88] and (2) the traditional family with both parents raising their children is now the exception rather than the rule. Both "facts" are wrong and reflect an ignorance of statistics, compounded by a gullible acceptance of those beliefs which are consonant with the vision of the anointed.

Marriage Patterns

Washington Post writer Haynes Johnson, Texas governor Ann Richards, and feminist writer Barbara Ehrenreich are just some of the many to repeat the claim that half of all marriages end in divorce.[89] In a given year, the number of divorces may well be half as large as the number of marriages that year, but this is comparing apples and oranges. The marriages being counted are only those marriages taking place within the given year, while the divorces that year are from marriages that took place over a period of decades. To say that half of all marriages end in divorce, based on such statistics, would be like saying that half the population died last year if deaths were half as large as births. Just as most people were neither born nor died last year, so most marriages did not begin or end last year. Yet, on the basis of such gross misconceptions of statistics, the anointed not only assume airs of superiority but claim the right to shape public policy.

According to census data for 1992, 11 percent of all adults who had ever been married were currently in the status of divorced persons.[90] If 50 percent overstates the divorce rate, 11 percent does not include people who had been divorced but were now remarried, or those who were never married. However, these census statistics are relevant to the claim that traditional marriages are disappearing, for remarriages are still marriages. Married couples outnumbered unmarried couples by about 54 million to 3 million.[91] Most of the people who had never married were under the age of 25. Marriage statistics, which count everyone over the age of 15, of course include many people whom no one would expect to be married. But, by the time people reach middle age, the great majority have been married. In the 45- to 54-year-old bracket, for example, people who were married and currently living with their spouse outnumbered the

never-married by more than fifteen to one.[92] That is not even counting those people who had been married but were now separated, widowed, or divorced. Traditional marriages have become an anachro-
nism only in the vision of the anointed. People are getting married
later—about five years later, as compared to 1890[93]—but they are
still getting married.

Within these general patterns there are substantial differences
between racial groups which should not be ignored. However, what
should also not be ignored is how relatively recent these racial differences are. In every decennial census from 1920 through 1960,
inclusive, at least 60 percent of all black males from age 15 on up
were currently married. Moreover, the difference between black and
white males in this respect was never as great as 5 percentage
points during this entire era. Yet, by 1980, less than half of all black
males in these age brackets were currently married—and the gap
between black and white males was 17 percentage points.[94] By
1992, that gap had widened to 21 percentage points.[95] Like other
negative social trends—in crime, welfare dependency, venereal disease, and educational test scores, for example—this trend represented a reversal of a previous positive trend. From the census of
1890 through the census of 1950, there was an increase in the proportion of both men and women currently married, among both
blacks and whites.[96]

"Ozzie and Harriet" Families

A member of the Institute for Human Development at the University of California at Berkeley voiced a widespread view among the
intelligentsia when she said:

> After three decades of social upheaval, the outlines of a new family
> are beginning to emerge. It's more diverse, more fragile, more fluid
> than in the past.[97]

This was taken as representing the "passing of the Ozzie and Harriet family."[98]

While the proportion of children living with both parents has been declining over the decades, still the 1992 statistics from a census survey showed that more than two-thirds—71 percent, in fact—of all people under the age of 18 were still living with both their parents. Fewer than one percent were living with people who were not relatives. In particular segments of the population, especially in urban ghettos, the situation was drastically different. Nationwide, a majority—54 percent—of all black children were living only with their mothers in 1992. However, this was not a "legacy of slavery" as sometimes claimed. As recently as 1970, a majority of black children were still living with both parents.[99] The sharp decline in marriage rates among black males in recent decades has obviously taken its toll on black children being raised without a father.

If most American children are still living with both parents, how can the traditional or Ozzie and Harriet family be said to be "passing"? Like so many statistical misconceptions, this one depends on confusing an instantaneous picture with an ongoing process. Because human beings go through a life cycle, the most traditional families—indeed, Ozzie and Harriet themselves—would be counted statistically as not being a traditional family. Before Ozzie met Harriet, and even after they married, they would not be counted in the Census Bureau's "Married Couple Family with Own Children Under 18" category until in fact they had their first child. In later years, after the children were grown and gone, they would again no longer be in that statistical category. Moreover, in old age, when one spouse dies first the other would obviously no longer be counted as a married couple. What this means is that innumerable people who have had the most traditional pattern of marriage and child rearing would at various times in their lives be counted in statistics as *not* in the category popularly known as the "traditional family" of parents and their children. Depending on their life span and the span of their childbearing years, some individuals in the most traditional families would be counted as *not* being in such families for most of their adult lives.

Because most 16-year-olds have not yet married, because married couples do not continue to have children living with them all their lives, and because every elderly widow or widower does not remarry, does not mean that the traditional family has been repudiated—except perhaps by some of the anointed.

The family is inherently an obstacle to schemes for central control of social processes. Therefore the anointed necessarily find themselves repeatedly on a collision course with the family. It is not a matter of any subjective animus on their part against families. The anointed may in fact be willing to shower government largess upon families, as they do on other social entities. But the preservation of the family as an *autonomous decision-making unit* is incompatible with the third-party decision making that is at the heart of the vision of the anointed.

This is not a peculiarity of our times or of American society. Friedrich Engels' first draft of the *Communist Manifesto* included a deliberate undermining of family bonds as part of the Marxian political agenda,[100] though Marx himself was politically astute enough to leave that out of the final version. Nor has this war against the autonomy of the family been confined to extremists. The modern Swedish welfare state has made it illegal for parents to spank their own children and, in the United States, a variety of so-called "children's advocates" have urged a variety of government interventions in the raising of children[101]—going beyond cases of neglect or abuse, which are already illegal. In New Zealand, a whole campaign of scare advertisements during the 1980s promoted the claim that one out of eight fathers sexually abused their own daughters, when in fact research showed that not even one out of a hundred did so.[102]

As in so many other areas, the ascendancy of the vision of the family which now prevails among the anointed began in the 1960s. A 1966 article in the *Journal of Social Issues* epitomized the rationalistic view that the family was just one of a number of alternative lifestyles and an arbitrary "social preference" which defined "illegitimacy" as a social problem:

> The societal preference for procreation only within marriage, or some form of socially recognized and regulated relationship between the sexes, is reinforced by laws and customs which legitimize coition as well as births and denote some responsibility for the rearing of chil-

dren. It is within this context that value judgements may be regarded as the initial and formal causes of social problems. Without the value judgments which initially effected and now continue to support the legitimation of coition and births, illicit parenthood would not be regarded as a problem. In fact, by definition, it would not exist.[103]

Thus the "disproportionate publicity and public concern about teen-age unwed mothers"[104] is simply a matter of how people choose to look at things. As in the case of early discussions of rising crime rates, it was suggested that "more inclusive and improved counting of non-white illicit births" may have caused a statistical change without a real change.[105] In short, everything depended on how we chose to look at things, rather than on an intractable reality. Teenage pregnancy was only a socially defined problem in this view, while "the more generic problem of *unwanted pregnancy*"[106] was what needed to be addressed. Here "needs for counseling"[107] were taken as axiomatic and "it is quite pointless to continue debating whether youth should receive sex education"[108] for this too was axiomatic and inevitable, with only the particular channels of this education being open to rational discussion. In a similar vein, a later publication of the Centers for Disease Control declared that "the marital status of the mother confers neither risk nor protection to the infant; rather, the principal benefits of marriage to infant survival are economic and social support."[109] This rationalistic picture overlooked what is so often overlooked, that different kinds of people have different values and behavior patterns—and that these values and behaviors have enormous impacts on outcomes. But to say this would be to get into the forbidden realm of personal responsibility and away from the vision of a benighted "society" needing to be reformed by the anointed, who reject "consensus romanticism about the family,"[110] as it was put by Hillary Rodham (later Clinton).

CHAPTER 4

THE IRRELEVANCE
OF EVIDENCE

> *Facts are stubborn things; and whatever may be
> our wishes, our inclinations, or the dictates of our
> passions, they cannot alter the state of facts and
> evidence. . . .*
>
> —John Adams[1]

Factual evidence and logical arguments are often not merely lacking
but ignored in many discussions by those with the vision of the
anointed. Much that is said by the anointed in the outward form of an
argument turns out not to be arguments at all. Often the logical structure of an argument is replaced by preemptive rhetoric or, where an
argument is made, its validity remains unchecked against any evidence, even when such evidence is abundant. Evidence is often particularly abundant when it comes to statements about history, yet the
anointed have repeatedly been as demonstrably wrong about the past
as about the present or the future—and as supremely confident.

TEFLON PROPHETS

One of the more remarkable feats of those with the vision of the
anointed has been the maintenance of their reputations in the face of
repeated predictions that proved to be wrong by miles. Examples are
all too abundant. A few of the more obviously false but teflon
prophets include such individuals as John Kenneth Galbraith and
Paul Ehrlich, and such institutional prophets as the Club of Rome

and Worldwatch Institute. In each case, the utter certainty of their predictions has been matched by the utter failure of the real world to cooperate—and by the utter invulnerability of their reputations.

John Kenneth Galbraith

The best known of Professor Galbraith's many books has been *The Affluent Society*, which popularized a previously arcane adjective. One of the central themes of this book was that the rising prosperity of relatively recent times had banished from the political agenda and from public concern questions about the distribution of income.

According to Professor Galbraith, "few things are more evident in modern social history than the decline of interest in inequality as an economic issue."[2] This "decline in concern for inequality" was not due to any successful egalitarian redistributive measures, according to Galbraith, but was instead a factor in the absence of such measures.[3] Inequality had simply "faded as an issue."[4] Galbraith did not agree with this trend and, in fact, cited some of the usual misleading statistics on *family* income[5] to show a social problem. But the "poverty at the base of the income pyramid" simply "goes largely unnoticed," while "increasing aggregate output" has become "an alternative to redistribution" and "inequality has been declining in urgency."[6]

Since 1958, when this was written, there have followed decades of some of the most intense preoccupation with inequality and income distribution in the history of the republic. From the political rostrum to the pulpit, from the mass media to academic journals, and from the halls of Congress to the chambers of the Supreme Court, "equality" has been the cry of the times.

Another theme appearing in *The Affluent Society*, and amplified in Galbraith's later book *The New Industrial State*, was that big corporations had become immune to the marketplace. "The riskiness of modern corporate life is in fact the harmless conceit of the modern corporate executive," according to Galbraith, for "no large United States corporation, which is also large in its industry, has failed or been seriously in danger of insolvency in many years."[7] General

Motors is "large enough to control its markets"[8] according to Galbraith—but not according to Toyota, Honda, and other Japanese automakers who proceeded to take away substantial parts of that market in the years that followed this pronouncement. By the early 1990s, Honda produced the largest selling car in the United States and Toyota produced more cars in Japan than General Motors did in the United States.

Since Galbraith's sweeping pronouncements about corporate invulnerability were written, the country's leading magazine, *Life*, stopped publishing and was resurrected later as a shadow of its former self. The W. T. Grant chain of retail stores, once a pioneer in the industry, went out of existence—as did the Graflex Corporation, which had dominated the market for press cameras for decades. Pan American was perhaps the best known of the many airlines that folded. Venerable newspapers were obliterated in cities across the country. The Chrysler Corporation was saved from extinction only by a government bailout. Despite Galbraith's later assurance in *The New Industrial State* of "the impregnable position of the successful corporate management,"[9] corporate takeovers and corporate shake-ups spread throughout the American economy, with heads rolling in corporate suites across the land. Conversely, despite Galbraith's sneers at the idea of a lone entrepreneur starting up a pioneering new company,[10] Steve Jobs created Apple computers and Bill Gates created the Microsoft Corporation, both companies rising into the Fortune 500 inside of a decade, with both men becoming multibillionaires. Nor were these isolated flukes. Nearly half the firms in the Fortune 500 in 1980 were no longer there just ten years later.[11]

None of this has made a dent in Galbraith's reputation, his self-confidence, or his book sales. For no one has been more in tune with the vision of the anointed or more dismissive of "the conventional wisdom"—another term he popularized as a designation for traditional beliefs and values. If there is any single moral to the Galbraith story, it might be that if one is "politically correct," being factually incorrect doesn't matter. But he is just one of many examples of the same principle.

Paul Ehrlich

While John Kenneth Galbraith may be the best known of those who are often wrong but never in doubt, Paul Ehrlich is perhaps preeminent for having been wrong by the widest margins, on the most varied subjects—and for maintaining his reputation untarnished through it all. The prologue to his best-known book, *The Population Bomb*, first published in 1968, begins with these words:

> The battle to feed all of humanity is over. In the 1970s and 1980s hundreds of millions of people will starve to death in spite of any crash programs embarked upon now.[12]

Now that the 1970s and 1980s have come and gone, it is clear that nothing faintly resembling Ehrlich's prediction has come to pass. Moreover, such local famines as struck sporadically had nothing to do with overpopulation and everything to do with the disruption of local food distribution systems, due usually to war or other manmade disasters. As with so many other predictions of catastrophe—"famine and ecocatastrophe" in Professor Ehrlich's words[13]—there is, as the bottom line, a power agenda by which the vision of the anointed is to be imposed on the masses. According to Ehrlich, we must "take immediate action" for "population control"—"hopefully through changes in our value system, but by compulsion if voluntary methods fail."[14] The supreme irony is that this campaign of hysteria over population came at a time when the world's population growth rate was declining,[15] both in the industrial and the nonindustrial world,[16] when producers of toys, diapers, and baby food were diversifying into other fields,[17] and when hospital maternity wards were being closed or were being used for nonmaternity patients, in order to fill the empty beds.[18]

The Population Bomb is a textbook example of a scare book in another way—the unbridled extrapolation. As Ehrlich says, "the population will have to stop growing sooner or later"[19] or a variety of catastrophic scenarios will unfold. By the same token, if the temperature has risen by 10 degrees since dawn today, an extrapolation will show that we will all be burned to a crisp before the end of the month, if this trend continues. Extrapolations are the last refuge of a groundless argument. In the real world, everything depends on where we are now, at what rate we are moving, in what direction, and—most important of all—what is the specific nature of the process generating the numbers being extrapolated. Obviously, if the rise in temperature is being caused by the spinning of the earth taking us into the sunlight, then the continuation of that spinning will take us out of the sunlight again and cause temperatures to fall when night comes. But both the logical and the empirical test are consistently avoided by the "population explosion" theorists.

Contrary to their theory of a declining standard of living with population growth, the standard of living was rising when Malthus first wrote, two hundred years ago. It rose during his lifetime and it has been rising since then. The population bombers cannot name a single country where the standard of living was higher when its population was half of what it is today. Instead, they must resort to extrapolations and ominous rhetoric about "standing room only" and the like. In reality, the entire population of the world today could be housed in the state of Texas, in single-story, single-family houses—four people to a house—and with a typical yard around each home.[20] Moreover, the most thinly populated continent—Africa—is also the poorest. Japan has more than twice the population density of many African nations and more than ten times the population density of sub-Saharan Africa as a whole.[21] In medieval Europe as well, the poorest parts of the continent—notably Eastern Europe and the Balkans—were also the most thinly populated. A large influx of Germans, Flemings, and other Western Europeans cleared and developed much of the fertile but empty land of Eastern Europe, raising the economic level of the region.[22] For the nations of the world, there is no correlation between population density and income level. While there are costs associated with crowding, there are other and huge costs associated with trying to provide electricity, running water, sewage systems, and other services and infrastructure in a thinly populated area, where the cost per person is vastly greater than in a more densely populated area.

Is there some ultimate limit to how many people can live on the planet? Probably. But to see how meaningless and misleading such a question is, consider the fear of the young John Stuart Mill that a finite number of musical notes meant that there was some ultimate limit to the amount of music possible.[23] Despite the young Mill's melancholy over this, at that point Tchaikovsky and Brahms had not yet been born, nor jazz even conceived. Nor was there any sign that we are running out of music more than a century later.

The starvation of "hundreds of millions" is not the only Ehrlich prediction to have missed by miles. He was equally certain, equally wrong, and equally unblemished by his predictions about the exhaustion of natural resources. In 1980, economics professor Julian Simon challenged anyone to a bet as to whether various natural resources would or would not become more expensive over time—as would happen if they were in fact becoming more scarce. Professor Simon offered to allow anyone to pick any resources he wished, and any time period he wished, in which to test the theory that resources were becoming more scarce or approaching exhaustion. In October 1980, Ehrlich and other like-minded predictors of natural resource exhaustion bet $1,000 that a given collection of natural resources would cost more in ten years than when the bet was made. The Ehrlich group chose copper, tin, nickel, tungsten, and chrome as the natural resources whose combined prices (in real terms) would be higher after a decade of their continued extraction from the earth. In reality, not only did the combined prices of these resources fall, *every single resource selected by Ehrlich and his colleagues declined in price.*[24]

How could a decade of extracting these minerals from the earth not lead to a greater scarcity and hence a higher price? Because supply and demand are based on *known reserves* and these can just as easily increase as decrease. For example, the known reserves of petroleum in the world were more than twice as large in 1993 as they were in 1969, despite massive usage of oil around the world during the intervening decades.[25] One of the fatal flaws in the vision of the anointed is the implicit assumption that knowledge is far more extensive and less costly than it is. In some abstract sense, there is indeed a fixed amount of any natural resource in the earth and usage obviously reduces it. But no one knows what that fixed amount is and, since the process of discovery is costly, it will never pay anyone to discover that total amount. Depending on various economic factors, such as the interest rate on money borrowed to finance exploration, there is a variable limit to how much it pays to discover as of any given time—no matter how many more untold centuries' worth of supply may exist. By dividing the currently known reserves by the annual rate of usage, it is always possible to come up with a quotient—and to use that quotient to claim that in ten years, fifteen years, or some other time period we will "run out" of coal, petroleum, or some other natural resource.

A textbook example of this kind of hysteria by arithmetic was provided by Vance Packard in his 1960 best-seller, *The Waste Makers:*

> In oil, the United States is clearly approaching depletion. At today's rate of consumption—not tomorrow's—the United States has proved reserves of oil sufficient to meet the nation's needs for thirteen years.[26]

When this was published, the proved reserves of petroleum in the United States were not quite 32 billion barrels. At the end of the allotted 13 years, the proved reserves were more than 36 billion barrels.[27] Nevertheless, the simple formula of hysteria-by-quotient has been creating alarms—and best-selling books—for more than a century. Meanwhile, known reserves of many vital natural resources have been increasing, driving down their prices.

MISCELLANEOUS MISTAKEN MESSIAHS

Ralph Nader

There is perhaps no more sacrosanct figure among the contemporary anointed than Ralph Nader, usually identified as the premier "consumer advocate." Yet one of Nader's first published writings, in *The Nation* magazine in 1959, revealed the mind-set behind consumer advocacy when he said, "the consumer must be protected at times from his own indiscretion and vanity."[28] Once again, the role of the anointed was to preempt other people's decisions, for their own good.

The book that put Ralph Nader on the map—*Unsafe at Any Speed*, denouncing the safety records of automobiles in general and the Corvair in particular—also exhibited another characteristic of the anointed, the ignoring of trade-offs. Nader's thesis was that automobile safety was deliberately being neglected by the car manufacturers in favor of other considerations, such as styling and cost. He then proceeded to enumerate the safety deficiencies of various cars, but especially the Corvair, and mentioned gory accidents presumably caused by such deficiencies.

A moment's reflection on the implications of trade-offs makes it clear that *inevitably*, beyond some point, safety will be sacrificed with *any* product in the sense that unlimited sacrifices of other features— including affordability—for the sake of safety would of course make that particular product somewhat safer. If the paper on which these words are written were made flameproof, that might well save someone a burn somewhere or perhaps even prevent a house from catching fire. Similarly, automobiles could of course be built to tank-like sturdiness at a sufficiently high price, which is to say, by making them unaffordable to many or most people. Carrying safety-first to such extremes on all the millions of products in the economy would raise costs in general and correspondingly lower the real income and living standard of the public. Nor is it clear that this would even increase safety, on net balance, since higher real incomes reduce death rates, whether one compares rich and poor in a given society or wealthy and poverty-stricken societies internationally.

Sacrificing real income for the sake of reducing remote dangers is a trade-off that would have to be justified on its merits in each specific case—if one were thinking in terms of trade-offs. But Nader scorned what he called "abject worship of that bitch-goddess, cost reduction."[29] The very notion of trade-offs was dismissed as "auto industry cant."[30] *Unsafe at Any Speed* is a classic of propaganda in its ability to use distracting or dismissive rhetoric to evade a need to confront opposing arguments with evidence or logic. Throughout the book, automobile manufacturers were denounced for such things as "neglect" of safety,[31] "industrial irresponsibility,"[32] and "unconscionable" behavior.[33] To Nader, "safety features lying unused on the automobile companies' shelves"[34] were virtual proof that they should have been used. Cost considerations—including the costs of changing the overall design of a car to accommodate these safety features, as well as the direct costs of the specific features themselves—were dismissed out of hand by Nader. Sometimes he counted only the modest cost of the particular feature in isolation,[35] but at other times he brushed aside the effect of design changes that might make the car less attractive to the consumer. The design engineer was considered by Nader to "shirk his professional duty" when he considered "cost reduction and style."[36] Automobile company representatives who pointed out that the industry cannot produce features that the consumers do not want, or are unwilling to pay for, were scorned by Nader for treating the issue as "wholly one of personal consumer taste instead of objective scientific study."[37]

Like so many who invoke the name and the mystique of science in order to override other people's choices, Nader offered remarkably little hard data to back up his claims, whether on the overall safety of the automobile over time, or of American automobiles versus cars from other countries (including socialist countries where "corporate greed" was presumably not a problem), or of the Corvair compared to similar cars of its era. The whole issue was conceived in categorical rather than incremental or comparative terms.

Despite Nader's argument that automakers paid little attention to safety, motor vehicle death rates per million passenger miles fell over the years from 17.9 in 1925 to 5.5 in 1965, the year *Unsafe at Any Speed* was published, and this trend continued to a rate of 4.9 five years later,[38] after federal legislation on automobile safety, inspired by Nader and his followers. Naderites and the federal safety regulations they inspired have been widely credited with subsequent reductions in auto fatality rates,[39] usually by those who are either unaware of, or who choose to ignore, the long-standing downward trend which had already produced a reduction of two-thirds in fatalities per million passenger miles before Nader ever appeared on the scene. Moreover, the earlier reductions in automobile fatalities occurred while the average highway speed of cars was increasing.[40] In short, the era of corporate greed and the presumably ignorant and helpless consumer saw dramatic improvements in safety, before the anointed came to the rescue.

As for the Corvair, it did indeed have safety problems growing out of its rear-engine design. It also had safety advantages growing out of that same design, notably better traction on slippery surfaces. The salient question is whether *on net balance* it was any less safe than similar cars of its era. Extensive tests by the U.S. Department of Transportation showed that it was not.[41] An independent academic researcher likewise noted, along with the Corvair's greater tendency to have certain kinds of accidents, "its less than average number of accidents in other categories."[42] In other words, it was a trade-off.

Although Nader represented the Corvair as a car difficult to handle,[43] Consumers Union's 1960 evaluation of the Corvair noted a "sandstorm of controversy" about the steering of rear-engine cars but concluded that "prospective buyers need not be unduly concerned."[44] A woman who was both a race car driver and a writer on automobiles was quoted against the Corvair in Nader's book *Unsafe at Any Speed* but, when questioned by Senator Abraham Ribicoff's congressional committee, she replied that the Corvair she drove "was one of the sweetest handling, most pleasant-to-drive production cars I had experienced." Moreover, she added, the way that Nader had quoted from her article "led me to suspect that he didn't know too much about cars."[45] Another automotive expert interviewed by the Ribicoff committee, at the suggestion of a member of one of Nader's organizations, said that he not only found the Corvair a safe-handling vehicle but even had sufficient confidence in its ease of handling to buy one for his own daughter, whose left hand was paralyzed by polio. This confidence was vindicated later, when a tire blew out while his daughter was driving the Corvair at over 80 miles per hour and she was still able to bring it to a safe stop.[46]

Whatever the outcome of the battle of facts, Nader won the battle of the media and the battle of politics. The alarm spread about the

Corvair caused sales to drop to the point where General Motors discontinued the car. This alarm also promoted more federal intervention in the design and manufacturing of automobiles. This episode also promoted the emergence of "consumer advocates" in general on the national scene to make similar claims about other products and to spawn more federal legislation.

The technique of many "consumer advocates" remained that pioneered by Ralph Nader in *Unsafe at Any Speed:* sweeping charges, selective examples, selective quotes, purple prose, dismissals of trade-offs, and an attribution of malign or irresponsible behavior to others. "Doctors, lawyers, engineers and other specialists have failed in their primary professional ethic,"[47] Nader's book charged, and the answer was collectivized decisions by "society."[48] His earlier article in *The Nation* likewise charged "widespread amorality among our scholarly elite" because "researchers are reluctant to stray from their scholarly and experimental pursuits."[49] In other words, it is "amoral" to disagree with Ralph Nader on the role of a scholar.

One of the problems faced by "consumer advocates" in general is how to make the consumers' own preferences disappear from the argument, since consumer sovereignty conflicts with moral surrogacy by the anointed. It is also not good politics to attack consumers. Here too *Unsafe at Any Speed* showed how artful phrasing can make the consumer's preferences evaporate from the discussion, as a prelude to making his autonomy disappear in laws proposed by so-called "consumer advocates." Arguing that the Corvair would be safer with higher pressure in the tires, Nader condemned the engineers for having "succumbed to the great imperative—a soft ride."[50] Clearly this was only the consumer's imperative. General Motors would not make one dollar more or one dollar less at different tire pressures unless the consumers preferred one kind of ride to another, though Nader chose to depict this consumer preference as "the car makers' obsession with the soft ride."[51] Displacing responsibility from the consumer to the producer has been a crucial part of consumer advocacy. "The American automobile is produced exclusively to the standards which the manufacturer decides to establish," according to Nader,[52] though what the automaker actually decides, with millions of dollars at stake, is far less likely to reflect some personal caprice than what consumers are apt to buy.

What the Nader approach boils down to is that third parties should preempt the consumer's choice as to whether he wants to sacrifice a comfortable ride in order to make a remote danger slightly more remote. Considering that the tiredness that comes from uncomfortable rides can also affect safety, it is by no means obvious that there would be greater safety on net balance by creating a harder ride.

In a sense, however, discussions of facts and logic are irrelevant. Nader achieved his political objectives, established his own image, and put his targets on the defensive. Nader's image has been aptly described by a biographer as "a combination of the best qualities of Lincoln of Illinois and David of 1 Samuel 17."[53] A somewhat different view of Nader was offered by a congressional committee chairman quoted in *Newsweek:* "Ralph's a bully and know-it-all, consumed by certainty and frequently in error."[54] It is one of the signs of Nader's continuing sacred status that this statement was made anonymously.

Gasoline Price Control and Decontrol

The confidence of the anointed in their own articulated "reason" has as its counterpoint their complete distrust in systemic social processes, operating without their guidance and intervention.[55] Thus the operation of a free market is suspect in their eyes, no matter how often it works, and government control of economic activity appears rational, no matter how many times it fails. As bitterly resented as the gasoline lines of the 1970s were under government price controls, there were widespread predictions of skyrocketing gasoline prices if these controls were abolished. For example, Congressman John Dingell considered it "obvious that gasoline could reach at least $2 a gallon after decontrol." So did Senator Howard Metzenbaum. Lester Brown of Worldwatch Institute declared that "gas will cost $2 per gallon within a few years and $3 per gallon during the vehicle's lifetime." Senator Dale Bumpers likewise predicted, "gasoline will soon go to $3 a gallon."[56]

Airs of condescension pervaded criticisms of those who believed otherwise and who relied on a free market. For example, the *New York Times* commented on Ronald Reagan's views:

> Ronald Reagan brushed aside energy issues during the campaign, insisting that shortages could be overcome by unleashing private enterprise. But not even his most fervent supporters in the energy business share that optimism. Virtually all private forecasts predict declining domestic oil production and liquid fuel shortages during the next decade.[57]

In a similar vein, President Jimmy Carter said:

> There is a dwindling supply of energy sources. The prices are going to rise in the future no matter who is President, no matter what party occupies the administration in Washington, no matter what we do.[58]

President Carter blamed the benighted masses for not facing up to the situation as seen by the anointed. "The American people," he said, "have absolutely refused to accept a simple fact. We have an energy crisis. . . . We are going to have less oil to burn and we are going to have to pay more for it."[59] *New York Times* columnist Tom Wicker pronounced Carter's statements to be "unquestioned truths."[60]

Disregarding the anointed, in this as in other things, the newly elected President Ronald Reagan issued an Executive Order during the first month of his administration, ending oil price controls. Within four months, the average price of a gallon of unleaded gasoline fell from $1.41 to 86 cents.[61] Refineries' average cost of buying crude oil fell from more than $30 a barrel in 1981 to less than half of that by March 1986.[62] Contrary to predictions of oil or gasoline shortages by President Carter's energy secretary James Schlesinger, by Senator Bumpers, and others,[63] the world's known crude oil reserves were 41 percent higher at the end of the decade of the 1980s than at the beginning.[64] In the post-Reagan years, the low price of gasoline made it a special target for taxation, which artificially forced up its price at the pump, though still not to the levels predicted when decontrol came in a decade earlier. The real cost of the gasoline itself—net of taxes and adjusted for inflation—reached an all-time low in 1993.[65]

How much the hysteria over oil price decontrol represented genuine misunderstandings of economics, and how much a cynical scare tactic to get more government control, may never be known. However, many of those pushing continued government control of oil prices were longtime promoters of other extensions of government power. Among these was Senator Edward Kennedy, who said: "We must adopt a system of gasoline rationing without delay," in "a way that demands a fair sacrifice from all Americans."[66] Needless to say, the anointed would define what was "fair" for others, while enhancing their own power, as distinguished from letting the marketplace reduce the sacrifice for everyone with lower prices.

The Club of Rome

Perhaps the most famous mistaken prediction in recent times was the "Club of Rome" prediction that economic growth would grind to a halt, around the world, during the latter part of the twentieth century. Both industrial output per capita and food per capita were to decline, along with a long-run decline in natural resources.[67] In this model the "death rate rises abruptly from pollution and from lack of food."[68] Like so many wrong economic predictions, it was buttressed with all sorts of graphs, tables, and mathematical models. It also relied on extrapolations—and on putting the burden of proof on others: "In postulating any different outcome from the one shown in table 3, one must specify which of these factors is likely to change, by how much, and when."[69] In other words, you cannot say that the emperor has no clothes until you have designed a whole new alternative wardrobe.

Just how threadbare the current wardrobe was was demonstrated by resort to the ultimate finiteness argument which misled John Stuart Mill about music and Paul Ehrlich about population:

> There may be much disagreement with the statement that population and capital growth must stop *soon*. But virtually no one will argue that material growth on this planet can go on forever.[70]

Abstract ultimate limits are neither the theoretical nor the practical issue. What the Club of Rome report sought was collective coercive powers *now* to head off some impending catastrophe. They were discussing such scenarios as "stopping population growth in 1975 and industrial capital growth in 1985."[71] They wanted "society" to make choices[72]—i.e., collective decision making, through surrogates like themselves, in "a world forum where statesmen, policy-makers, and scientists" would decide what needed to be done.[73] Such "concerted international measures and joint long-term planning will be necessary on a scale and scope without precedent."[74] This call for super-socialism on a global scale used the shopworn arguments that the alternative to "a rational and enduring state of equilibrium by planned measures" was leaving things to "chance or catastrophe."[75] The report warned: "A decision to do nothing is a decision to increase the risk of collapse."[76] This neat dichotomy between collective decision making and doing "nothing" circumvents the very possibility of systemic adjustments through the ordinary functioning of prices and other social forces, such as were in fact reducing the birth rate around the world even as this alarum was being sounded.

Like most prophecies of doom, the Club of Rome report had an agenda and a vision—the vision of an anointed elite urgently needed to control the otherwise fatal defects of lesser human beings. Long after the Club of Rome report has become just a footnote to the long history of overheated rhetoric and academic hubris, the pattern of its arguments, including its promiscuous display of the symbols of "science"—aptly characterized by Gunnar Myrdal as "quasi-learnedness"[77]—will remain as a classic pattern of orchestrated hysteria in service to the vision of the anointed. Moreover, this was not the isolated act of a given set of people. What made the Club of Rome report politically important was its consonance with widespread views and visions among the anointed. Economist Robert Lekachman, for example, declared: "The era of growth is over and the era of limits is upon us"[78]—all this on the eve of the longest peacetime expansion in history.

FICTITIOUS HISTORY

Anyone can be wrong about the future. Often the variables are so numerous, and the interactions so complex, that the only real mistake was to have predicted in the first place. Being wrong about the past is something else. Here the anointed's pattern of being often wrong but never in doubt cannot be explained by the difficulties of interpreting numerous causal factors, because the end results are already known and recorded. That the record was not checked is only another sign of the great confidence of those with the vision of the anointed—and the groundlessness of that confidence.

Among the areas in which the contemporary anointed have made sweeping assumptions about the past, based on their vision rather than on the actual record of the past, have been two in which the record contradicting their assumptions is particularly clear and obvious. One has been the practice of attributing such social pathology as broken families in the black community to "a legacy of slavery." Another has been the practice of attributing the soaring national debt and other economic difficulties of recent years to the past policies of the Reagan administration. There has also been a more general use of history to pooh-pooh those present concerns which the anointed do not share by showing that people voiced similar concerns in the past—the implicit assumption being that these past expressions of concern were groundless.

The "Legacy of Slavery"

Nothing so turns the tables on critics of social pathology in the black community as invoking the painful history of slavery. But because slavery has left bitter legacies, it does not follow that any particular bitter experience among blacks today can automatically be attributed to slavery. Cancer is indeed fatal, but every fatality cannot be attributed to cancer—and certainly not after an autopsy has shown death to be due to a heart attack or gunshot wounds.

One of the key misfortunes within the contemporary black community, from which many other misfortunes flow, is the breakdown of the family, or the failure to form a family in the first place. As of 1992, more than half of all black adults had never been married, quite aside from an additional 16 percent who had been either divorced or widowed. By contrast, only 21 percent of white adults had never been married.[79] More than half of all black children—57 percent—were living with only one parent and another 7.5 percent were not living with either parent.[80] Thus, only a little more than a third of black children were living in traditional two-parent households. The great majority of those black children who were living with only one parent were living with their mothers, and more than half of these mothers were unmarried.[81] The all too common, and all too tragic, situation was the teenage mother—"children having children." Of 190,000 black children whose parents were currently still teenagers, only 5,000 were living with both parents.[82] This of course does not include all those children whose mothers were teenagers when they were born but whose mothers were 20 years old or older at the time the Census Bureau collected the statistics. In short, it underestimates the extent of teenage motherhood and the consequences that continue long after the mother has reached 20 years of age.

Children having children is a deadly situation, whether from the standpoint of physical health—babies born to teenage mothers being prone to more medical disabilities—or from the standpoint of the inability or unwillingness of teenage mothers to raise those children with the knowledge, skills, and values necessary for them to become productive and law-abiding adults. Since many of these teenage girls are high school dropouts and are otherwise lacking in the discipline, knowledge, and maturity necessary to raise a child, they can hardly be expected to give the child what they themselves do not have. The tragedy of the situation is too obvious to require elaboration.

As in other areas where violations of societal norms have led to disasters, the first order of business for the anointed has been to turn the tables on society, which must itself be made to feel guilty for what it complains of. Blaming "a legacy of slavery" for the high levels of unwed teenage pregnancy among blacks, and the abdication of responsibility by the fathers of the children, clearly performs that function. Whether it is actually true is another question—and one receiving remarkably little attention.

Going back a hundred years, when blacks were just one generation out of slavery, we find that the census data of that era showed that a slightly *higher* percentage of black adults had married than had white adults. This in fact remained true in every census from 1890 to 1940.[83] Prior to 1890, this question was not included in the census, but historical records and contemporary observations of the Reconstruction era depicted desperate efforts of freed black men and women to find their lost mates, children, and other family members—efforts continuing on for years and even decades after the Civil War.[84] Slavery had separated people, but it had not destroyed the family feelings they had for each other, much less their desire to form families after they were free. As late as 1950, 72 percent of all black men and 81 percent of black women had been married.[85] But the 1960 census showed the first signs of a decline that accelerated in later years—as so many other social declines began in the 1960s. This new trend, beginning a century after Emancipation, can hardly be explained as "a legacy of slavery" and might more reasonably be explained as a legacy of the social policies promoted by the anointed, especially since similar social policies led to similarly high rates of unwed motherhood in Sweden, where neither race nor slavery could be held responsible.

Looking more closely at the history of broken homes and female-headed households in the United States, we find that both have long been more prevalent among blacks than among whites, although the differences were not always as dramatic as they are today. The higher levels of broken homes among blacks in the past were due in part to higher mortality rates among blacks, leaving more widows and widowers, but there were also more family breakups.[86] None of this was unique to blacks, however. The Irish went through a similar social history in nineteenth-century American cities. But the female-headed households of an earlier era, whether among blacks or whites, were seldom headed by teenage girls. As of 1940, among black females who headed their own households, 52 percent were 45 years old or older. Moreover, only 14 percent of all black children were born to unmarried women at that time.[87] The whole situation was radically different from what it is today. Whatever factors caused the changes, these were clearly twentieth-century factors, not "a legacy of slavery."

The Reagan Administration

Few histories have been rewritten so completely and so soon as the history of the Reagan administration. From innumerable outlets of the anointed—the media, academia, and the lecture platform— poured the new revised history of the Reagan administration, that its reductions in tax rates in the early 1980s—"tax cuts for the rich" being the popular phrase—had brought on record federal deficits. Yet this revisionist history of the 1980s is easily refuted with widely available official statistics on the federal government's tax receipts, spending, and deficits during the eight years of the Reagan administration. The year before Ronald Reagan became president, the federal government took in $517 billion in tax revenues, which was the all-time high up to that point. The record of tax revenues and expenditures during the Reagan years, from 1981 through 1988, is shown in the following table.

YEAR	RECEIPTS (billions)	OUTLAYS (billions)	DEFICIT (billions)
1981	$599	$ 678	$ 79
1982	618	746	128
1983	601	808	208
1984	666	851	185
1985	734	946	212
1986	769	990	212
1987	854	1,004	149
1988	909	1,064	155

Source: *Budget of the United States Government: Historical Tables* (Washington, D.C.: U.S. Government Printing Office, 1994), p. 14. (Rounding causes some deficit numbers to be off by one.)

Contrary to the notion that deficits have resulted from reduced tax receipts by the federal government,[88] those receipts in fact reached new record highs during the Reagan administration. Every year of that administration saw the federal government collect more money than in any year of any previous administration in history. By the last year of the Reagan administration in 1988, the federal government collected over $391 billion *more* than during any year of the Carter administration—in percentage terms, the government took in 76 percent more that year than it had ever collected in any year of any other administration.[89] The idea that tax cuts—for the rich or otherwise—were responsible for the deficit flies in the face of these easily obtainable statistics. Spending increases simply outstripped the rising volume of tax receipts, even though hundreds of billions of dollars more were pouring into Washington than ever before. But of course there is no amount of money that cannot be overspent.

The very idea of "tax cuts" reflects verbal ambiguities of the sort so often exploited by the verbally adept among the anointed. Except for one year, *tax receipts* never fell during the two Reagan administrations (and even that one year, tax receipts were higher than they had ever been in any previous administration). It was *tax rates* that were cut. As for "the rich," even if we accept the popular definition of them as people currently above some given income level, those in the top income brackets paid larger sums of money after the Reagan *tax rate* cuts than before. They even paid a higher percentage of all the taxes paid in the country, according to a report of the House Ways and Means Committee, controlled by Democrats.[90] What bothered the liberals was that "the rich" paid a smaller percentage of their rising incomes than before. But, whatever the metaphysics of "fairness," revisionist history can be checked against hard data—and it fails that test.

Corresponding to the notion that "tax cuts for the rich" caused the rising national debt has been the notion that "cutbacks in spending on social programs" were responsible for much social pathology, including the growth of homelessness. However, as liberal scholar Christopher Jencks has pointed out, actual federal spending on housing increased throughout the years of the Reagan administration. What declined were appropriations—the legal authorization of future spending.[91] In other words, hypothetical money declined but hard cash increased. Since it is hard cash that pays for housing, homelessness has its roots in other factors besides government spending on housing.

While there were some social programs that were actually cut during the Reagan administration, most "cutbacks in social programs" were reductions in projected levels of future spending. That is, if program X were spending $100 million a year before the Reagan administration took office and was seeking to expand to $150 million a year, an actual expansion to $135 million would be called a "cutback" in spending of $15 million, even though the program received $35 million more than it had ever received before. This is Washington Newspeak rather than anything that most people would regard as a "cutback" anywhere else.

For many of the anointed, it was never sufficient to declare the Reagan administration's economic, social, or foreign policies mistaken, malign, or even dangerous. It was necessary to ridicule them as the products of a consummately stupid president—an "amiable dunce," as Democratic elder statesman Clark Clifford called him.[92] This denigration of Ronald Reagan began even before he became president, and was in fact one of the reasons why his chances of becoming even the Republican nominee, much less president, were considered nil. As *Washington Post* editorial board member Meg Greenfield recalled the mood she saw among Washington insiders in 1980:

> It was the wisdom of the other contenders and of most Republican Party leaders, too, not to mention of practically everyone in Democratic politics, that Reagan was: too old, too extreme, too marginal and not nearly smart enough to win the nomination. The Democrats, in fact, when they weren't chortling about him, were fervently hoping he would be the nominee. When he carried the convention in Detroit, people I knew in the Carter White House were ecstatic.[93]

This assessment of Reagan remained, even after he defeated President Carter in a landslide in the 1980 elections. This view of him remained unchanged as he got major legislation—the "Reagan revolution"—through Congress over the opposition of those who disdained him, despite the fact that the Republicans were never a majority in both houses of Congress during the first Reagan administration and were not a majority in either house during the second. In a 1987 essay full of condescending references to "Ronnie," Gore Vidal used as the crowning example of President Reagan's being out of touch with reality the following quotation from the president: "I believe that communism is another sad, bizarre chapter in human history whose last pages even now are being written."[94] The later sudden collapse of communism in the Soviet bloc was foreseen by very few of the anointed who ridiculed Reagan.

The point here is not to reassess the Reagan administration—a task that can be left to future historians—but to examine the role of evidence for the anointed. Here, as elsewhere, the criteria they used were not pragmatic criteria of success, whether at the polls, in Washington politics or on the international stage. The overriding criterion was consonance with the vision of the anointed, and Ronald Reagan had to fail that test, because no president in half a century was so completely out of step with that vision. The choices facing the anointed were abandonment of a cherished vision or depicting Ronald Reagan as a bumbling idiot, even if that meant treating concrete evidence as irrelevant.

Pooh-Pooh History

Complaints about the declining standards of the younger generation, about rising crime rates, or about any of a number of other concerns have been ridiculed by the anointed, by quoting people who voiced similar concerns and perhaps dire predictions in the past. Not only does this tactic relieve the anointed of any responsibility to debate the specific merits of the particular issue at hand, it further reinforces their more general picture of an irrational public, whose views need not be taken seriously.

Those who complained about the rising crime rates that followed the judicial expansion of criminals' "rights" in the 1960s were ridiculed by quoting people who had complained about coddling criminals in earlier times, and who had predicted dire consequences. Complaints about the declining behavioral standards of the younger generation go even further back into history—into Roman times, for example—and so are even more useful for purposes of pooh-poohing such complaints today. It is seldom considered necessary to offer any evidence that (1) these complaints were without foundation, or that (2) the failure of the degeneration to reach the dire conditions warned against was not due to those warnings and the actions they spurred to forestall disaster and turn the situation around. One historical example may illustrate the point—and while one example is seldom decisive for a whole spectrum of issues, it is a salient demonstration of the pitfalls of reaching sweeping conclusions without evidence.

In early nineteenth-century America, there were many public alarms about drunkenness, violence, and crime. Moreover, empirical evidence suggests that these alarms were well-founded. As a result, massive campaigns against these social ills were launched by numerous organizations at both local and national levels. These included a temperance movement that swept across the country, along with religious revivals, and the creation of the Young Men's Christian Association, with a moral message accompanying its athletic and other activities. Organized and uniformed police departments were created in big cities, replacing more haphazard methods of law enforcement. Employers began to ask job applicants for evidence of church membership. Volunteer organizations began placing homeless urban street urchins with farm families. In short, there was an all-out effort on many fronts against social degeneracy.[95] Moreover, those efforts paid off. Per capita consumption of alcohol began declining in 1830 and by 1850 was down to about one-fifth of what it was in 1829.[96] A decline in crime began in the mid-nineteenth century and continued on into the early twentieth century.[97]

While there were as always "many factors" at work, one of the more obvious being a changing age composition of the population, this change was found to account for only a small fraction of the declining crime rates.[98] More fundamentally, from the standpoint of evaluating pooh-pooh history, there was a very real problem to begin with, very real efforts to deal with it, and very real progress following those efforts. It was not simply that the benighted voiced unfounded hysteria for the anointed to pooh-pooh.

The era in which trends in crime, drunkenness, and other social degeneracy were turned around was of course the era of "Victorian morality," so much disdained by the anointed of later times. Its track record, however, compares favorably with the later track record of the opposite approach.

ARGUMENTS WITHOUT ARGUMENTS

There are too many discussion tactics that substitute for substantive arguments to permit a comprehensive survey. Half a dozen common substitutes may be illustrative, however. They are (1) the "complex" and "simplistic" dichotomy; (2) all-or-nothing rhetoric; (3) burying controversial specifics in innocuous generalities; (4) shifting to the presumed viewpoint of someone else, in lieu of supporting one's own assertions with evidence or logic; (5) declaring "rights"; and (6) making opaque proclamations with an air of certainty and sophistication.

The "Complex" Complex

One of the most frequently recurring buzzwords of the contemporary anointed is "complex," often said with a sense of superiority toward those who disagree with them—the latter being labeled "simplistic."

The real world is, of course, more complex than any statement that anyone can make about it, whether that statement is in three words or in three volumes. An exhaustive description of a watch, for example, including its internal mechanisms, the various sources of the materials from which it was produced, as well as the principles of physics which determine how the watch keeps time, not to mention the conceptual complications in the notion of time itself (wrestled with by Albert Einstein and Stephen Hawking, among others), would fill volumes, if not shelves of volumes—quite aside from the economic complications involved in the financing, production, and worldwide distribution of watches in very different economies. Yet, despite all this, most of us would find nothing wrong with the simple statement that Joe was wearing a watch, so that he could tell what time to stop work and go home. Nor would we question its validity on grounds that it was "simplistic."

A truly exhaustive description being never-ending, we necessarily accept less than exhaustive descriptions all the time. What is truly simpleminded is to use that fact *selectively* to dismiss unpalatable conclusions, without having to offer either evidence or logic, beyond the bare assertion that these conclusions are "simplistic" in general or, more specifically, because they left out some particular element. Demonstrating that the omitted element changes the relevant conclusion in some fundamental way is the real task—a task often avoided merely by using the word "simplistic."

Sometimes there is an underlying assumption that complex social phenomena cannot have simple causes. Yet many of the same people who reason this way have no difficulty accepting a theory that a giant meteorite striking the Earth—a very simple event, however catastrophic—could have had ramifications that included dust clouds obscuring the sun, leading to falling temperatures all over the planet and expansion of the polar ice cap, resulting in migrations and extinctions of whole species.

With social phenomena as well, a simple act can have complicated repercussions. A federal law saying simply that no interest rate in the United States could exceed 4 percent per annum would have enormously complicated repercussions, from the stock market to the construction industry, from oil exploration to credit card availability. Whole occupations, firms, and industries would be devastated. Organized crime, with its loan sharks, would flourish. Massive international capital movements would derange trade and payments between nations, disrupting economies around the world and straining relations among regional and global power blocs. All these complications—and more—would result from a law written in one short sentence, simple enough to be understood by any 10-year-old.

Complex phenomena may, of course, also have complex causes. But the *a priori* dogma that they cannot have simple causes is part of the "complex" complex. It is one more way of seeming to argue, without actually making any argument. It is also one more example of the presumption of superior wisdom and/or virtue that is at the heart of the vision of the anointed. As a tactical matter, this dogma enables them to deny, on purely *a priori* grounds, that their various "compassionate" interventions in legal, economic, or social systems could have been responsible for the many counterproductive consequences which have so often followed.

Despite attempts to dismiss unpalatable conclusions on grounds that they are "oversimplified," nothing is *over*simplified unless it is wrong—and wrong specifically for the purpose at hand. The ancient Ptolemaic conception of the universe has long since been rejected as incorrect, in favor of the more sophisticated Copernican system, but the Ptolemaic system continues to be used by modern astronomers to compute the times and durations of eclipses—and it does so with accuracy down to fractions of a second. The points on which the Ptolemaic system is wrong simply do not affect these kinds of calculations. Since its assumptions are simpler than those of the Copernican system, it is easier to use for calculation, without sacrificing accuracy. For other purposes, such as sending a spacecraft to Mars or Venus, the Ptolemaic conception of the universe must give way to the Copernican conception—because the latter gives more accurate information *for that purpose.*

Since all theories of complex phenomena must be simplified, in order to be completed within the lifetime of the analyst, the question as to whether a particular theory is *over*simplified is ultimately an empirical question as to whether it leads to demonstrably false conclusions for the purpose at hand. Demonstrating the falsity of the conclusions—not of the assumptions, which are always false, at least in the sense of being incomplete—is a precondition for determining that a theory is oversimplified. Merely labeling an analysis "oversimplified" on *a priori* grounds puts the cart before the horse, by evading responsibility for first demonstrating the falsity of its conclusions.

If there are hundreds of factors involved in some phenomenon— whether physical or social—and someone claims to be able to predict that phenomenon with a high degree of accuracy by using only three of those factors, then the question as to whether this is madness or genius is ultimately a question as to whether he can actually do it. It is not a question as to whether it seems plausible. The theory of mercantilism may seem more plausible than Einstein's theory of relativity, but Einstein's theory has been verified—most notably at

Hiroshima and Nagasaki—while mercantilism has failed repeatedly over the centuries, though still surviving politically on the basis of its plausibility.

The most fundamental reason for not using plausibility as a test is that what seems plausible is a function of our existing assumptions, and so cannot be a test of those assumptions. To dismiss opposing arguments on the *a priori* ground that they are "simplistic" is to seal off the prevailing vision from feedback.

An appreciation of the many complexities involved in resolving controversial issues might suggest that the existence of alternative (or opposing) conclusions is something quite reasonable to expect among intelligent and informed individuals who read the complicated evidence differently, or who weigh the intricate factors or the perplexing probabilities differently. From this perspective, complexity suggests intellectual or ideological tolerance. Yet that is seldom the conclusion drawn by the anointed. Despite their emphasis on complexity, the issue is almost never considered *that* complex. It is just complex enough that intelligent and compassionate individuals should clearly be on one side, while those on the other side are considered deficient in at least one of these qualities. This attitude was epitomized in *New York Times* columnist Anthony Lewis' view of the much-debated—and indeed complex[99]—death penalty issue. Capital punishment will continue, he said, "until, perhaps, someday, reason overtakes primitive emotion."[100] Could anything be more self-congratulatory? In a similar vein, Justice Harry Blackmun wrote in one of his Supreme Court opinions: "I fear for the darkness as four justices anxiously await the single vote necessary to extinguish the light."[101] In other words, those of his colleagues who differed from him were the forces of darkness. In a similar vein and on a different set of issues, Ralph Nader declared: "The issues are black and white" and "No honest person can differ."[102]

All or Nothing

Most differences that matter in real life are differences of degree—even when these are extreme differences, such as that between an undernourished peasant, owning only the rags on his back, and a maharajah bedecked in gold and living in one of his several palaces. Yet a polemical tactic has developed which enables virtually any general statement, however true, to be flatly denied, simply because it is not 100 percent true in all circumstances. The simplest and most obvious statement—that the sky is blue, for example—can be denied, using this tactic, because the sky is not *always* blue. It is reddish at sunset, black at midnight, and gray on an overcast day. Thus, it is "simplistic" to say that the sky is blue. By the same token, it is "simplistic" to say that the ocean is water, because there are all sorts of minerals dissolved in the ocean, which also contains fish, plant life, and submarines, among other things.

This trivializing tactic is widely, but selectively, used to deny whatever needs denying, however true it may be. Even in the days of Stalin, to make a distinction between the Communist world and the free world was to invite sarcastic dismissals of this distinction, based upon particular inadequacies, injustices, or restrictions found in "the so-called 'free world,'" as the intelligentsia often characterized it, which kept it from being 100 percent free, democratic, and just. This tactic persisted throughout a whole era, during which millions of human beings in Europe and Asia fled the lands of their birth, often leaving behind their worldly belongings and severing the personal ties of a lifetime, sometimes taking desperate chances with their own lives and the lives of their children—all in order to try to reach "the so-called 'free world.'" This verbal tactic continued, even as some Communist nations themselves chose to undergo political convulsions and economic chaos, in order to try to become more like "the so-called 'free world.'"

All-or-nothing reasoning allows the anointed to say that such things as crime, child abuse, and alcoholism occur in *all* classes, that *all* segments of society are susceptible to AIDS, and otherwise obfuscate the very large and very consequential differences in all these areas. All-or-nothing rhetoric has likewise served as a substitute for arguments in many other contexts. Attempts to resist the escalating politicization of courts, colleges, and other institutions have been met with similarly derisive dismissals, on grounds that these institutions are *already* political, so that it is "hypocritical" to protest their politicization now, merely because of the ascendancy of political ideas with which one disagrees.[103] This all-or-nothing argument has become a standard response to any resistance to the escalating politicization of any institution or organization.

Obviously, if there is not complete anarchy, there must be some political structure, and the institutions within the society must in some way be linked to those structures, if only by obeying the laws of the land. No institution in any society can possibly be nonpolitical in the ultimate sense of being hermetically sealed off from governmental authority. Yet centuries of struggle and bloodshed have gone into the effort to create zones of autonomy, constitutional limitations on government, and institutional traditions, all in order to insulate individuals and organizations from the full impact of political activity and governmental power. The separation of church and state, the sanctity of the doctor-patient relationship, the lifetime appointments of federal judges, and the exemption of spouses from testifying against one another in court are just some of the examples of these attempts to provide insulation from governmental power and the political process.

Nevertheless, all-or-nothing rhetoric has been used to deny that any institution is nonpolitical, thereby justifying such things as turning classrooms into propaganda centers and judges disregarding the written law, in order to substitute their own social theories as a basis for judicial rulings. At the very least, one might debate the specific merits or consequences of such actions, rather than have the whole issue preempted by the trivializing argument that educational institutions or courts are *already* "political"—in some sense or other. Extreme differences of degree are commonly understood as differences in kind, as when we refer to a maharajah as "rich" and a hungry peasant as "poor," even though each owns something and neither owns everything.

A special variant of the all-or-nothing approach is what might be called tactical agnosticism. Law professor Ronald Dworkin, for example, objected to application of laws against inciting to riot because "we have no firm understanding of the process by which demonstration disintegrates into riot."[104] Apparently society must remain paralyzed until it has definitive proof, which of course no one has with most decisions, personal or social.

All-or-nothing tactics are almost infinitely adaptable as substitutes for arguments and evidence on a wide range of issues. For example, any policy proposals to which the anointed object can be dismissed as "no panacea." Since nothing is a panacea, the characterization is always correct, regardless of the merits or demerits of the policy or its alternatives. This categorical phrase simply substitutes for logic or evidence as to those merits or demerits. Conversely, when a policy promoted by the anointed turns out to create more problems than it solves (if it solves any), attempts to show how the previous situation was far better are almost certain to be dismissed on grounds that opponents are nostalgic for a "golden age" which never existed in reality. Golden ages being as rare as panaceas, this truism again serves to preempt any substantive argument about the merits or demerits of alternative policies.

The all-or-nothing fallacy is also used to deal with analogies used for or against the vision of the anointed. Because all things are different, except for the similarities, and are the same except for the differences, any analogy (however apt) can be rejected by those who find it a sufficient objection that the things being analogized are not "really" the same. By the same token, any analogies favored (however strained) can be defended on grounds that those things analogized involve the same "underlying" or "essential" principle. Ice and steam are chemically the same thing, though of course they are not physically the same thing. Just as it is possible to make or deny an analogy between ice and steam, so any other analogy can be selectively made or denied. Similarly, anything can be said to have "worked" (as Lincoln Steffen said somewhat prematurely of the Soviet Union), or to have failed (as critics said of the Reagan administration's policies), because *everything* works by sufficiently low standards and everything fails by sufficiently high standards. Such

statements are not arguments. They are *tactics* in lieu of arguments—
and they are accepted only insofar as they are consonant with the
prevailing vision.

A special variant of the all-or-nothing principle is the view that
either one knows *exactly* what particular statements mean or else one
is free to engage in adventurous reinterpretations of the words. In literature this is called "deconstruction" and in the law it is called
"judicial activism." Proponents of judicial activism, for example,
make much of the fact that the Constitution of the United States in
some places lacks "precision" or is not "exact."[105] Ultimately, nothing is exact—not even physical measurements, for the instruments
themselves cannot be made 100 percent accurate. In the real world,
however, this theoretical difficulty is resolved in practice by establishing tolerance limits, which vary with the purpose at hand. A precision optical instrument that is off by half an inch may be wholly
unusable, while a nuclear missile that lands 5 miles off the target has
virtually the same effect as if it had landed directly in the center of
the target. However, in the vision of the anointed, the absence of precision becomes an authorization for substituting the imagination. In
reality, however, the question is not what *exactly* the Constitution
meant by "cruel and unusual punishment" but whether the death
penalty, for example, was included or excluded. Precision is a red
herring.

All-or-nothing arguments are not mere intellectual errors. They
are tactics which free the anointed from the constraints of opposing
arguments, discordant evidence, or—in the case of judicial
activism—from the constraints of the Constitution. Most important of
all, they are freed from the feedback of uncooperative reality.

Innocuous Generalities

Yet another technique for arguing without actually using any arguments is to bury the specifics of one's policy preferences in a vast
generality, so diffuse that no one can effectively oppose it. For example, many people say that they are for "change"—either implying or
stating that those opposed to the specific changes they advocate are

against change, as such. Yet virtually no one is against generic "change."

The staunchest conservatives advocate a range of changes which differ in specifics, rather than in number or magnitude, from the changes advocated by those considered liberal or radical. Milton Friedman wrote a book entitled *The Tyranny of the Status Quo* and the policy changes of the 1980s have been called "The Reagan Revolution." Edmund Burke, the patron saint of conservatism, said: "A state without the means of change is without the means of its conservation."[106] Change, as such, is simply not a controversial issue. Yet a common practice among the anointed is to declare themselves emphatically, piously, and defiantly in favor of "change." Thus, those who oppose their particular changes are depicted as being against change in general. It is as if opponents of the equation $2 + 2 = 7$ were depicted as being against mathematics. Such a tactic might, however, be more politically effective than trying to defend the equation on its own merits.

Change encompasses everything from genocide to the Second Coming. To limit the term to beneficial change—to "progress"—is to be no more specific. Quite aside from whether the result anticipated will actually follow from the policies advocated, there are often serious differences of opinion as to whether a given empirical result is in fact morally or socially desirable. Everyone is for a beneficial outcome; they simply define it in radically different terms. *Everyone* is a "progressive" by his own lights. That the anointed believe that this label differentiates themselves from other people is one of a number of symptoms of their naive narcissism.

In academic circles, the equally vast generality is "diversity," which often stands for a quite narrow social agenda, as if those who reiterate the word "diversity" endlessly had no idea that diversity is itself diverse and has many dimensions besides the one with which they are preoccupied. Advocates of diversity in a race or gender sense are often quite hostile to ideological diversity, when it includes traditional or "conservative" values and beliefs.

"Innovative" is another of the generalities used in place of arguments, and "making a difference" is likewise promoted as something desirable, without any specific arguments. However, the Holocaust was "innovative" and Hitler "made a difference." The anointed, of course, mean that their particular innovations will be beneficial and that the differences their policies make will be improvements. But that is precisely what needs to be argued, instead of evading the responsibility of producing evidence or logic by resorting to preemptive words.

The Shifting Viewpoint

Often discussions of political controversies begin in the conventional forms of an argument, examining opposing assumptions, reasons, logic, or evidence—and then shift suddenly to presenting the opaque conclusions of one side. This tactic is yet another way for the anointed to appear to argue, without the responsibility of actually producing or defending any arguments.

During the student riots of the 1960s, for example, columnist Tom Wicker's reply to those who charged that reason and civility were being violated on university campuses was, "all too often, as today's students see things, 'reason and civility' merely cloak hypocrisy and cynicism, and they aim to 'strike through the mask.'" As regards the student seizure of a building at Harvard, Wicker said:

> Who really abandoned "reason and civility," students asked—the students who seized a building to protest the Harvard Corporation's retention of R.O.T.C. or the administrators who called in police to evict the protesters with what was widely regarded as excessive violence?[107]

This verbal sleight-of-hand not only enabled Wicker to put forth justifications without having to justify, but also to transform a vocal and violent minority into spokesmen for students in general:

Students everywhere volubly hold to the belief that an "Establishment"—political, social, economic, military—manipulates society for
its own ends, so that the popular rule of the people is a myth. The war
goes on, racism continues, poverty remains, despite the familiar
American preachments of peace, democracy, prosperity, and the rule
of reason.[108]

If Wicker had said on his own that the failure of American society—
like every other society on Earth—to solve all its problems was justification for violence, he would have been expected to produce some
logic or evidence of his own. Instead, he was able to shift to the viewpoint of "students everywhere" and to characterize them as "idealis-
tic youth."[109] In general, to say that "it appears to some observers"[110]
that this or that is true is meaningless as a justification, because
there would obviously be no issue in the first place unless some other
observers saw things differently.

Illegitimate as it is to evade the responsibility for one's conclusions by shifting to someone else's viewpoint, it is doubly illegitimate when that is merely a *presumed* viewpoint, contradicted by
what the others you are relying on actually said. In the wake of the
Los Angeles riots of 1992, for example, many of the anointed justified the violence and destruction by shifting to the presumed viewpoint of "the black community"—when in fact 58 percent of blacks
polled characterized the riots as "totally unjustified."[111] Justifying
criminal activity by shifting to the presumed viewpoint of others
extends far more widely in time and space. Ramsey Clark, for example, declared: "Nothing so vindicates the unlawful conduct of a poor
man, by his light, as the belief that the rich are stealing from him
through overpricing and sales of defective goods."[112] Not a speck of
evidence was presented to show that the typical poor person in fact
saw things this way "by his light" or by the light of Ramsey Clark,
for that matter.

Even in scholarly—or at least academic—studies, the shifting
viewpoint has substituted for both logic and evidence. For example,
historian David Brion Davis said, "Emerson recognized the eco-

nomic motive in British emancipation" of slaves in its empire,[113] thus relieving himself of the formidable task of substantiating this conclusion in the teeth of massive evidence to the contrary. Words like "recognized" or "admitted," attached to selected quotations, shift both the viewpoint and the burden of proof.

Often a shifting to the individual, in an issue that reaches far beyond that individual, takes the more specific form of what logicians call "the fallacy of composition"—the assumption that what applies to a part applies also to the whole. For example, it is true that one person in a stadium crowd can see the game better if he stands up but it is not true that, if they all stand up, everyone will see better. Those who focus on the effects of any particular government policy or judicial ruling on particular individuals or groups often implicitly commit the fallacy of composition, for the whole point of government policies and judicial rulings is that they apply very broadly to many people—and what happens as a consequence to those who are ignored is no less important than what happens to those who have been arbitrarily singled out by an observer.

New York Times columnist Anna Quindlen, for example, responded to criticisms of disruptions by gay activists demanding more money for AIDS by saying: "If I could help give someone I loved a second chance, or even an extra year of life, what people think would not worry me a bit."[114] In other words, the desires of the arbitrarily selected group are made the touchstone, not the consequences of such behavior on other people whose money is to be commandeered for their benefit—or the consequences for society in making mob rule the mode of social decision making. In a similar vein, Quindlen referred to letters from other readers on other issues saying, "Thank you for speaking our truth."[115] However lofty and vaguely poetic such words may seem, the cold fact is that the truth cannot become private property without losing its whole meaning. Truth is honored precisely for its value in *interpersonal* communication. If we each have our own private truths, then we would be better off (as well as more honest) to stop using the word or the concept and recognize that nobody's words could be relied upon anymore. The more subtle insinuation is that we should become more "sensitive" to some particular group's "truth"—

that is, that we should arbitrarily single out some group for different standards, according to the fashions of the times or the vision of the anointed.

"Rights" Rites

One of the most remarkable—and popular—ways of seeming to argue without actually producing any arguments is to say that some individual or group has a "right" to something that you want them to have. Conceivably, such statements might mean any of a number of things. For example:

1. Some law or government policy has authorized this "right," which is somehow still being denied, thereby prompting the reassertion of its existence.
2. Some generally accepted moral principle has as its corollary that some (or all) people are entitled to what the "right" asserts, though presumably the fact that this right needs to be asserted suggests that others have been slow to see the logical connection.
3. The person asserting the particular "right" in question would like to have some (or all) people have what the right would imply, even if no legal, political, or other authorization for that right currently exists and there is no general consensus that it ought to exist.

In the first two cases, where there is some preexisting basis for the "right" that is claimed, that basis need only be specified and defended. Still, that requires an argument. The third meaning has become the more pervasive meaning, especially among those with the vision of the anointed, and is widely used as a substitute for arguments. Take, for example, the proposition, "Every American has a right to decent housing." If all that is really being said is that some (or all) of us would prefer to see all Americans living in housing that meets or exceeds whatever standard we may have for "decent housing," then there is no need for the word "rights," which conveys no

additional information and which can be confused with legal autho-
rizations or moral arguments, neither of which is present. Moreover,
if we are candid enough to say that such "rights" merely boil down to
what we would like to see, then there is no need to restrict the statement to Americans or to housing that is merely "decent." Surely we
would all be happier to see every human being on the planet living in
palatial housing—a desire which has no fewer (and no more) arguments behind it than the "right" to "decent" housing.

However modest a goal, "decent" housing does not produce itself,
any more than palatial housing does. Be it ever so humble, someone
has to build a home, which requires work, skills, material resources,
and financial risks for those whose investments underwrite the operation. To say that someone has a "right" to any kind of housing is to
say that others have an obligation to expend all these efforts on his
behalf, without his being reciprocally obligated to compensate them
for it. Rights *from* government interference—"Congress shall make
no law," as the Constitution says regarding religion, free speech,
etc.—may be free, but rights *to* anything mean that someone else has
been yoked to your service involuntarily, with no corresponding
responsibility on your part to provide for yourself, to compensate others, or even to behave decently or responsibly. Here the language of
equal rights is conscripted for service in defense of differential privileges.

More important, from our current perspective, all this is done
without arguments, but merely by using the word "rights," which
arbitrarily focuses on the beneficiary and ignores those whose time
and resources have been preempted. Thus, for example, health care
was declared by Bill Clinton during the 1992 election campaign to
be "a right, not a privilege"[116]—a neat dichotomy which verbally
eliminates the whole vast range of things for which we work, precisely because they are neither rights nor privileges. For society as a
whole, nothing is a right—not even bare subsistence, which has to be
produced by human toil. Particular segments of society can of course
be insulated from the necessities impinging on society as a whole, by
having someone else carry their share of the work, either temporarily

or permanently. But, however much those others recede into the background in the verbal picture painted by words like "rights," the whole process is one of differential privilege. This is not to say that no case can ever be made for differential privileges, but only that such a case needs to be made when privileges are claimed, and that the arguments required for such a case are avoided by using words like "rights."

Health care is only one of innumerable things for which such tactical evasions have been used. Housing, college, and innumerable other costly things have been proclaimed to be "rights." *New York Times* columnist Tom Wicker encompassed all economic goods by proclaiming a "right to income."[117] Some have extended this reasoning (or nonreasoning) beyond material goods to such things as a right to "equal respect"—which is to say, the abolition of respect, which by its very nature is a differential ranking of individuals according to some set of values. To say that we equally respect Adolf Hitler and Mother Teresa is to say that the term respect has lost its meaning.

The language of "rights" has other ramifications. Rights have been aptly characterized as "trumps"[118] which override other considerations, including other people's interests. For the anointed to be announcing rights for particular segments of the population is for them to be choosing others as their mascots—and to be seeking to get the power of the state to ratify and enforce these arbitrary choices, all without the necessity of making specific arguments.

General Proclamations

Perhaps the purest example of an argument without an argument is to say that something is "inevitable." This is an inherently irrefutable argument, so long as any time remains in the future. Only in the last fraction of a second of the existence of the universe could anyone refute that claim—and perhaps they would have other things on their mind by then.

Whether particular policies are favored or opposed, there are opaque proclamations of this sort which substitute for arguments.

And whether a policy is favored or opposed, it may be currently existing or nonexistent. In each of these four cases, there are proclamations that substitute for arguments, as illustrated below:

	EXISTING	NON-EXISTING
FAVORED	"Here to stay"	"Inevitable"
OPPOSED	"Outmoded"	"Unrealistic"

It is one of the signs of our times that such proclamations are so widely accepted in lieu of arguments—but only when used in support of the prevailing vision of the anointed.

PENETRATING THE RHETORIC

Perhaps a few suggestions might be in order for seeing through much of the rhetoric of the anointed. Some of the things discussed in previous chapters, as well as in this one, illustrate some general principles of common sense, which are nevertheless often widely ignored in the heat of polemics:

1. All statements are true, if you are free to redefine their terms.
2. Any statistics can be extrapolated to the point where they show disaster.
3. A can always exceed B if not all of B is counted and/or if A is exaggerated.
4. For every expert, there is an equal and opposite expert, but for every fact there is not necessarily an equal and opposite fact.
5. Every policy is a success by sufficiently low standards and a failure by sufficiently high standards.
6. All things are the same, except for the differences, and different except for the similarities.
7. The law of diminishing returns means that even the most beneficial principle will become harmful if carried far enough.
8. Most variables can show either an upward trend or a downward trend, depending on the base year chosen.
9. The same set of statistics can produce opposite conclusions at different levels of aggregation.

10. Improbable events are commonplace in a country with more than a quarter of a billion people.

11. You can always create a fraction by putting one variable upstairs and another variable downstairs, but that does not establish any causal relationship between them, nor does the resulting quotient have any necessary relationship to anything in the real world.

12. Many of the "abuses" of today were the "reforms" of yesterday.

CHAPTER 5

THE ANOINTED VERSUS THE BENIGHTED

Every man, wherever he goes, is encompassed by a cloud of comforting convictions, which move with him like flies on a summer day.

—Bertrand Russell[1]

Thus far, we have noted some of the consequences and tactics of those with the prevailing vision, but we have not yet come to grips with the specific underlying assumptions of that vision. What kind of world exists inside the minds of the contemporary anointed, and what kind of individual and social causation activates that world? The question here is not about what kind of world they wish to create, but what kind of world they think exists already.

THE UNDERLYING VISION

The vision of the anointed may stand out in sharper relief when it is contrasted with the opposing vision, a vision whose reasoning begins with the tragedy of the human condition. By tragedy here is not meant simply unhappiness, but tragedy in the ancient Greek sense, inescapable fate inherent in the nature of things, rather than unhappiness due simply to villainy or callousness. The two visions differ in their respective conceptions of the nature of man, the nature of the world, and the nature of causation, knowledge, power, and justice.

These differences can be presented schematically, as below:

	THE TRAGIC VISION	THE VISION OF THE ANOINTED
Human capability	severely and inherently limited for all	vast for the anointed
Social possibilities	trade-offs that leave many "unmet needs"	solutions to problems
Social causation	systemic	deliberate
Freedom	exemption from the power of others	ability to achieve goals
Justice	process rules with just characteristics	just (equalized) chances or results
Knowledge	consists largely of the unarticulated experiences of the many	consists largely of the articulated intelligence of the more educated few
Specialization	highly desirable	highly questionable
Motivation	incentives	dispositions
Process costs	crucial	incidental
Decision-making mechanism preferred	systemic processes that convey the experiences and revealed preferences of the many	deliberate plans that utilize the special talents and more advanced views of the few
Kinds of decisions preferred	incremental	categorical

These differences are not random happenstances. They are systematic differences that follow logically from fundamental differences in underlying assumptions, beginning with assumptions about the nature of human beings and the range of possibilities open to them. All these particular differences between the two visions turn ultimately on differences about human limitations and their corollaries. The more ambitious definitions of freedom and of justice, for example, in the vision of the anointed are consistent with the expansive sweep of human capabilities they assume. By the same token, the emphasis on specialization by those with the tragic vision reflects their sense of the inherent limitations of the human mind and the corresponding dangers in attempting to bite off more than anyone can chew. It is not merely that the engineer cannot perform surgery, the judge in his decisions cannot venture very far beyond his narrow expertise in the law without precipitating disasters when he attempts to become a social philosopher who can make law the instrument of some grander vision of the world.

The conflicts between those with the tragic vision and those with the vision of the anointed are virtually inevitable. Clearly, those who assume a larger set of options are unlikely to be satisfied with results deriving from a smaller set of options. Thus, those with the vision of the anointed, who assume an expansive range of choices, repeatedly find themselves in conflict with those who have the tragic vision and who consequently assume a much smaller set of choices. While these conflicts pervade contemporary ideological politics, they are not peculiar to our times. Both visions have a long history, encompassing many individuals of historic stature. Those with the vision of the anointed are particularly prone to think of their own philosophy as new, and therefore as adapted to contemporary society, but their framework of assumptions goes back at least two centuries—as does the framework of those with the tragic vision.

Both visions also have internal coherence. Those who follow the assumptions of a particular vision as regards law tend also to follow that vision as regards economics. Thus Judge David L. Bazelon, whose role and philosophy as regards expanding criminals' rights have already been noted in Chapter 2, believed in the socioeconomic sphere that "inequality of riches in our affluent society" was one of "a host of inequities,"[2] that government should provide people's "basic needs as rights," that income, education, and medical care should be "matters of right, not of grace."[3] Conversely, Adam Smith not only had opposite views from Judge Bazelon on government's role in the economy, but also on the application of the criminal law. For Smith, "mercy to the guilty is cruelty to the innocent."[4] A similar coherence of vision is found across many other issues, with environmentalists and their opponents often taking opposite positions on military defense as well, for example. As a contemporary writer has noted:

> Liberalism in America and worldwide has great faith in modifying human behavior by adjusting "underlying social conditions" to make people desire the right thing instead of the wrong thing. In its clearest form, this is the response to crime control by liberals, who are not much interested in tougher sentences, improved security devices, better-armed and equipped police, more escape-proof prisons—they seek to change society or the malefactors, so that people will not want to commit crime. This is also the form of the liberal solution to most foreign policy problems—we should behave in a better manner and reorder the world so that the urge to war will be reduced, and mankind will live in better harmony.[5]

Police, prisons, etc., represent only trade-offs, while creating a society in which crime is prevented from arising in the first place is a solution. Hence the former approach is consistent with the tragic vision and the latter approach is in keeping with the vision of the anointed. Not only today, but for more than two centuries, both crime and war have been seen, by those with the vision of the anointed, as things to be deterred by changing people's dispositions rather than by confronting them with retaliatory capabilities that provide incentives against crime or war. William Godwin's 1793 treatise, *Enquiry Concerning Political Justice*, remains one of the most systematic elaborations of the vision of the anointed and in it crime and war are approached in precisely the same way as among 1960s liberals and their later followers. Dispositions and understanding are seen by the anointed as the key to crime control, for example: "It is impossible that a man would perpetrate a crime, in the moment when he sees it in all its enormity,"[6] according to Godwin, just as Ramsey Clark was to say in the twentieth century, "healthy, rational people will not injure others."[7] In both cases, it is the failure of "society" that causes crime, with the criminal being the victim of circumstances. Much the same story can be found in other eighteenth-century figures such as Condorcet and Holbach.

Similarly with war. The way for a country to avoid war, according to Godwin, is to behave with "inoffensiveness and neutrality" toward other countries and to avoid the kind of "misunderstanding" that leads to war.[8] Nearly a century and a half later, this same theory was being expounded and put into practice by British Prime Minister Neville Chamberlain, who repeatedly blamed such subjective factors as fears, suspicions, and misunderstandings for war,[9] and who therefore put great weight on "personal contacts"[10] between himself and other nations' leaders as a way of dissipating such negative subjective factors. Just as Godwin thought neutrality a source of peace, so Chamberlain espoused a policy of "impartiality,"[11] and practiced it by trying to "keep the balance even between the two sides"[12] in the Spanish civil war while Hitler and Mussolini helped Franco's insurgents, by referring to Japan's invasion of China as "this unhappy conflict"[13] and similarly referring to "the unhappy Sudetenland"[14] where local Nazis were carrying out Hitler's orchestrated campaign of subversion and where Chamberlain condemned only "extremists on both sides."[15]

The important point here is that these were not simply isolated misjudgments on Chamberlain's part. They were logical corollaries of a particular set of assumptions about the world, a vision with a coherence and a pedigree, as well as with intellectual progeny who would later repeat many of the same beliefs and even phrases during the long history of the "cold war." Many latter-day adherents to the vision of the anointed urged neutrality in the face of Soviet-backed insurgencies around the world, practiced moral equivalence, resisted defense buildups, and were euphoric over "personal contacts" that were now called "summit meetings." Half a century after Chamberlain, *New York Times* columnist Tom Wicker attributed Soviet-American conflicts to the fact that "both sides" had a "dangerous hostility" toward one another in the 1950s.[16]

The tragic vision, in which incentives matter more than dispositions, has looked on foreign policy and war in a wholly different way.

No document represents the tragic vision of man more starkly than *The Federalist Papers,* where John Jay said, "nations in general will make war whenever they have a prospect of getting anything by it."[17] Within the context of this vision, it was not preventing "misunderstandings" but maintaining military deterrence that was crucial. In both the 1930s and the 1980s, those with this tragic vision of the world in general—Winston Churchill and Ronald Reagan being the most prominent examples—espoused foreign policies that were likewise radically different from the policies espoused by those with the vision of the anointed. We now know from history that the foreign policies based on the tragic vision were different both in their assumptions and in their ultimate outcomes.

DIFFERENTIAL KNOWLEDGE AND WISDOM

One of the most important questions about any proposed course of action is whether we know how to do it. Policy A may be better than policy B, but that does not matter if we simply do not know how to do policy A. Perhaps it would be better to rehabilitate criminals, rather than punish them, *if we knew how to do it.* Rewarding merit might be better than rewarding results *if we knew how to do it.* But one of the crucial differences between those with the tragic vision and those with the vision of the anointed is in what they respectively assume that we know how to do. Those with the vision of the anointed are seldom deterred by any question as to whether anyone has the knowledge required to do what they are attempting. As we have already seen, when President Lyndon Johnson spoke of addressing the conditions that breed urban violence, he said:

> All of us know what those conditions are: ignorance, discrimination, slums, poverty, disease, not enough jobs.[18]

Similarly, when the *New York Times* editorially expressed dismay at statistics on high infant mortality rates in the United States, it declared: "America already knows how to make the rate drop again."[19] With these and innumerable other issues, the question for the anointed is not knowledge but compassion, commitment, and other such subjective factors which supposedly differentiate themselves from other people. The refrain of the anointed is *we already know the answers, there's no need for more studies,* and the kinds of questions raised by those with other views are just *stalling* and obstructing progress. "Solutions" are out there waiting to be found, like eggs at an Easter egg hunt. Intractable problems with painful trade-offs are simply not part of the vision of the anointed. Problems exist only because other people are not as wise or as caring, or not as imaginative and bold, as the anointed. If there was one defining moment of the 1960s, it might well have been at the judicial conference in 1965 when Justices Brennan and Warren roared with laughter as a law professor poured scorn and ridicule on the concerns of a former police commissioner about the effects of recent judicial rulings on law enforcement and public safety.[20] It was the anointed in their classic role of disdaining the benighted—and dismissing the very possibility that the unintended ramifications of morally inspired decisions might make matters worse on net balance.

Far more important than particular reckless policies, even those with such deadly consequences as weakening the criminal law, is a whole mind-set in which omnicompetence is implicitly assumed and unhappy social phenomena are presumed to be unjustified morally and remediable intellectually and politically. Inherent constraints of circumstances or people are brushed aside, as are alternative policy approaches which offer no special role for the anointed. The burden of proof is not put on their vision, but on existing institutions.

The notion that "society" must justify itself before the bar of "reason" presupposes that there is some individual or group capable of such encyclopedic knowledge and such mastery of the structured principles of so many disciplines as to make such judgments across a broad spectrum and at a speed that would fit all these judgments into one lifetime. Those with sweeping schemes for "reconstructing society" seldom pause to ask about the sufficiency of anyone's knowledge for such a task. Karl Menninger, for example, said:

The immediate task of our time seems to be to think out our economic organization in dynamic terms and according to a strategy which will so co-ordinate the now prevailing tendencies that they will no longer conflict. The political problem, therefore, is to organize human impulses in such a way that they will direct their energy to the right strategic points, and steer the total process of development in the desired direction.[21]

In other words, the only problem is political mobilization and social imagination, so as to result in a solution in which current tendencies "will no longer conflict," rather than a mere trade-off in which their continuing conflicts will be dealt with as best one can. Nor was any time wasted worrying about the presumption of some people in preempting the decisions of others, these others' decisions being treated as mere "impulses" for the anointed to "organize" and direct toward what the anointed define as "the right strategic points." Indeed, the whole process was analogized to engineering problems, with the designing of another type of human being included in this engineering for, as Menninger noted: "No economic order can be brought into existence as long as the corresponding human type does not emerge."[22] In short, not only is the external world to be redesigned, so are the people who are to inhabit it. Were this merely the fantasy of one man, it would not be worth noting. But it is in fact part of the vision of the anointed as it has existed for centuries. The idea of creating the kind of people needed for a new society goes at least as far back as William Godwin's *Enquiry Concerning Political Justice* in 1793, where he spoke of "men as they may hereafter be made" through a process of "the improvement of mankind" which he thought would be "in the utmost degree simple."[23] Two centuries later, the task appears less simple and such expressions as "brainwashing" and "reeducation" camps have chilling overtones in the light of history, though that has not stopped indoctrination efforts in American schools and colleges, led by those who still have the vision of the anointed today.

By contrast, those with the tragic vision have long questioned whether anyone—themselves included—knows enough to engage in

sweeping social and political experiments. "We cannot change the
Nature of things and of men," Edmund Burke said, "but must act
upon them the best we can."[24] Adam Smith took a very similar position, while seeing the more general issue as a conflict of visions
between the doctrinaire with an "ideal plan of government" who
"seems to imagine that he can arrange the different members of a
great society with as much ease as the hand arranges the different
pieces upon a chess-board" and the more modest reformer who will
adjust his policies to "the confirmed habits and prejudices of the
people" and who, when he "cannot establish the right," will "not disdain to ameliorate the wrong."[25] Those with the tragic vision might
share the desire for social betterment without sharing the assumptions as to how much knowledge and control of social ramifications
exist. A succinct summary of the tragic vision was given by historians Will and Ariel Durant:

> Out of every hundred new ideas ninety-nine or more will probably be
> inferior to the traditional responses which they propose to replace.
> No one man, however brilliant or well-informed, can come in one
> lifetime to such fullness of understanding as to safely judge and dis-
> miss the customs or institutions of his society, for these are the wis-
> dom of generations after centuries of experiment in the laboratory of
> history.[26]

Severe limitations on the effectiveness of well-intentioned notions
were likewise seen by Justice Oliver Wendell Holmes, who said, "to
improve conditions of life and the race is the main thing—but how
the devil can I tell whether I am not pulling it down more in some
other place?"[27] Doing good on some problem right under one's nose
is not enough in a world of constrained options and systemic interactions, where the overlooked costs of immediate benevolence take
their toll elsewhere. Holmes exemplified the tragic vision of life,
based on a tragic vision of human limitations. He spoke disdainfully
of "the vain attempt to love one's neighbor as one's self,"[28] of "our
legislation to make other people better,"[29] and of attempts to "legis-
late bliss."[30]

In the tragic vision, individual sufferings and social evils are inherent in the innate deficiencies of all human beings, whether these deficiencies are in knowledge, wisdom, morality, or courage. Moreover, the available resources are always inadequate to fulfill all the desires of all the people. Thus there are no "solutions" in the tragic vision, but only trade-offs that still leave many desires unfulfilled and much unhappiness in the world. What is needed in this vision is a prudent sense of how to make the best trade-offs from the limited options available, and a realization that "unmet needs" will necessarily remain—that attempting to fully meet these needs *seriatim* only deprives other people of other things, so that a society pursuing such a policy is like a dog chasing its tail. Given this vision, particular solutions to particular problems are far less important than having and maintaining the right processes for making trade-offs and correcting inevitable mistakes. To those with the tragic vision, the integrity of processes is crucial—much more so than particular causes. As Jean-François Revel put it, in a free society "there is no single just *cause,* only just *methods.*"[31]

The vision of the anointed begins with entirely different premises. Here it is not the innate limitations of human beings, or the inherent limitations of resources, which create unhappiness but the fact that social institutions and social policies are not as wisely crafted as the anointed would have crafted them. As John Stuart Mill put it, the "present wretched education, and wretched social arrangements, are the only real hindrance" to happiness being widespread.[32] Mill's view in many ways epitomized the vision of the anointed.[33] When he spoke of "the best and wisest,"[34] it was with none of the sense of irony that the phrase "the brightest and the best" has acquired in our time. Great things could be achieved, Mill said, "if the superior spirits would but join with each other" for social betterment.[35] He called upon the universities to "send forth into society a succession of minds, not the creatures of their age, but capable of being its improvers and regenerators."[36]

A democracy can rise above mediocrity, according to Mill, only where "the sovereign Many have let themselves be guided (which in their best times they always have done) by the counsels and influ-

ence of a more highly gifted and instructed One or Few."[37] It is on
these latter—the "thinking minds,"[38] "the most cultivated intellects
in the country,"[39] "those who have been in advance of society in
thought and feeling"[40]—that social well-being and progress depend.
In short, it was *not* the case in this vision that all human beings were
incapable of leading society to substantially higher levels of understanding, behavior, and well-being. The "best and wisest"—the
anointed—were not only capable of it but had a duty to do it. Where
they lacked the political power to do so, then their duty was that of
"keeping alive the sacred fire in a few minds when we are unable to
do more," as Mill wrote to a friend.[41]

The hallmark of the vision of the anointed is that what the anointed
consider lacking for the kind of social progress they envision is will
and power, not knowledge. But to those with the tragic vision, what is
dangerous are will and power without knowledge—and for many
expansive purposes, knowledge is inherently insufficient.

In their haste to be wiser and nobler than others, the anointed have
misconceived two basic issues. They seem to assume (1) that they
have more knowledge than the average member of the benighted and
(2) that this is the relevant comparison. The real comparison, however, is not between the knowledge possessed by the average member
of the educated elite versus the average member of the general public,
but rather the *total* direct knowledge brought to bear through social
processes (the competition of the marketplace, social sorting, etc.),
involving millions of people, versus the secondhand knowledge of
generalities possessed by a smaller elite group. Moreover, the existing
generation's traditions and values distill the experiences of other millions in times past. Yet the anointed seem to conceive the issue as one
of the syllogistic reasoning of the past versus the syllogistic reasoning
of the present, preferring to believe that improvements in knowledge
and reason permit the former to be dismissed.

Differential Toleration

Much more candidly than the anointed of our times, Mill sought
differential toleration for intellectual elites. "Customs are made for

customary circumstances and customary characters," he said in *On Liberty*.[42] Most of the "men and women who at present inhabit the more civilized parts of the world" are only "starved specimens of what nature can and will produce" in later and better times.[43] According to Mill, "exceptional individuals, instead of being deterred, should be encouraged in acting differently from the mass."[44] As he said in *On Liberty*:

> In this age, the mere example of nonconformity, the mere refusal to bend the knee to custom, is itself a service. Precisely because the tyranny of opinion is such as to make eccentricity a reproach, it is desirable, in order to break that tyranny, that people should be eccentric. Eccentricity has always abounded when and where strength of character has abounded; and the amount of eccentricity in a society has generally been proportioned to the amount of genius, mental vigour, and moral courage which it contained.[45]

Mill's *On Liberty* has often been seen—mistakenly—as a plea for greater freedom of all from government, when it was in fact a plea for differential exemption of the anointed from *social* criticism. That is, the anointed should judge and influence the benighted, but not vice-versa. Mill saw government in the England of his day as no longer a major threat to freedom.[46] It was the social "tyranny of the majority"[47] and "the despotism of Custom"[48] that he opposed in *On Liberty*. What he considered to be desirable was that individuals be free to do as they like "without detriment to their estimation" in the eyes of others.[49] Today, that is called being "nonjudgmental"—and, very often in practice, it too is a principle applied selectively as between the anointed and the benighted.

Moral Surrogacy

Echoes of Mill's notion of one-way nonjudgmentalism and one-way moral surrogacy are found today in, for example, Ronald Dworkin's assertion that "a more equal society is a better society even if its citizens prefer inequality."[50] The anointed will define for these citizens what is better. Moreover, the exalted vision of themselves by the anointed is often matched by sweeping assumptions about the irrationality or immorality of ordinary people. Without either a speck of evidence or a moment's hesitation, the anointed speak of Americans' "love affair with the automobile," when in fact there are many quite rational reasons for preferring cars to the alternative modes of mass transportation incessantly being urged or imposed by elite opinion.[51] The issue here is not how the net advantages of alternative modes of transportation work out. The issue is precisely that *there is no issue* as far as the anointed are concerned, that mass irrationality may simply be assumed. What the Declaration of Independence called "a decent respect for the opinion of mankind" is not part of the vision of the anointed, which depends crucially on differential wisdom and virtue.

Given this perspective, systemic processes which depend upon the direct experiences and revealed preferences of millions of human beings, whether expressed in prices in the marketplace or through social self-selection of various sorts, are all treated as mere nuisances to be swept aside by public policy when these systemic processes impede the carrying out of the vision of the anointed. Even formalized and solemnized commitments, such as the Constitution of the United States, are treated as mere obstacles to be circumvented by flexible interpretation. Other people's decisions, through whatever processes those decisions have been made, are to be preempted by the decisions of the anointed.

Although followers of this tradition often advocate more egalitarian economic and social results, they necessarily seek to achieve those results through highly unequal influence and power, and—especially in the twentieth century—through an increased concentration of power in the central government, which is thereby enabled to redistribute economic resources more equally. While those with the vision of the anointed emphasize the knowledge and resources available to promote the various policy programs they favor, those with the tragic vision of the human condition emphasize that these resources are taken from other uses ("there is no free lunch") and that the knowledge and wisdom required to run ambitious social programs far exceed what any human being has ever possessed, as the unintended negative consequences of such programs repeatedly demonstrate.

Human limitations are moral, as well as intellectual, in the tragic vision—and these limitations too extend across the spectrum. As Alexander Hamilton put it:

> Look through the rich and poor of the community; the learned and the ignorant. Where does virtue predominate? The difference indeed consists, not in the quantity but kind of vices which are incident to the various classes. . . .[52]

To those whose reasoning begins with the tragedy of the human condition, evil is diffused throughout humanity, while those with the vision of the anointed tend to see evils more localized in particular "oppressors" of one sort or another, as expressed in "white racism," "male domination," or "capitalist exploitation," for example. This second set of evils, however severe, is more remediable than the kind of evil implied in the remark: "We have met the enemy and it is us." The logic of the two visions almost inevitably puts them at odds as to how much improvement can be expected from the political process. At the extreme, a revolutionary cannot believe in the tragic vision, for that would imply that all the sacrifices and sufferings incident to a revolution could easily result in largely cosmetic changes in personnel and style—or might even bring to power a worse despot. Conversely, it would be unconscionable to be conservative if that meant passively accepting unnecessary evils and *simultaneously* preventable sufferings.

To those with the tragic vision, institutions, traditions, laws, and policies are to be judged by how well they cope with the intellectual and moral inadequacies of human beings, so as to limit the damage they do, and to coordinate the society in such a way as to maximize the use of its scattered fragments of knowledge, as well as to correct inevitable mistakes as quickly as possible. But to those with the less constrained vision of the anointed, the goal is the liberation of human beings from unnecessary social inhibitions, so as to allow repressed creativity to emerge and the vast knowledge and talent already available to be applied to existing problems.

For the anointed, traditions are likely to be seen as the dead hand of the past, relics of a less enlightened age, and not as the distilled experience of millions who faced similar human vicissitudes before. Moreover, the applicability of past experience is further discounted in the vision of the anointed, because of the great changes that have taken place since "earlier and simpler times." Here the two visions clash again, for those with the tragic vision see no great changes in the fundamental intellectual or moral capacities of human beings, however much the material world may have changed or various institutions and customs may have developed through trial and error.

Justice Holmes saw modern man as being very much like his barbarian ancestors,[53] with the different conditions of life today being due to economic and social developments based on the very institutions, traditions, and laws which those with the vision of the anointed are anxious to supersede with untested theories. As Edmund Burke put it, we "should approach to the faults of the state as to the wounds of a father," with "awe and trembling solicitude"[54]—not as an "exciting" opportunity for experimentation. Beginning, like Holmes, with a vision of human nature little changing in its basic essentials, Burke expected no great benefit from speculative theories as a basis for public policy:

> We know that *we* have made no discoveries, and we think that no discoveries are to be made, in morality; nor many in the great principles of government, nor in the ideas of liberty. . . .[55]

To those with the tragic vision, barbarism is not some distant stage of evolution, but an ever-present threat when the civilizing institutions are weakened or undermined:

> Civilization is not inherited; it has to be learned and earned by each generation anew; if the transmission should be interrupted for one century, civilization would die, and we should be savages again.[56]

A similar sense of the fragility of civilization led Edmund Burke to regard the promotion of social experimentation and atomistic reason as a dangerous playing with fire:

> We are afraid to put men to live and trade each on his own private stock of reason; because we suspect that this stock in each man is small, and that the individuals would do better to avail themselves of the general bank and capital of nations and of ages.[57]

Neither Burke nor others in the tradition of the tragic vision were opposed to change, per se, and many of them in fact advocated major changes in their own day. The authors of *The Federalist Papers* were, after all, not only establishing a new government after overthrowing the old, but were also establishing a radically new *kind* of government, in a world ruled by monarchs. What made them different from those who led the French revolution was that their vision of human beings was radically different. The French revolution operated on assumptions much closer to those of the vision of the anointed.

Where the American revolution deliberately created a government of elaborate checks and balances, to constrain the evils inherent in human beings, the French revolution concentrated vast powers in its leadership, so as to allow those who were presumably wise and benevolent to effect sweeping changes with little hindrance. Condorcet, as an intellectual supporter of the French revolution, could see no reason for the American system of checks and balances, in which society was to be "jostled between opposing powers" or to be held back by the "inertia" of its constitution.[58] Indeed, even after the revolutionaries turned against him and threw him into prison, Condorcet still seemed not to understand the reason for limitations on government power.

The Benighted Public

For those with the vision of the anointed, it is not sufficient to discredit or denigrate proponents of the tragic vision. The general public must also be discredited, as well as the social processes through which the public's desires are expressed, individually or collectively, such as a market economy or social traditions. In short, all alternatives to the vision of the anointed must be put out of court, by one means or another. Nowhere is evidence considered so unnecessary as in making sweeping denigrations of the public. Mass psychoanalysis of "society" is a common pattern, exemplified by psychiatrist Karl Menninger's view of crime:

> Society secretly wants crime, needs crime and gains definite satisfactions from the present mishandling of it. We need criminals to identify ourselves with, to secretly envy, and to stoutly punish. They do for us the forbidden, illegal things we wish to do.[59]

Not only psychiatrists, but journalists as well, engage in mass psychoanalysis of the public. *New York Times* columnist Tom Wicker, for example, said that "Americans want to believe" that their president "is somehow immune to life's wounds." Those who questioned the introduction of controversial material on homosexuality into the public school curriculum were depicted by *New York Times* columnist Anna Quindlen as people who want children to grow up with "contempt and fear" of people unlike themselves.[60] Neither evidence nor even an awareness of a need for evidence accompanied this sweeping denigration of those who disagreed as not merely mistaken but malign. A headline on the cover of *U.S. News and World Report* proclaimed: "The War Against Women" and added: "Women are falling further behind in country after country—and their men like it that way."[61] No evidence was offered that men in general wished women ill, much less that "their men" wished the women connected with them ill—presumably their wives, sisters, mothers, and daughters. During the Vietnam war, celebrated journalist William L. Shirer declared that the American people "don't give a damn" about the bombing of Hanoi, because they were following football.[62] Yet people who attend the ballet or go to art galleries during a war or other national crisis are seldom, if ever, accused of being calloused brutes. But anything that paints the public as benighted requires neither consistency nor logic nor evidence. Back in 1960, Vance Packard wrote that "Americans have thus far chosen to suppress awareness" of a "dangerous decline in the United States of its supply of essential resources."[63] In other words, only a psychological state of "denial" could explain why the public did not exhibit the same hysteria that was so fashionable among the intelligentsia—and which would prove to be so false when actually put to the test, as Paul Ehrlich and others discovered.

President Jimmy Carter echoed a theme among the anointed when he said that there was "a longing for meaning" in the country.[64] Again, evidence was neither asked nor given. It is widely taken as axiomatic that ordinary people's lives lack meaning, which must be brought to them by the anointed via various political crusades or social activism. Later, this notion would be puffed up as "the politics of meaning" by Hillary Clinton.[65] Hopelessly naive beliefs on various subjects were also attributed to the public by Jimmy Carter—that "our armies were always invincible," that "our nation's resources were limitless," and so on.[66]

One of the high priorities of the anointed is to destroy the myths and illusions which they presume to abound among the public. Patriotism is a prime target. Anna Quindlen referred to patriotism during the Gulf War of 1991 as "Amerimania."[67] An internal memorandum of the Smithsonian Institution warned that an exhibit being put together on a leading American fighter plane of World War II should "avoid an overly heroic/cheer-leading/patriotic tone (the same goes for the music)."[68] Those who objected to various other examples of the trashing of American achievements were dismissed by another Smithsonian official as people who don't like exhibits which "undermine their fantasies" and who don't want to be "educated," but prefer instead a museum where they can be "distracted for a moment from the dailiness, the tedium, the fear of their lives."[69] The Smithsonian's own view of its mission was that it should "tell visitors immediately what we are about and how we'd like them to change."[70] In other words, the purpose of a taxpayer-supported institution is to express the ideologies of those who run it and to brainwash the visiting public with the vision of the anointed.

Contemporary denigrations of the masses echo a centuries-old tradition among the anointed, despite much rhetoric on the political left about "the people." Rousseau likened the masses of the people to "a stupid pusillanimous invalid,"[71] and Condorcet said that "the human race still revolts the philosopher who contemplates its history."[72] To eighteenth-century British radical writer William Godwin, the peasant had "the contemptible insensitivity of an oyster."[73] Fabian socialist George Bernard Shaw considered the working class to be "detestable" people who "have no right to live."[74] Edmund Wilson, despite his many left-wing causes—or perhaps because of them—exhibited only contempt toward ordinary people. While serving in the military during World War I, he wrote to a friend lamenting "the cruelty of ineptitude and waste" that he saw in the conduct of the war, but added, "I should be insincere to make it appear that the deaths of this 'poor white trash' of the South and the rest made me feel half so bitter as the mere conscription or enlistment of any of my friends."[75] Nor was this due to the racism of Southern whites, for Wilson himself referred to how distasteful Chattanooga was to him because of "the niggers and the mills."[76]

The benighted masses are also important as guinea pigs for particular social experiments, including the remaking of these masses themselves to be the kind of people that the anointed wish them to be. When William Godwin wrote, two centuries ago, of "men as they hereafter may be made,"[77] he was echoing a theme already sounded by Helvetius and Holbach, among others, and one that would still be apparent in such twentieth-century phenomena as "reeducation" camps and "brainwashing" programs in Communist countries, as well as in various counterparts within democratic countries of the massive propaganda apparatus of totalitarianism.

What is seldom part of the vision of the anointed is a concept of ordinary people as autonomous decision makers free to reject any vision and to seek their own well-being through whatever social processes they choose. Thus, when those with the prevailing vision speak of the family—if only to defuse their adversaries' emphasis on family values—they tend to conceive of the family as a *recipient* institution for government largess or guidance, rather than as a *deci-*

sion-making institution determining for itself how children shall be raised and with what values.

To those with the vision of the anointed, the public serves not only as a general object of disdain, but as a baseline from which to measure their own lofty heights, whether in art, politics, or other fields. Systemic processes which offer channels of expression of the public's views and values are to be circumscribed and circumvented. Art, music, and ballet are to be financed by compulsory exactions from the public, while ignoring or disdaining what the public itself wants or does not want. Similarly, so-called "public television"—taxpayer-subsidized television—is in fact the least responsive to the public's desires and most reflective of the vision of the anointed. Shamelessly one-sided propaganda for the environmentalist movement, for example, has become a staple of so-called "nature" programs on "public television" for years.

Failure to use tax money to finance things not liked by the taxpaying public is routinely called "censorship." If such terminology were used consistently, virtually all of life would be just one long, unending censorship, as individuals choose whether to buy apples rather than oranges, vacations rather than violins, furniture rather than mutual funds. But of course no such consistency is intended. This strained usage of the word "censorship" appears only selectively, to describe public choices and values at variance with the choices and values of the anointed. If a public library declines to buy some avant-garde book approved by the anointed, because either the librarian or the taxpaying public does not like it, that is called "censorship"—even though the book remains freely available to all who wish to buy it and no library can possibly purchase even a tenth of all the books published, so that discretionary preferences are inevitable and the First Amendment does not guarantee either an audience or money.

The presumed irrationality of the public is a pattern running through many, if not most or all, of the great crusades of the anointed in the twentieth century—regardless of the subject matter of the crusade or the field in which it arises. Whether the issue has been "overpopulation," Keynesian economics, criminal justice, or natural resource exhaustion, a key assumption has been that the public is so irrational that the superior wisdom of the anointed must be imposed, in order to avert disaster. The anointed do not simply *happen* to have a disdain for the public. Such disdain is an integral part of their vision, for the central feature of that vision is preemption of the decisions of others.

SOCIAL CAUSATION

Those with the tragic vision and those with the vision of the anointed not only have different conceptions of the limitations of human beings and of the limitations of resources, relative to the insatiable desires of people, but also have very different conceptions of cause and effect as it operates in social processes.

In the vision of the anointed, it is the dispositions, wisdom, intentions, talents, will, and commitment of social decision makers which are crucial. In the tragic vision, where human knowledge and foresight are very limited *for all*, causation more often operates in systemic ways, with innumerable interactions producing results controlled by no given individual or group, but falling into a pattern determined by the incentives and constraints inherent in the logic of the circumstances, rather than as a consequence of specifically articulated, syllogistic rationality.

Systemic causation operates in a wide spectrum of circumstances, whether in the world of nature or in human societies. Vegetation on a mountainside may fall into a pattern, not because any of the plants or trees sought to produce such a pattern, but because different temperatures at different heights favor the survival of different species. Even where human volition is involved, the overall pattern that emerges need not reflect anyone's volition. The Dow Jones industrial average may stand at 4086, not because anyone planned it that way, but because that was the net result of innumerable transactions by innumerable people seeking only their own individual advantage on the particular stocks they were trading.

More broadly, language arises out of gropings, accidents, experiences, and historical borrowings and corruptions of other languages.

No wise individual or council sat down and designed language—either as a general concept or as specific languages, except for artificial languages like Esperanto, which have languished in disuse. The richness, complexity, and subtleties of language have arisen systemically, from the experiences and interactions of millions of ordinary human beings, not from a top-down "plan" formulated by some elite. From time to time, linguistic practices are codified or modified by intellectuals, but this is an incidental part of a vast drama.

Systemic causation creates an order which arises as a consequence of individual interactions directed toward various and conflicting ends, not toward the creation of this order itself. The characteristics of such an order can be analyzed, even if they cannot be created—and this order may, in particular instances or in general, be superior to what can be created, as the case of artificial versus naturally evolving language suggests. The eighteenth-century school of French economists called the Physiocrats coined the term *laissez-faire* to express their view that "the natural order" that would emerge in a market economy was both discernible and more beneficial than attempts to control such complex interactions from the top. That has likewise been the central theme of the twentieth-century writings of Friedrich Hayek, who has sharply distinguished an emergent "order" from a contrived "design."[78] In short, systemic causation has been an enduring feature of the tragic vision, whether among economists, legal analysts, or social thinkers in various other fields.

Systemic causation takes many forms. Legal traditions, family ties, social customs, and price fluctuations in an economy are all systemic ways in which the experiences and preferences of millions of people powerfully influence the decisions of millions of other people. Where the tragic vision and the vision of the anointed differ most fundamentally is on the reality and validity of such systemic processes, which utilize the experiences of the many, rather than the articulated rationality of a talented few. Related to this difference is a sharp difference in the role of dispositions, intentions, or goals in the two visions.

The very terms of discourse among those with the vision of the anointed have historically reflected their preoccupation with dispositions, intentions, goals, whether these were "liberty, equality, fraternity" in the eighteenth century or "social justice," "compassion," or "women's liberation" today. By contrast, those with the tragic vision have emphasized process characteristics, often treating the dispositions, intentions, or goals of those operating within these processes as incidental or irrelevant. For example, although Adam Smith regarded the intentions of businessmen as selfish and anti-social,[79] he saw the systemic consequences of their competition as being far more beneficial to society than well-intentioned government regulation.[80]

Although the overall results of systemic interactions are not directly controlled by anyone, they are neither random nor unfathomable. Otherwise, there could be no such thing as economic analysis of market competition or scientific analysis of ecological or evolutionary patterns. Determining the particular characteristics of particular kinds of systems of reciprocal interaction can be a demanding task—but it is a task seldom undertaken by those with the vision of the anointed, who see little standing between intention and result, other than such subjective factors as compassion or commitment. Thus, systemic causation seldom plays a major role in the prevailing vision of the anointed, however important it may be in the tragic vision. Where the world is conceived in the tragic vision as a system of innumerable and reciprocal interactions, all constrained within the confines of natural and human limitations, individual problems cannot be solved one by one without adding to other problems elsewhere, if only by using up the resources available to deal with them.

A noted controversy among economists back in 1946 may illustrate more specifically and concretely the nature of systemic causation. The issue was whether raising the government-mandated minimum wage level would lead to higher pay for low-level workers or to a higher unemployment rate among such workers after their new pay levels reduced the number of such workers in demand by employers. This controversy, which raged in a leading economics journal (the *American Economic Review*) and was reprinted repeatedly in other places, was between an economist who saw the issue in intentional terms and others who saw it in systemic terms.

After surveying hundreds of employers with questionnaires asking whether they would lay off workers in the wake of an externally mandated increase in wages—and finding that most did not say that they would—Professor Richard A. Lester of Princeton University concluded that the prevailing economic analysis was wrong.[81] However, the economic analysis he was attacking was not about employer intentions but about systemic consequences. It might well be that every employer in the affected industries intended to maintain his employment—but the inherent constraints of consumer demand for the products could easily make it impossible for all the employers to do this, as their attempts to pass on their higher wage costs in higher prices reduce consumers' purchases of their products.

This was only one of many possible ways in which systemic results could differ radically from employer intentions or from the intentions of those who promoted minimum wage laws. But it is only after shifting the focus from intentions to systemic interactions that such counterproductive consequences become apparent in the analysis, without having to wait for painful social confirmation. In the wake of a minimum wage increase, the possible adjustment paths include the following:

1. Capital could be substituted for labor *intentionally* by individual employers buying machinery and laying off workers.
2. Capital could be substituted for labor *systemically* by a loss of profits and market share by the more labor-intensive firms, which are more hard hit by the minimum wage increase than the capital-intensive firms are.
3. Higher-skilled and higher-priced labor could be substituted for lower-priced labor *intentionally* by individual employers.
4. Higher-skilled and higher-priced labor could be substituted for lower-priced labor *systemically* by the greater loss of business by those firms more heavily dependent on the lower-skilled labor whose costs have been increased.
5. Marginally profitable firms could be forced out of existence, reducing industry employment, even without any reduction in employment by any of the surviving employers.

The specific path of adjustment in the industry is less important
than the fact that *the adjustment must be made* to higher labor costs
without a corresponding increase in revenue from product sales.
What employers intend does not matter, even in situation 5 above,
where the surviving firms may be able to maintain their employment
as planned. However, situation 5 has its pitfalls for those researchers
who survey employers before and after a minimum wage increase, for
the result may be that employment among surviving firms is as high
(or higher) than ever, even though industry employment has gone
down due to some companies going out of business. The fatal pitfall
in survey research is that one can only survey survivors. As a distinguished economist pointed out at the time of this controversy, by
using such research methods one can prove that no soldier was killed
in World War II.[82]

Incentives versus Dispositions

If systemic causation is the dominant social force, that leaves
much less of a role for the anointed, much less importance to the difference between their knowledge, wisdom, and virtue, on the one
hand, and the knowledge, wisdom, and virtue of ordinary people, on
the other. A downgrading of the importance of the special wisdom
and virtue of any elite has been a feature of the tragic vision for centuries, going back at least as far as Hobbes in the seventeenth century and remaining a dominant note in the twentieth-century writings
of Friedrich Hayek and others. According to Hobbes: "A plain hus-
band-man is more Prudent in the affaires of his own house, than a
Privy Counselor in the affaires of other men."[83]

This conclusion reflected in part a belief that the incentives facing
decision makers had much more to do with the quality of their decisions than differences in ability and virtue among them. It also suggested that these latter differences were exaggerated. Both beliefs
have remained common, for centuries, among those with the tragic
vision. Adam Smith thought that men differed from one another less
than dogs.[84] So did Friedrich Hayek two centuries later.[85] Oliver
Wendell Holmes likewise believed that great and conscientious

minds had less impact on the law than might be supposed. He acknowledged "the countless number of great intellects that have spent themselves in making some addition or improvement" in the law—"the greatest of which," he said, "is trifling when compared to the mighty whole."[86] Hayek applied this principle to social processes in general:

> Compared with the totality of knowledge which is continually utilized in the evolution of a dynamic civilization, the difference between the knowledge that the wisest and that which the most ignorant individual can deliberately employ is comparatively insignificant.[87]

The tragic vision of human limitations clearly applies to all, with no exception for any elite. Exempting the anointed from the systemic processes which produce legal traditions, social customs, market mechanisms, and other processes for expressing the life experiences of mankind becomes much more questionable in a world of systemic causation. The importance of the anointed's "compassion" or commitment to "social justice" is similarly reduced in a world where intentions are incidental and results depend much more on the kinds of social processes at work—and the incentives generated by such processes.

In their zeal for particular kinds of decisions to be made, those with the vision of the anointed seldom consider the nature of the *process* by which decisions are made. Often what they propose amounts to third-party decision making by people who pay no cost for being wrong—surely one of the least promising ways of reaching decisions satisfactory to those who must live with the consequences. It is not that the anointed advocate such processes, as such, but that their preoccupation with goals often neglects the whole question of process characteristics. The very standards by which social "problems" are defined tend likewise to be third-party standards. Thus "waste," "quality," and "real needs" are terms blithely thrown around, as if some third party can define them for other people. Government actions to enforce these third-party preemptions are often advocated in the form of bureaucracies to replace the systemic processes of the marketplace.

Such practices as judicial activism, intended to produce socially more beneficial results than a strict adherence to legal rules and traditions might produce, look very different within the framework of systemic causation. To derange a whole process, evolved from the experiences of millions of people over centuries of legal development, on the basis of the beliefs or feelings of a particular judge or set of judges about a particular issue before them, risks raising up humanity in one place and pulling it down in another, to use Holmes' analogy.

"Hard cases make bad law" is another way the tragic vision has been expressed. To help some hard-pressed individual or group whose case is before them, judges may bend the law to arrive at a more benign verdict in that particular case—but at the cost of damaging the whole consistency and predictability of the law, on which millions of other people depend, and on which ultimately the freedom and safety of a whole society depend. There cannot be a law-abiding society if no one knows in advance what law they are to abide by, but must wait for judges to create *ex post facto* legal rulings based on "evolving standards" rather than known rules. An expanding penumbra of uncertainty surrounding laws creates incentives for a growing volume of litigation, as well as for a blackmailing of law-abiding individuals and organizations into out-of-court settlements because they cannot be sure how some speculative charge against them will be viewed by judges operating under "evolving standards."

In a system of human interactions, the incentives generated by those systems—whether economic systems or legal systems, for example—are crucial to those with the tragic vision. But those with the vision of the anointed see dispositions as crucial, and hence emphasize the inculcation of the proper attitudes through schools, the media, and otherwise. Whether the issue is child rearing, criminal justice, or foreign policy, those with the tragic vision tend to rely on incentives while those with the vision of the anointed tend to rely on creating favorable dispositions. Those with the vision of the anointed often advocate the settlement of international differences through "diplomacy" and "negotiation," rather than by "force"—as if diplomacy and negotiation were not dependent on a surrounding

set of incentives, of which the credible threat of military force is crucial. Yet unilateral military cutbacks have often been advocated by
those who favor diplomacy and negotiation. Indeed, such policies
were not only advocated but followed by Western democracies for a
dangerously long time during the period leading up to the outbreak
of World War II.

Among the social incentives of systemic interactions, generated
more or less spontaneously, are personal ties within families, within
communities, or among citizens of a given nation. All these systemically generated ties have been treated as precious sources of motiva-
tion and cohesion by those with the tragic vision, who see such ties
as countering the inherent selfishness of individuals. Yet these same
ties have aroused less enthusiasm, often suspicion, and sometimes
even disdain or hostility by those with the vision of the anointed, to
whom such particularistic ties are seen as obstacles to broader social
interests or to being a "citizen of the world." Once again, these different conclusions go back to underlying differences in the way the
world is conceived and corresponding differences in what ranges of
options are assumed to be available. To those with the vision of the
anointed, the alternative to particularistic ties are universalistic ties,
while to those with the tragic vision the alternatives are individual
egotism and mob psychology.

Within the framework of systemic causation, proclamations of
high principles and deep compassion are irrelevant distractions
which promote a dangerous confusion between what you would like
and what is likely to happen if what you advocate is put into practice. But those with the vision of the anointed tend automatically to
attribute statistical differences between groups to intentional reasons (discrimination) or to dispositional reasons (racism, sexism),
with seldom a serious thought about systemic reasons, such as age
differences, cultural differences, or differences associated with
childbearing and homemaking. It is considered an act of generosity
if the latter reasons are not dismissed out of hand but are accorded
a "perhaps"—and all this without a speck of evidence being used
to distinguish between these possibilities and those possibilities
whose only superior claims are based on their being part of the

intentional and dispositional reasons at the heart of the vision of the anointed.

Nowhere does the difference between systemic causation and intentional causation show up more dramatically than in discussions of racial issues. With such negative phenomena as racism, as with such positive phenomena as compassion, *systemic* causation does not depend simply on whether these dispositions exist but on the situational incentives and constraints within which they exist. An owner of a professional basketball team and an owner of a symphony orchestra may be equally racist, but it would be financially suicidal for the former to refuse to hire black basketball players, while the relatively few black symphonic musicians could be denied jobs with much less effect on the overall quality of a symphony orchestra or its financial viability. While these examples are hypothetical, empirical research in countries around the world shows repeatedly that discrimination is in fact more severe in those sectors of the economy where the costs incurred by the discriminators are less.[88] Even in South Africa under apartheid, where racism among white employers was buttressed by legal discrimination against black workers, those very employers often defied or evaded the apartheid laws to hire more blacks, and in higher positions, than permitted by the government.[89] The South African housing market produced such racial integration, in defiance of the law, that whites were in some cases a minority in areas legally designated as being for whites only.[90] Yet this whole field of the economics of discrimination has been dismissed as "a lot of hot air" by an academic whose sole evidence was a Federal Reserve study of mortgage lending in Boston[91]—a study whose fatal flaws have already been noted in Chapter 3. For many others with the vision of the anointed, no evidence at all is necessary for asserting that racism and discrimination underlie statistical disparities.

In contrast to the vision of the anointed, systemic causation says that there are often underlying and quite rational reasons for decisions, even if the expression of those reasons are neither obvious nor well articulated. In short, *there is an underlying reality* reflected through systemic processes, however imperfectly. It is not simply a matter of subjective dispositions. This reasoning can be taken a step further: A fundamental reality is not vitiated by the fact that different human beings see it differently, even if some respond irrationally.

For example, in nineteenth-century Japan, the fundamental reality was that the Japanese were technologically far behind the Western industrial nations—and that this had enormous implications for the country's military vulnerability, political subordination, and chances of survival as an independent nation. A wide spectrum of Japanese recognized this and acted upon it, ultimately creating the scientific, technological, and economic foundation for Japan's emergence a century later as one of the leading industrial nations of the world. However, not every Japanese was perfectly rational about their initial shock at discovering how far behind they were, compared to the West. Among the reactions were these:

> Associations were formed to promote the use of Roman letters in the writing of Japanese and to abandon the kanji and kana characters. Suggestions were made that the kimono be abolished along with many Japanese foods. One man, Yoshio Takahashi, even published a book, *The Improvement of the Japanese Race,* in which he claimed that the Japanese were physically and mentally inferior to westerners, and he urged that all Japanese males divorce their wives and marry western women who would bear children with superior characteristics, and so improve the Japanese stock! A song composed in 1878 for children as they played with a ball, called the *Civilisation Ball Song,* was designed to impress on their young minds how superior western technology was. At each bounce of the ball, they had to recite the names of ten objects that would improve their country: "Gas lamps, steam engines, horse-drawn carriages, cameras, telegrams, lightning conductors, newspapers, schools, letter post and steamships."[92]

Nothing would be easier than to ridicule some of these attitudes. Certainly no one today could consider the Japanese race mentally inferior, for example, after their remarkable achievements in overtaking Western nations technologically in just one century. But a sweeping dismissal of the concerns behind even these extreme reactions in nineteenth-century Japan would be as mistaken in general as these reactions were on particular points. *There was an underlying reality,* however varied and sometimes irrational the subjective responses were to it. It was not just a matter of subjective dispositions, nor would psychological reeducation of the Japanese, or redefining the backwardness of nineteenth-century Japan out of existence with cultural relativism, have made a dent in that underlying reality. Everything cannot be reduced to psychological attitudes or "perceptions."

Systemic causation does not presuppose perfect rationality on the part of human beings. On the contrary, its rationality is a systemic rationality, such that any professional basketball team owner who refused to hire black players under competitive market conditions would simply not continue to survive as an owner. Similarly, systemic causation would not explain the highly varying proportions of female employees in different industries and occupations by the subjective attitudes of men in those particular industries and occupations, but by the varying situations in those sectors of the economy where women are prevalent or rare. It would, in fact, be an incredible coincidence if men's attitudes toward women should continue to be radically different from one industry to another, over a span of time sufficient for a complete turnover of the men in all the industries.

The point here is not to resolve issues involving women or minorities in the labor market. The point is to illustrate the difference between seeking systemic explanations of social phenomena and presupposing that subjective dispositions provide a sufficient causal explanation. A spectrum of subjective responses to any situation is virtually inevitable and these responses will almost invariably include both wise and foolish reactions, as well as reactions well articulated and clumsily expressed. Nothing would be easier, *on any issue,* than to seize upon foolish, malign, or confused statements or actions, in order to present a social problem as due to subjective dispositions which differ from the superior dispositions of the anointed. But, if causation is seen as systemic rather than dispositional, then the task is to discover the underlying reality behind the varied subjective expressions. Perceptions are like mirrors which reflect the real world with varying degrees of distortion, but proving distortion does not disprove the existence of a reality which cannot be talked away.

Trade-offs versus "Solutions"

Perhaps the most fundamental difference between those with the tragic vision and those with the vision of the anointed is that the former see policy-making in terms of trade-offs and the latter in terms of "solutions." This is not merely a difference in words or in optimism, but a difference in procedures. To those with the vision of the anointed, the question is: What will remove particular negative features in the existing situation to create a solution? Those with the tragic vision ask: What must be sacrificed to achieve this particular improvement? As the distinguished economist Herbert Stein said of evaluating a political candidate:

> There are always conditions that one could wish were different or better than they are. The relevant question is whether there is a cure for the condition which the candidate knows and can put into effect and which will not have consequences that are worse than the initial condition.[93]

Implicit in these different approaches to policymaking are different assumptions as to whether other people are so irrational as to have set up unhappy situations for no reason, so that costless improvements are now available. Belief in such differential wisdom and rectitude is more congenial to the vision of the anointed, for whom potential solutions abound, requiring only the discernment to discover them and the power to put them into practice.

No one denies the existence of constraints, though the vision of the anointed does not incorporate these constraints as a central feature and ever-present ingredient in its thinking, while the tragic vision does. Moreover, the trade-offs made necessary by constraints are seen differently by the two visions. To those with the vision of the anointed, it is simply a question of choosing the best solution, while to those with the tragic vision the more fundamental question is: *Who* is to choose? And by what process, and with what consequences for being wrong? As already noted in Chapter 2 (and as will be seen in subsequent chapters), it is so easy to be wrong—and to persist in being wrong—when the costs of being wrong are paid by others.

Often, those with the vision of the anointed more or less automatically collectivize decisions and then take on the role of deciders themselves, whether the issue is sex education, subsidizing the arts, health insurance, or innumerable other social issues. However, there is no *a priori* reason why different individuals should not have different trade-offs in all these areas—which is to say, there is no necessity for the anointed to preempt and collectivize these decisions.

A simple example may illustrate concretely the difference between seeking a solution and seeking a trade-off. When a baby was killed in a tragic airplane crash in 1989 by being ripped out of its mother's arms by the force of the impact and being sent hurtling through the cabin, a political "solution" was proposed by having a federal law requiring babies to be strapped into their own seats on airplanes. But a study by economists indicated that such a law, requiring parents to purchase an extra seat, would divert a portion of the traffic to cheaper alternative modes of transportation on the ground—most of which have higher mortality rates than airplanes. Over a period of a decade, there would be an estimated saving of one baby's life in airplane crashes, a loss of nine lives in alternative ground transportation, and an additional cost of $3 billion.[94]

Few people would regard this as a reasonable trade-off. But it is only by analyzing the issue *as a trade-off* that we avoid the dangerous and deceptive appearances of a "solution."

The proposed legislation to increase airline safety by requiring a separate seat for children was a perfect example of what Justice Holmes referred to as raising humanity in one place while pulling it down in another. Nothing is easier than to increase safety in some arbitrarily defined sector in some arbitrarily chosen way, in disregard of what this does to safety elsewhere and in other ways. Unfortunately, this kind of thinking is all too congenial to the vision of the anointed—and to politicians.

More generally, political attempts to "solve" various "problems" *seriatim* ignore the costs created by each "solution" and how that exacerbates other problems. It is by no means impossible to solve downtown parking problems in any city, for example, by building more parking garages, either above ground or underground, but the resources required for such a task would leave many municipalities dangerously lacking in policemen and fire protection, municipal hospitals, and public schools. It is no answer to suggest raising local taxes or getting federal grants, for these actions simply *relocate* the trade-off, without getting rid of it. It is like infinite regress. If the parking problem is worth eliminating, even at the large and inescapable costs of doing so, then clearly it should be done. But no one should imagine that this is a "solution" rather than a trade-off.

Much of political rhetoric is concerned with presenting issues as isolated problems to be solved—not as trade-offs within an overall system constrained by inherent limitations of resources, knowledge, etc. The issue is posed as one of providing "affordable housing," "decent jobs," "adequate health care," and the like. The cost problem is often waved aside by some such general statement as, "Surely a country that can put a man on the moon . . . " or fight a war in the Persian Gulf, or build a nationwide highway system, etc., can afford to do whatever is proposed. From a trade-off perspective, however, all these expensive activities of the past are reasons why we have *less* to spend on other things, not reasons why we can spend more. We cannot undo the flight to the moon, unfight the Gulf War, or unbuild the national highway system. One of the most severe constraints is the constraint that time moves in only one direction. Trade-offs that should have been made differently in the past are now irrelevant.

What can be afforded *seriatim* vastly exceeds what can be afforded simultaneously. Simple and obvious as this should be, it is often ignored in denunciations of government inaction on various festering social problems or "unmet needs." But even an ideal set of trade-offs must—and should—leave a whole spectrum of unmet needs, because the cost of wiping out the last vestige of any problem is leaving other problems in more dire condition. In short, trade-offs must be incremental rather than categorical, if limited resources are to produce optimal results in any social system as a whole.

Despite the importance of incremental trade-offs, the language of politics is filled with categorical rhetoric about "setting *priorities*," "providing basic *necessities*," or "assuring *safety*" in foods, medicines, or nuclear power. But incremental decisions differ as much from categorical decisions as trade-offs differ from solutions. If faced with a categorical choice between food and music, every sane person would choose food, since one can live without music but not without food. But if faced with an incremental choice, the decision could easily be just the opposite. If food were *categorically* more important than music, then we would never reach a point where we were prepared to sacrifice resources that could be used to produce food, in order to produce music. Given this premise, Beethoven, Brahms, and Bach should all have been put to work growing potatoes, instead of writing music, if food were categorically more important.

A world where food had a categorical priority over music would be a world of 300-pound people, whose brief lives would never be brightened by a song or a melody. The fact that no one would advocate such an absurd and disastrous outcome, in such an obvious case, does not mean that people will not advocate equally absurd and disastrous outcomes in more complicated cases, where the connections are harder to follow and where the categorical language of "priorities," "necessities," or "safety" is set in the concrete of law or public policy—and where the consequences are either left unmonitored or are monitored by agencies with a vested interest in the continuation of the laws and policies which justify their own existence, money, and power.

Put differently, many a sound and beneficial principle becomes a dangerous absurdity when it becomes a fetish. That is why any categorical principle must be assessed not only in terms of its soundness as a principle, but also in terms of what happens when that principle is applied categorically. Laws tend to be categorical, as do court determinations of what is and is not "unconstitutional." That is fine when the law prohibits murder or kidnapping, for example, since virtually everyone is against these things in virtually all cases. But when laws and court decisions become the chosen instruments of social trade-offs, then it is not enough to examine the good intentions or even the sound principles behind the policies chosen, without examining also the effect of pursuing those policies through a categorical process. As already noted in the case of mandating separate airline seats for babies, policies chosen for the sake of safety can in fact make life more dangerous.

Looked at more broadly, the pursuit of safety in disregard of costs means a degree of sacrifice of economic prosperity—and economic prosperity is itself one of the key factors in longevity. More prosperous individuals, classes, and nations tend to have lower death rates around the world, simply because of their greater ability to guard against diseases and against such natural disasters as earthquakes and floods. The costliness of first-rate medical care and medical research requires no elaboration. Earthquakes in San Francisco or Los Angeles do not kill nearly as many people as earthquakes that hit Third World cities. Flood conditions can be detected sooner and evacuations begun and carried out more quickly where there are ample resources to produce all the cars, planes, and other vehicles needed to move huge numbers of people out of danger. All these things are made possible by the material wealth which is often treated so disdainfully by those promoting "safety." But to kill the goose that lays the golden egg is, in effect, to kill people.

None of this means that safety laws and policies must be rejected categorically. On the contrary, it means that such laws and policies must be either accepted or rejected *incrementally*, in the light of what is being sacrificed in the specific instance. But that in turn means that the incremental trade-off must be made through institutions and processes capable of such incremental decision making, as courts of law or government bureaucracies seldom are. For example, if the costs of smokestack emissions must be paid in emissions fees or fines by those who own the smokestack, then their incentives will be to reduce those emissions in the most efficient way possible—to the point where the cost of further reductions would exceed the fees or fines. This is likewise the optimum trade-off for society, which gains

nothing by further reductions at costs exceeding the damage done by
the remaining emissions.

To eliminate another thousand dollars' worth of emissions at a cost
of a million dollars is to make the society $999,000 worse off. Yet
this can easily happen when laws, regulations, or court rulings categorically force cutbacks in emissions in some arbitrarily specified
way to some arbitrarily specified level of "safety." Often the officially
specified way of reducing pollution is not the most efficient way of
doing so, or may have been the most efficient way when the laws,
regulations, or court rulings were made but is no longer, as technology advances. Were the same goal being pursued incrementally
through market processes, not only would polluters have incentives
to reduce their pollutions in the most efficient way, but others would
also have an incentive to keep trying to find still better ways to do so.
But, once official categorical edicts have specified a particular way
of reducing emissions, there is less incentive for others to find alternative technologies for accomplishing the same purposes, when the
costs and uncertainties of gaining official acceptance for the new
technology reduce its prospective profitability.

In many other ways as well, market economies often find it easier
to decide issues incrementally. When an insurance company, for
example, seeks additional customers for its fire insurance, it must
determine incrementally how much risk it is prepared to accept in
order to get the additional business and how much it must condition
its insurance policies on certain actions by the customer, in order to
reduce the risks of an outbreak of fire. Make the conditions too strin-
gent and another insurance company gets the customer; make them
too lenient and losses from fires will exceed the premiums paid by
the additional customers. But when a government agency attempts to
insure against various disasters, either directly or by providing "disaster relief" after the fact, it seldom weighs such considerations
incrementally or imposes constraints on the creation of risks.
Instead, dangerous locations or behavior are subsidized at taxpayer
expense, and the media often applaud the "courage" of those who
choose to continue to live in harm's way in areas prone to flooding,
hurricanes, fire, or other natural hazards.

Because inherent limitations of human knowledge are among the most severe constraints, decision making often involves not simply a trade-off of known consequences of alternative courses of action, but instead a weighing of varying probabilities of various outcomes. A certain level of pesticide residues in the soil creates a certain level of probability of a given increase in particular diseases, while banning the use of such pesticides creates a certain level of probability that other, insect-borne diseases will increase—as, for example, a resurgence of malaria followed bans on DDT. Thus, the issue is not one of categorical "safety"—or even safety to some arbitrarily specified level—but rather of weighing alternative probabilities of alternative consequences. To say that pesticides, nuclear power, medicines, automobiles, or other things must be "safe"—either absolutely (which is impossible) or within some specified level of risk—is to say that only one set of probabilities will be weighed. Put differently, to minimize the overall dangers to human life and health is to *accept* specific, preventable dangers rather than follow policies which would create worse preventable dangers. The issue thus is not whether nuclear power is "safe" but whether its dangers are greater or less than the dangers of supplying the same power from coal, oil, hydroelectric dams, or other ways of generating electricity, or the dangers in reducing the availability of electricity. Fewer or dimmer lights are almost certain to increase both accidents and crime, for example, and brownouts and blackouts create other dangers when people get trapped in elevators or fire alarm systems no longer function.

To say that particular dangers on one end of a spectrum are intolerable, either absolutely or beyond some specified risk level, is to say that alternative dangers on the other end of the spectrum are acceptable in whatever open-ended ways they work out. People die when life-saving medicines are kept out of the United States because those medicines have not met the specified safety standards of the Food and Drug Administration. Laws to protect orphans from being adopted into unfit homes condemn more orphans to institutional care or to repeatedly disruptive movements through a whole series of foster homes, both of which can do lasting damage. Banning police use of certain forceful methods of subduing people resisting arrest will indeed lead to a reduction in the number of people injured or killed while being taken into custody—at the cost of an increase in the number of policemen injured or killed in these confrontations. There are no solutions; there are only trade-offs.

The language of politics, and especially of ideological politics, is often categorical language about "rights," about *eliminating* certain evils, *guaranteeing* certain benefits, or *protecting* certain habitats and species. In short, it is the language of solutions and of the unconstrained vision behind solutions, the vision of the anointed. Indirectly but inexorably, this language says that the preferences of the anointed are to supersede the preferences of everyone else—that the particular dangers they fear are to be avoided at all costs and the particular benefits they seek are to be obtained at all costs. Their attempts to remove these decisions from both the democratic process and the market process, and to vest them in obscure commissions, unelected judges, and insulated bureaucracies, are in keeping with the logic of what they are attempting. They are not seeking trade-offs based on the varying preferences of millions of other people, but solutions based on their own presumably superior knowledge and virtue.

CHAPTER 6

CRUSADES OF THE ANOINTED

Beware the people who moralize about great issues; moralizing is easier than facing hard facts.

—John Corry[1]

It is not only the consummated policies of the anointed which reflect their vision. So do their crusades still in progress. The pattern of thinking involved in this vision shows up as strongly in trivial crusades against particular kinds of maps as in crusades over something as deadly serious as AIDS. The function of the vision in enhancing the self-esteem of the anointed is also revealed in the particular groups chosen as targets and in the particular beneficiary groups chosen to symbolize their moral stances. The symbolic function of these latter groups is much like that of team mascots. A mascot's own well-being is not so crucial as its role in enabling others to "make a statement." Many social groups are treated as the human mascots of the anointed, whether or not that ultimately works out to the benefit of those groups themselves. After a general survey of the kinds of crusades to which the anointed are attracted and the kinds of reasoning used in them, the discussion will turn to the targets and the mascots of the anointed.

GENERAL CRUSADES

Safety Crusades

Few issues are so perfectly adapted to the vision of the anointed—and to politics—as issues involving safety. Such issues lend themselves to the rhetoric of "solutions" rather than trade-offs, and to categorical statements, such as: "Not one human life should be sacrificed for the sake of profits," thereby establishing the moral superiority of the anointed over the benighted. On the surface, where most political battles are fought, those opposed to policies or legislation for greater safety seem to have an impossible task. It is only when these issues are examined more closely, within a framework of constrained options, that the heedless proliferation of safety rules can be seen as counterproductive—which is to say, dangerous. People are dying from such "safety."

Perhaps the most obvious examples are the Food and Drug Administration safety rules which make it illegal for Americans to use various life-saving pharmaceutical drugs which have been in use in Europe for years. Americans die while waiting for these drugs to pass elaborate "safety" requirements. The underlying problem with this approach is that it seeks a categorical "solution" in some arbitrarily specified level of drug safety, rather than a trade-off between the dangers of the drug and the dangers of not using the drug. Clearly, with no safety requirements at all, needless deaths from untested drugs would be numerous and unconscionable. But, beyond some point, the residual increment of safety from more years of testing declines to the point where it is outweighed by the lives that continue to be lost through delay. Safety can be fatal.

The same reasoning applies to pesticides, vaccines, and other substances which have both positive and negative effects on human health. The banning of DDT was followed by a resurgence of malaria, a fatal disease to many. Even a small country like Ceylon had 2.8 million people infected with malaria in 1948, before DDT was used. This fell to less than a hundred cases by 1962, after large-scale DDT programs were instituted—and rose again to 2.5 million cases by

1969 after DDT was banned.[2] Although the dangers of DDT have been exaggerated—even professional sprayers, with many times the concentration of DDT in their bodies as the average person, show no medical ill effects—nevertheless, sufficiently massive doses can be harmful.[3] If DDT were 100 percent safe, it would be the only 100 percent safe thing on the planet. The relevant question is the trade-off between the toxic effects of DDT and the effects caused by insect-borne diseases. A very similar question must be asked about vaccines. More than 3 million Americans are vaccinated against whooping cough annually, preventing an estimated 300,000 cases of the disease, including an estimated 400 fatal cases. Yet this same vaccine is also responsible for an estimated 30 cases of brain damage annually.[4] Clearly there is no "solution" in such situations but only a trade-off. It would be obscene to speak of solutions to the parents of brain-damaged children. This is the tragedy of the human condition in its starkest form.

The trade-off approach, however, means that there is no special role for the anointed to play, unless they choose to seize upon one particular kind of safety and make it preemptive over other kinds of safety.

Maps

Perhaps nothing so captures the mind-set of the anointed as a tempest in a teapot created over a common map of the world used for centuries and called the Mercator Projection. This map has been objected to, not by professional map-makers or for scientific reasons, but by liberal-left organizations and individuals for ideological reasons. Because of the methods by which it is produced, a Mercator map shows areas near the equator relatively smaller than similar-sized areas nearer the poles. Thus, Greenland appears larger than Australia on a Mercator Projection, even though Australia is in fact more than three times the size of Greenland. However, this particular distortion is not what has created the controversy. Because so many of the poorer nations of the world are in or near the tropics, their areas seem smaller on the Mercator map, relative to the nations of Europe and North America.

"In our society," a critic claimed, "we unconsciously equate size with importance and even with power, and if the Third World countries are misrepresented, they are likely to be valued less."[5] The source of this revelation about other people's unconscious was of course not revealed. However, a maverick map-maker in Germany named Arno Peters has denounced the Mercator Projection as an example of "European arrogance," since it makes Europe look relatively larger than Third World countries and this has been taken to imply intentional efforts to foster Eurocentric and even imperialist attitudes.[6] In the United States, the National Council of Churches has endorsed and published Peters' alternative map of the world and some United Nations agencies have likewise switched to the Peters map. Textbook publishers have been forced by the Texas Education Agency to include in their books sold in that state a disclaimer concerning the accuracy of the Mercator Projection and to include comparisons of other maps. The fact that most professional map-makers have been highly critical of the Peters alternative map carries no weight with the anointed.

"The political implications of this map are true, whereas the political implications of the Mercator map are false," according to a spokesman for the National Council of Churches' publishing organization.[7] "The question for the church is not primarily one of scientific reliability," he said in defense of the Peters map. "We see this map as being very central to establishment of a correct world view."[8] In short, the integrity of yet another profession is to be violated for the sake of "political correctness."

As with so many other issues involving the vision of the anointed, this ideological uproar turns on a failure to understand the nature of trade-offs and a willingness—or even eagerness—to read malign intentions into others. *All maps necessarily distort the globe* for the simple reason that there is no way to accurately represent a three-dimensional planet on a two-dimensional piece of paper. Something has to give. Some maps have the areas correct but the directions wrong, while others have just the reverse, and still others have other problems.[9]

Choices of map projections, like all other choices, can only be made among the alternatives actually available—and an accurate map of the world has never been one of those alternatives. In map-making, as in other decision-making processes, there are no "solutions" but only trade-offs, which in this case permit one kind of accuracy to be achieved only at the expense of other kinds of accuracy. Finally, to complete the parallel with so many other kinds of misunderstandings by the anointed, maps do not exist for symbolic or ideological purposes but to meet some concrete practical need. One of the most enduring and most important needs met by maps is for finding places, particularly for navigation by ships and later by planes. Given this imperative, which was a matter of life and death to sailors for centuries, the Mercator Projection became a commonly used map because its directions were made accurate—at the expense of distorting the relative size of areas. Given that the users of these maps were far more concerned with arriving alive at their destinations than with comparing real estate, the Mercator Projection reigned supreme as a world map.

Enter the anointed. For them, all this history and the scientific principles of map-making have been blithely ignored and yet another opportunity for moral preening created instead.

The Generic "He"

When someone says that a flock of geese is flying overhead, no one believes that this is an all-female flock, with no ganders among them. It is just that the female name—goose—is used generically to denote the whole species. With people, the male name—man—is used to denote the species, while ships and countries are usually referred to as "she." How all this arose historically is lost somewhere in the mists of time. But just as no one means to exclude ganders when referring to a flock of geese, or to suggest that some female made the decision when Russia decided that *she* would invade the Caucasus, so no one intended to exclude women when the generic "he" was used. One can look through writings from centuries past and see general principles about "man" illustrated by examples of how mothers treat their children or how housewives manage a household.

Simple and obvious as all this should be, a whole crusade has been launched, requiring that clumsy phrases like "he/she" or "s/he" or "he or she" be used, leading to such constructions as "When anyone decides that he or she should have his or her house painted, then he or she should go to a painter and ask him or her how much it will cost." All this is supposed to demonstrate that we are part of the anointed who believe in the equality of the sexes, rather than the benighted who betray anti-female animus by using the generic "he." This cluttering of the English language conveys no additional information in the statement itself, however much it may serve as a shibboleth identifying the anointed. It connotes also false information, namely that those who preferred a less cluttered way of writing were secretly harboring malign thoughts toward women—or "self-hate" where these writers were women themselves. As with so many verbal and other fetishes of the anointed, it serves primarily to circumvent a need for either logic or evidence.

Trivial as such crusades may seem, they have been very successful in changing the way people talk in the media, in academia, and in government. Not only is the generic "he" taboo in many quarters, the speech controllers have pressed on to new conquests, attacking such words as "layman," "craftsman," "actress," or "matron," which violate their unisex view of the world, and also proscribe such phrases as "to master a language" because it uses a sex-specific word.[10] These examples are from an official guidebook put out by the Australian government, which shows how far such crusades have spread. An American guidebook, distributed internationally, declares that there is "a perfectly scientific, completely foolproof, and highly theoretical model for avoiding sexism on the job."[11] As so often happens, pretensions of "science" are the last refuge of those who offer neither the evidence nor the logic that are integral to science.

The net effect of all this is that young women, especially in educational institutions where they are bombarded with radical feminist propaganda, are led to believe that every use of the generic "he" in books of the past is proof of disdain or hostility toward women, when in fact such usage simply avoided cluttering up the language or forcing writers into strained constructions and awkward phrases. In short, the anointed are helped to make yet another group feel like victims and to regard the anointed as their rescuers.

MASCOTS OF THE ANOINTED

The ideals of "a government of laws and not of men" and "equal protection of the law" are at the heart of American constitutional law and the democratic process. Yet, increasingly, government has come to be seen as a way of benefitting particular groups adopted as mascots, often without much regard for what that does to other groups or to the integrity of the system as a whole. Groups disliked, distrusted, or feared by the general public are particularly eligible to become mascots who symbolize the superior wisdom and virtue of the anointed.

Even for judges, where impartiality has been the treasured ideal for centuries, this arbitrary singling out of beneficiaries has been held up as a new ideal. During Judge David H. Souter's confirmation hearings to become a Supreme Court justice, a member of the Senate Judiciary Committee urged him to be a "champion" of "the less fortunate," declaring this to be "the role assigned to the Court in our system."[12] Nor was this simply the aberration of one senator. The notion that judges, including Supreme Court justices, are to align themselves on various "sides" has reached the Supreme Court itself. Justice William O. Douglas referred to previous court decisions as "good tidings to the moneyed interests" and described these decisions as making clear "on which side the Court was aligned."[13] In a similar vein, New York Times columnist Linda Greenhouse characterized Justice Harry Blackmun's changing criteria of legal interpretation over the years as a changing of sides on social issues, in which the "defender of a comfortable status quo became a questioner and then a challenger."[14] One of Blackmun's former law clerks likewise praised him as someone who had "learned that Justices must take sides."[15]

Those who urge such championing or taking sides are suggesting something for which even an umpire would be considered disgraced beyond redemption. An umpire cannot become a "champion" of pitchers, except at the expense of batters and vice versa—and in either case at the expense of the integrity of the game. Nevertheless, this view has grown and, in many cases, prevailed in practice. Among the mascots chosen by the anointed have been vagrants, criminals and carriers of contagious diseases.

Vagrants or "the Homeless"

A textbook example of someone with anti-social behavior being turned into a mascot by a judge with the vision of the anointed was Richard F. Kreimer, a vagrant who made a nuisance of himself in a New Jersey public library. During the late 1980s, a number of homeless people began coming into this library in the small town of Morristown, New Jersey, disturbing both the other library users and the staff by their behavior and their body odors. Richard F. Kreimer in particular often exhibited offensive and disruptive behavior, including talking loudly to himself and to others and, on at least one occasion, was so belligerent toward a librarian as to cause her to call the police.[16] Some librarians resigned rather than put up with it.[17]

Theft of property, smoking, and using drugs and alcohol were just some of the homeless people's activities complained of by the library officials. On May 16, 1989, a notice was posted, limiting the use of the library to persons "engaged in normal activities associated with the use of a public library" and specifically banning people who "annoy others" in various ways and whose "personal hygiene" was not acceptable.[18] This policy was challenged in court by Kreimer, with the aid of the American Civil Liberties Union and others who literally made this a federal case—one costing the town more than a quarter of a million dollars in legal fees.[19]

Federal District Court Judge H. Lee Sarokin ruled in favor of Kreimer. Declaring the library to be a "public forum," defined as "an available public space where citizens communicate their ideas through the spoken word," Judge Sarokin declared it covered by the First Amendment.[20] It was a place where people have a "right to receive ideas."[21] The library's "drastic exclusion" denies "access" to reading materials for "the poor and homeless who are without the funds to purchase even a single newspaper."[22] Judge Sarokin declared the library policy "vague" and brushed aside the claim that Kreimer and others were annoying other people: "Conduct that annoys some people does not annoy others."[23] Moreover, a hygiene test has "a disparate impact on the poor."[24] In short, the library rules "unreasonably frustrate, infringe, or obstruct the expressional and associational rights of individuals," according to Judge Sarokin.[25]

In a classic expression of the vision of the anointed, Judge Sarokin lectured the community on its attitude toward the homeless: "If we wish to shield our eyes and noses from the homeless, we should revoke their conditions, not their library cards."[26] In other words, it is society's fault that people end up like Richard Kreimer—and it is within society's capability to change their conditions. In reality, Kreimer was born into a middle-class family and inherited with his brother an estate worth $340,000.[27] What society was supposed to do to prevent Kreimer—an able-bodied white male—from becoming a bum was unspecified. Yet other people's legal rights were to be disregarded or held hostage pending the carrying out of Judge Sarokin's social vision.

Just as Kreimer was treated as a mascot, so the other library users were treated as expendable, and the law-abiding and taxpaying citizens of the town were treated as targets. In addition to having to spend more than a quarter of a million dollars defending against a lawsuit, the town ultimately had to settle out of court, paying Kreimer $150,000, in order to prevent its policemen's homes from being in jeopardy of being taken away from them to satisfy an adverse court judgment.[28]

Here, as elsewhere, the anointed show what Jean-François Revel has called "a pitiless ferocity toward some" and "a boundless indulgence toward others."[29] Both the particular mascots chosen and the particular targets chosen serve the same purpose—to demonstrate the superiority of the anointed over the benighted. To put themselves solidly on the side of the supposed underdogs, the anointed often place permanent labels on people, on the basis of transient circumstances. Richard Kreimer was not born "homeless." In fact, he inherited a home and sold it.

Most homeless people are by no means as fortunate as Kreimer, either in their initial circumstances or in finding a judge so ready to adopt them as mascots, in order to engage in moral preening. However, there are similar attitudes in the intellectual community in general and in the mass media in particular. The thesis that the homeless are "people just like us" who happen to have fallen victim to misfortune has been repeated endlessly in the media and the television camera has often presented as typical what is most atypical among the homeless: normal, intact families forced into homelessness by some unexpected injury, plant shutdown, or other unavoidable catastrophe. Politicians promoting various programs to solve the homeless problem likewise have a vested interest in presenting the atypical as typical, in an effort to gather political support behind their programs. Homeless advocates report such requests as: "We need a witness for a hearing. Can you get us a homeless family: mother, father—father out of work in the past four months from an industrial plant—white?"[30]

Despite such image-making, a substantial component of the homeless are mentally ill people, often either biologically so or made so by drugs and alcohol. An estimated one-third of the homeless fall into the mentally ill category and another third into the category of alcohol and drug abusers.[31] All have been adopted as mascots of the anointed, though in different ways. For example, lawyer-activists have made it increasingly difficult and costly to confine the mentally ill to institutions, rather than let them roam the streets.[32] Costly lawsuits and the threat of large damage awards add to the incentives for local officials to discharge the mentally ill from hospitals.

The premise behind all this is that "society" is to blame for the things it chooses to call mental illness. It is assumed that either there is no such thing as mental illness, aside from society's arbitrary condemnation of certain behavior,[33] or else where there is a genuine problem, it is regarded as either a product of bad child rearing or of more general social malaise requiring political "solutions." Either way, the problem is due ultimately to the fact that other people are not as wise or as virtuous as the anointed, and the solution is to impose this superior wisdom and virtue, whether on the family or on the whole society. In short, the mentally ill are mascots of the anointed, enabling the latter to "make a statement."

Notions of social causes of mental illness have had to retreat before growing scientific evidence of biological malfunctions affecting the brain. However, this better understanding of the biology of much mental illness has led to medications which provide another rationale for opening the mental hospitals and sending mental patients back home—or out onto the streets, as the case may be. However, even those mentally ill individuals who can be helped by medication often stop taking the medication, once they are no longer living under supervision, and retrogress to delusions and incoherence. Those who are sleeping on the streets on bitterly cold winter nights are as much mascots of the anointed as Richard Kreimer. In both cases, they serve to enable the anointed to score points against a benighted society, whether or not this proves ultimately to be a benefit to the mascots themselves.

Incidentally, Judge H. Lee Sarokin was elevated to the Circuit Court of Appeals by President Clinton in 1994.

Criminals

For at least 200 years, those with the vision of the anointed have been claiming that criminals have been misunderstood by the public and mistreated by the law. A product of social circumstances and societal failures, criminals should not be punished but rehabilitated, according to this view, found in such eighteenth-century figures as Condorcet and Godwin.[34] In addition to questioning the morality of punishing people for circumstances beyond their control, the anointed tend to believe that punishment does not work but that rehabilitation does. This belief is part of a wider pattern among the anointed of emphasizing dispositions rather than incentives, whether discussing criminals, international diplomacy, or child rearing.

The conclusions of those with this vision are as logical as the opposite conclusions of those with the tragic vision. It is the impervi-

ousness of the anointed to any argument or evidence, and their readi-
ness to dismiss and condemn those with different views, which have
made criminals mascots symbolizing the superiority of the anointed.
An episode in San Jose, California, illustrates this mind-set. The federally funded Alternatives to Incarceration program sent selected
imprisoned criminals to colleges to complete their sentences there
instead of behind bars. After a series of rapes at San Jose State University, the city's police chief discovered that imprisoned rapists had
been released to that institution and that "convicted felons routinely
stalked women in dark streets in the vicinity of the university in
downtown San Jose."[35] What is revealing is the response when he
expressed his concern to the director of this particular project:

> When I complained, the project director said the "clients" were
> screened and that California had declared it an exemplary program.
> Actually, we later found out that the program screened applicants only
> on the basis of academic scores. Federal rules prevented consideration
> of their criminal records. And California had declared the program
> exemplary only because it submitted quarterly reports on time.
>
> When my complaints about the program became public, I was cen-
> sured by the students and faculty and advised by my superiors in city
> hall to go easy. After all, this was an exemplary, federally funded pro-
> gram to reduce recidivism.[36]

Note that it was not considered sufficient for the anointed to disagree with the police chief's assessment of the danger; it was necessary
to condemn him for expressing such concerns. Moreover, the *intentions*
of the program—to reduce recidivism—were considered weighty in
themselves. Then, a few months later, came the tragic denouement
when the police "arrested an honor student in the program for brutally
torturing, raping, and murdering two women near the university." He
was "articulate and the project had often used him to show how wonderful it was that bright people could get a college education instead of
languishing in prison." Nor was this an isolated failure. During the
entire decade of this program, not one "client" actually graduated from
the university but a number were arrested for crimes against women.[37]

The point here is not simply that some people were mistaken in their beliefs and hopes for this particular program, but that they barricaded themselves against all beliefs to the contrary and morally condemned those who expressed such beliefs. It is this pattern which has been all too characteristic of the anointed, on this and other issues, over a very long span of time. Moreover, such patterns can be found among the anointed from the local level to the Supreme Court of the United States.

Most of the U.S. Supreme Court's landmark decisions expanding—or creating—"rights" for criminals occurred during the 1960s, but another landmark decision of national importance originated earlier in the Circuit Court of Appeals for the District of Columbia, a court aptly characterized as having "a more-liberal-than-thou posture" that made it "the darling of the *Washington Post*."[38] This was Judge David L. Bazelon's 1954 decision expanding the "insanity" defense in criminal law, an expansion which reverberated far beyond the legal jurisdiction of this particular court, becoming by imitation in other jurisdictions the law of the land. It was thus not simply the view of one judge or of one court. It was an expression of the vision of the anointed.

Before Judge Bazelon's decision, American courts tended to follow the same legal principle used in British law in the nineteenth-century *McNaughten* case:

> . . . the jurors ought to be told in all cases that every man is to be presumed to be sane, and to possess a sufficient degree of reason to be responsible for his crimes, until the contrary be proved to their satisfaction; and that, to establish a defense on the ground of insanity, it must be clearly proved that, at the time of the committing of the act, the party accused was labouring under such a defect of reason, from disease of the mind, as not to know the nature and quality of the act he was doing, or, if he did know it, that he did not know he was doing what was wrong.[39]

This was not good enough for Chief Judge Bazelon. In the *Durham* decision of 1954, he repudiated the *McNaughten* test by shifting the

burden of proof to the prosecution, when the defense claimed that
the defendant was not guilty by reason of insanity, and by allowing
much more expansive psychiatric speculations to be introduced as
evidence in the trial. In his decision in the *Durham* case, overturning
the burglary conviction of a man with a long history of crimes—
including writing bad checks, which hardly suggests a lack of reasoning ability—Judge Bazelon spoke of "the science of psychiatry"
and "the science of psychology"[40] as reasons for letting speculations
from these fields deflect the criminal punishments that would otherwise fall on the defendant. No longer did the defendant have to be
insane. It was enough if there was "some evidence" that the accused
"suffered from a diseased or defective mental condition."[41]

The nebulous notion of "defective mental condition" evolved in
later cases into saying that someone "suffering from an abnormal
condition of the mind"[42] was not responsible for his crime. To follow
this logic, the more horrible the crime, the further the criminal
departed from civilized norms and by definition the more "abnormal"
his mental condition. By such reasoning, every violation of law
should be excused. But of course nothing as straightforward as this
was proposed. Instead, the speculations of psychiatrists and psychologists were to be accepted as "science" and criminals acquitted
whenever these "scientists" raised sufficient doubts in the minds of
jurors. It was not necessary to *convince* the jury that the defendant
was insane or even had an abnormal mental condition, because the
burden of proof was on the prosecution and insanity was no longer
necessary. Congressional legislation in 1984 shifted the burden of
proof back to defense attorneys who claimed that their clients were
suffering from mental defects, and judicial interpretations are still
evolving. But the decisive turn in criminal justice was abandoning a
straightforward standard for nebulous speculations, the latter requiring vastly more knowledge than anyone possesses, as so often happens in the vision of the anointed.

Despite much talk about "science" in discussions of psychiatric
and psychological speculations—usually speculations about people
who were never patients of those making sweeping statements about
their mental condition as of the time of a crime that the speculators

never witnessed—the key scientific procedure of empirical verification has been not merely lacking but almost totally ignored. A psychiatrist or psychologist may testify hundreds of times as an "expert witness" in criminal cases without once being challenged as to the actual consequences of his previous testimony that turned criminals loose into the community. His "expertise" is never put to the crucial test of a record as to how often he has been wrong—and at what cost in money, violence, or lives. As in so many other areas, the *word* "science" is used as a *substitute* for logic and evidence. In short, the essence of science is ignored in favor of its appearance.

Many have claimed that the "insanity" defense is not a serious problem because it is used in only a fraction of criminal cases, and used successfully in a smaller fraction. This understates its full impact as another factor delaying trials and providing grounds for appeals after conviction in an already overburdened court system. Moreover, the demoralization of the public, as it sees horrible crimes go unpunished and violent criminals turned loose again in their midst because of psychiatrists' speculations, is not a small consideration. Riots broke out in San Francisco after a multiple murderer was let off with a lenient sentence because of speculation that his eating "Twinkies" might have made him more excitable.[43] But, whether or not public outrage takes this form or some other forms, there are numerous signs of a loss of confidence in the courts and in the ability of the society to protect the public from criminals and other antisocial individuals who have become mascots of judges.

It is not only psychiatric testimony which tempts judges into decisions which presuppose far more knowledge than anyone has ever possessed. Ordinary petty criminals have learned how to manipulate the arrogant gullibility of judges. A series in the *Washington Post* in 1994 included this vignette of one of many court appearances by a woman with a long history of petty crimes:

Rosa Lee had chosen her clothes carefully when she appeared two months earlier before Commissioner John Treanor on Nov. 13, 1990. She wanted to look as poor as possible to draw his sympathy.

She had worn an ill-fitting winter coat, gray wool overalls and a

white wool hat pulled back to show her graying hair. She had removed
her upper dental plate, giving her a toothless look when she smiled.
"My homey look," she called it. "No lipstick. No earrings. No
nothing!"[44]

The net result of all this was a suspended sentence for a woman
with a lifelong history of shoplifting (which she taught her children)
and drug addiction, the mother of children and grandchildren who
have been in prison. The fundamental problem was not that the
judge was taken in but that he imagined himself capable of knowing
enough to disregard the penalties of the law and play Solomon or
social worker instead. Although the reporter who covered the story
was well aware of how phony the act was—the woman asked him,
right in the courtroom, "Was I good?" and was pleased when he said
"Yes"—nevertheless the series blamed "society." The first story in
the series said of Rosa Lee: "Her life spans a half-century of hard-
ship in blighted neighborhoods not far from the majestic buildings
where policy-makers have largely failed in periodic efforts to break
the cycle of poverty that has trapped her and so many other Americans for so long."[45]

Criminals are the most obvious, and most resented, of those for
whose benefit judges have stretched the law, in an attempt to achieve
the cosmic justice of compensating for preexisting disadvantages.
Chief Judge Bazelon, who played such a key role in the evolution of
criminal law, was quite clear that the kind of legal principles he advocated were designed to "compensate for the disparities that produce
unequal access to constitutional rights" among those people "stunted
by many circumstances, including the accident of birth" and to "give
the stunted a box to stand on to reach our own eye level."[46] Convinced
that "poverty is the root cause of crime,"[47] Judge Bazelon expressed a
widespread view of the 1960s, and a long-standing assumption of the
anointed, that sufficient knowledge already existed, when he said:

The circumstances that lead some of these people to crime are no
mystery. They are born into families struggling to survive—if they
have families at all. They are raised in deteriorating, overcrowded

housing. They lack adequate nutrition and health care. They are sub-jected to prejudice and educated in unresponsive schools. They are denied the sense of order, purpose, and self-esteem that makes law-abiding citizens. With nothing to preserve and nothing to lose, they turn to crime for economic survival, a sense of excitement and accom-plishment, and an outlet for frustration, desperation, and rage.[48]

That most people born in poverty did not become criminals, and that people born in more fortunate circumstances sometimes did, was acknowledged by Judge Bazelon,[49] but this acknowledgment made no real difference in his conclusions or his judicial decisions. Corre-lation was causation.

Such reasoning might make sense if human beings were born into the world already civilized, so that some special explanation was necessary as to why they later engaged in barbaric behavior. But when everyone is born into the world today as uncivilized as the bar-barians of ancient times, there is nothing mysterious about the later behavior of those whose parents did not bother to civilize them. Nor is it surprising that such irresponsible parents have not developed, either in themselves or in their children, the skills, attitudes, and discipline necessary to rise out of poverty. At the very least, the direction of causation cannot automatically be assumed to be from poverty to crime, especially after decades in which massive govern-ment programs to alleviate poverty have seen crime rates rising to new heights.

The isolated views of one judge would hardly be worth noticing, except that (1) such views were echoed throughout the media, which lionized Judge Bazelon, (2) the U.S. Supreme Court made similar views "the law of the land" in its decisions during the 1960s and 1970s, and (3) both federal and state courts across the country went on similar judicial adventures, interpreting laws to mean whatever they wished them to mean, typically in consonance with the vision of the anointed. Perhaps the most dramatic examples came from the California Supreme Court when Rose Bird was its chief justice.

In more than 60 consecutive death penalty cases—every such case to reach the California Supreme Court during her tenure—Chief

Justice Bird voted to overturn the penalty, on grounds that the defendant had not had a fair trial as required by the Constitution. Either there was not a single judge in the entire state of California who ever gave a murderer a fair trial or else Rose Bird was simply using this claim as a pretense to enforce her own personal opposition to the death penalty. Since the state constitution explicitly stated that trial verdicts were not to be overturned by appellate courts unless the legal errors in those trials resulted in a real "miscarriage of justice,"[50] Chief Justice Bird's votes implied that these 60 consecutive trials not only contained technical legal errors, but also that these errors were of such a magnitude and nature that they created a miscarriage of justice in every case. The initial implausibility of this happening 60 consecutive times becomes even more incredible after a look at the particulars of some of these cases.

In one of the cases that came before the Bird court, a man went to a store not only to commit an armed robbery but also with a list of people who worked at that store whom he planned to kill. He proceeded methodically down his list, murdering the workers with shotgun blasts and pausing to reload, so that premeditation was not an issue. Yet, because the trial judge's instructions to the jury failed to mention premeditation as a requirement for a first-degree murder conviction, Chief Justice Bird voted to overturn the death penalty.[51] Death penalties in other premeditated murder cases were likewise reversed by the California Supreme Court on the same grounds. Because some judges may not have wanted to insult the jurors' intelligence by discussing premeditation in cases where it was so blatantly obvious, this technicality was taken as a sufficient reason for declaring that the murderer was a victim of a miscarriage of justice.

Another murderer had his death penalty overturned on grounds that his attorney had failed to make an insanity defense.[52] The California Supreme Court did not claim that the murderer was in fact insane, but simply second-guessed the defense attorney's strategy and pronounced it inadequate, thereby making this a de facto denial of the defendant's right to counsel. Here again, we see the insanity defense having an impact well beyond the cases in which it is attempted or sustained. Similar ingenuity was used by Rose Bird to vote against every death penalty that came before her.

Again, the idiosyncracies of one judge or even one court are significant primarily because they are indicative of the *zeitgeist* among elites. When Rose Bird's reelection was challenged in 1986, much of the national media, as well as much of the California media, sprang to her defense. *New York Times* columnist Tom Wicker defended her invariable vote to overturn death penalty cases by claiming that "in every single instance of a death-penalty reversal, the Bird court has found a constitutional infirmity"[53]—as if the court could possibly have claimed anything else, regardless of how tenuous that claim was. The death penalty cases were an "emotional issue,"[54] according to Wicker, using the standard term for any principle of concern to the benighted, while Rose Bird's position on the side of the anointed was a matter of principle—"the rule of law,"[55] no less. The *Los Angeles Times* likewise claimed that the Bird court "reversed death sentences because of errors they found in the records in the courts below"— that they were trying to "enforce justice even when it is unpopular."[56] A *New York Times* editorial claimed that Rose Bird's opponents were "politicizing" the judiciary[57]—not that it was she who had turned the court into an enforcer of her own ideology, rather than the law. Columnist Anthony Lewis depicted the campaign against Bird as an attack on "an independent judiciary."[58] Others in the media chimed in with support for Chief Justice Bird, usually not mentioning the number of consecutive reversals or the egregious specifics of the court's straining after technicalities, in defiance of the constitutional requirement that a substantive miscarriage of justice was necessary for a reversal.

That Rose Bird was a symbol of the anointed was further demonstrated in the judicial elections of 1986. Although no California Supreme Court justice had ever lost an election before, Rose Bird was defeated at the polls in 56 out of 58 counties, finding such electoral support as she had concentrated in bastions of the anointed. She carried San Francisco County with 65 percent of the vote and Alameda County—home of the University of California at Berkeley—with 51 percent. The closest she came to a majority elsewhere was 45 percent

of the vote in Santa Cruz County, home of the "politically correct"
University of California at Santa Cruz, and the same percentage of the
vote in Marin County, an affluent and trendy suburb of San
Francisco.[59] In character to the end, in her last week as chief justice,
Rose Bird voted in favor of paroling a cop-killer featured in the book
and movie *The Onion Field*.[60]

Those for whose benefit the law is stretched by judges—the mascots—include not only criminals but also a wide range of groups
looked on with disfavor by others, whether for valid or invalid reasons. That such people would be adopted as mascots by those with
the prevailing vision is completely consistent with the role in which
the anointed cast themselves, as being nobler and wiser than others.
Anybody can condemn criminals, so there is no distinction in it. But
to come up with rationales, rights, and "solutions" expressing solicitude for criminals is far more consistent with being one of the
anointed with special insights. For similar reasons, all sorts of other
groups are depicted as victims whom the anointed are to rescue from
the benighted. Given the imperfections of human beings, some of
these groups have in fact been given a bad deal, though it by no
means follows that what is proposed in the vision of the anointed will
make things better on net balance.

Disease Carriers

A classic example of the rights of particular mascot groups overriding the rights of others are cases involving people with contagious diseases, including fatal contagious diseases. The landmark Supreme
Court case in this area involved an elementary school teacher with
active tuberculosis, who was fired because of fears that she might
infect the children she taught. The teacher sued, charging discrimination against the handicapped, in violation of the Rehabilitation Act of
1973.

A majority of the U.S. Supreme Court ruled that it was indeed discrimination because tuberculosis could be considered a handicap.
Although the school board argued that the teacher was fired not
because of *her* impairment but because her presence threatened the

health of others, Justice Brennan, writing for the majority, refused to accept that distinction:

> Arline's contagiousness and her physical impairment each resulted from the same underlying condition, tuberculosis. It would be unfair to allow an employer to seize upon the distinction between the effects of a disease on others and the effects of a disease on a patient and use that distinction to justify discriminatory treatment.[61]

The bending of the law for mascots has as its counterpoint the presumptive guilt of target groups, such as employers, who would "seize upon" excuses to fire people. The fate of innocent third parties, such as schoolchildren, carries little weight when taking sides with mascots against targets. As in so many other contexts, such taking sides provided an occasion for assertions of the superior virtue and wisdom of the anointed as compared to the benighted. In Justice Brennan's words, the law's purpose was to "combat the effects of erroneous but nevertheless prevalent perceptions about the handicapped,"[62] to "ensure that handicapped individuals are not denied jobs or other benefits because of the prejudiced attitudes or the ignorance of others."[63] He repeatedly characterized others' responses in such terms as "reflexive reactions,"[64] "mythology,"[65] and "prejudice, stereotypes, or unfounded fear."[66]

Since the term "handicapped" covers such a wide range of conditions, even in its normal usage—quite aside from Justice Brennan's extension of the term to people with tuberculosis—almost any blanket statement about "the handicapped" is virtually certain to be wrong. So is any blanket statement about how mistaken or malign the benighted are in their particular assessments of the individual cases they encounter firsthand. But, although the term "handicapped" is, if anything, even less precise than "vagrant," there is no danger that laws favoring the handicapped would be declared unconstitutional as "void for vagueness," for such laws promote the vision of the anointed and laws against vagrancy go counter to it.

Even if medical experts were to certify that the tubercular teacher in question was a danger to the health of the children, thereby permitting her to be removed from the classroom, the law protecting the handicapped required that she be considered for other assignments for which she was "otherwise qualified." The Supreme Court sent the case back to the District Court to determine whether the teacher in question was "otherwise qualified" to be kept employed by the school system.[67]

Homosexual activists greeted this Supreme Court decision with approval, because of its possible implications for those with AIDS. Although AIDS was not at issue in this particular case, Justice Brennan in a footnote left open the question whether AIDS carriers might also be considered as "handicapped" people entitled to the same legal protections.[68]

Judges, by and large, have adopted this same vision of the anointed in dealing with cases involving AIDS. While public health officials have for decades traced the sources of other infectious diseases to those individuals who were carrying such diseases and spreading them, tracing AIDS to its sources has been declared a violation of federal laws protecting the "handicapped."[69] A jail inmate with AIDS who was kept separated from other prisoners was awarded $155,000 in damages.[70] A three-judge panel ruled that the Department of Health and Human Services could cut off $107 million in federal funds to a medical center which merely restricted the duties of a pharmacist with AIDS.[71] In courtrooms as elsewhere, AIDS carriers have become mascots of the anointed.

No group has so polarized the anointed from the benighted as people infected with the AIDS virus. In keeping with their having performed this vital role, AIDS carriers are treated as the most sacred of the mascots.

In contrast to the identification, and sometimes even quarantine, of people infected with other deadly and contagious diseases, AIDS carriers have been guaranteed anonymity by both law and policy as they mingle with unsuspecting members of the general public. From the beginning, various medical and other public officials have been preoccupied with reassuring the public on how they *cannot* get AIDS. As late as 1983, people were being reassured that their chances of catching AIDS from transfusions of untested blood were "extremely remote."[72] Secretary of Health and Human Services Margaret Heckler went on nationwide television on July 3, 1983, to "assure the American people that the blood supply is 100% safe."[73] But, just one year later, the Centers for Disease Control began reporting dozens of cases of people who caught AIDS from blood transfusions[74] and, just two years after that, the AIDS deaths from blood transfusions were in the thousands.[75] More than half of the nation's 20,000 hemophiliacs were infected with the AIDS virus as a result of the numerous blood transfusions they require.[76] The long incubation period of the disease proved to be like a time bomb.

The problem was not simply with what medical authorities did not know at the time but with what they presumed to know and to proclaim to the benighted—to those who, in Secretary Heckler's words, had "irrational fears" and "unwarranted panic."[77] Looking back on this period, years later, a feature story in *U.S. News and World Report* noted:

> Americans have long believed the blood supply to be safer than it is. In a 1983 joint statement, for example, the Red Cross and two trade groups representing most other blood banks—the American Association of Blood Banks and the Council of Community Blood Centers—put the risk of getting AIDS from a transfusion at about 1 in a million. In fact, it was at least 1 in 660—and up to 1 in 25 in high-exposure cities like San Francisco.[78]

Mistaken beliefs about the safety of untested blood did not originate with the public but with the anointed elites. This was only one of the many ways in which these elites pooh-poohed the dangers from AIDS. San Francisco nurses who used masks and gloves while handling AIDS patients were punished by hospital authorities for doing so in 1985,[79] though such precautions later became accepted and then officially recommended in federal guidelines.[80] It was at one time triumphantly proclaimed that no health-care worker had ever contracted AIDS from patients, but by September 1985 there were the first of many cases of nurses, lab workers, and others who caught the disease from AIDS patients[81] and by 1991 there were cases of

patients who caught AIDS from a dentist.[82] As *Newsweek* noted: "Just
a year ago most authorities on AIDS considered it virtually impossible for an AIDS-infected physician or dentist to pass the virus on to
patients."[83]

Precautions to protect the public from AIDS carriers have repeatedly been *backed into* only after new revelations devastated previous
reassurances. The fundamental issue in all this is not why medical
authorities were repeatedly mistaken but why this disease was
approached in a way directly the opposite of the way other contagious
and potentially fatal diseases have been approached. Instead of erring
on the side of caution in defense of the public, as with previous
deadly and infectious diseases, "responsible" officials approached
the spread of AIDS by making the protection of the AIDS carrier from
the public paramount. One political reason has been fear of offending
the organized, zealous, single-issue homosexual organizations and
their allies in the media, in the American Civil Liberties Union, and
in other liberal bastions. But this only raises the further question as to
why the interests of carriers of a deadly, incurable, and contagious
disease should be regarded in such circles as preemptive over the
rights of hundreds of millions of other people. The answer to this more
fundamental question seems to be that AIDS carriers meet the criteria
for a mascot group sharply differentiating the anointed from the
benighted.

One of the arguments for maintaining the anonymity of AIDS carriers is that otherwise they will be "driven underground" and
become more dangerous. But anonymity laws make them "underground" to begin with—and maintain them in that situation even
when some others discover that they carry a dangerous disease but
are deterred by heavy legal penalties from warning anyone else. One
rationale has been that the "counseling" received by AIDS carriers
as part of their treatment will make these carriers more careful not
to spread their disease to other people. This view, expressed by the
New York Times among others,[84] would certainly be in keeping with
the vision of the anointed, as contrasted with relying on incentives,
as in the tragic vision. Since the AIDS carriers are already fatally

infected, the only incentives likely to be effective are those operating on the healthy population, who have every incentive to safeguard their own health—if the anointed do not prevent them from doing so.

Some indication of how much havoc can be wreaked by just one person with AIDS who does not choose to respond to "counseling" can be illustrated by the case of a homosexual airline steward who flew around the country infecting others with AIDS in gay bathhouses. As of 1982, at least 40 of the first 248 homosexual men found to have AIDS had either had sex with this steward or with someone else who had.[85] He lived for two more years, with an active sex life, despite knowing that he was infected with AIDS and despite entreaties, warnings, and even threats.[86] After having sex in the dim lights of a gay bathhouse, he would turn up the lights to show his partner the lesions on his skin and say: "I've got gay cancer. I'm going to die and so are you."[87] Although medical authorities in both the United States and Canada knew who he was and what he was doing, they were legally prohibited from warning anyone.

Other AIDS carriers also continued to have sex and some have deliberately bitten prison guards, or policemen trying to arrest them, in order to infect them.[88] Once infected, the incentives to stop were zero, except for those with consciences. Again, doctors and others fully aware of what they are doing are prevented by severe penalties of the law from warning anyone. Yet the *New York Times* editorially supported parole boards' decisions to parole various AIDS-infected prisoners as soon as they served the minimum term for eligibility for parole—"but only if they disclose their condition to those on the outside who might be imperilled."[89] How anyone could enforce such a requirement was left undisclosed. Feasibility questions often have a low priority in the vision of the anointed and mascots have a high priority.

Many of the same people who spread alarm over remote possibilities of dangers from pesticides or nuclear energy are among those most willing to accept dangers from AIDS carriers. Mascots are treated differently from targets.

TARGETS OF THE ANOINTED

Just as the logic of their vision guides the anointed in their choices of mascots, so it guides their selection of targets. The prime requisite for both mascots and targets is that they must distinguish the anointed from the benighted. Just as groups disdained by others become eligible to be mascots of the anointed, so groups respected by others are eligible to become targets. These include business people, physicians, and other professionals, members of religious communities, policemen, and others whose social roles or financial success engender respect or influence in the society at large. Just as the law is stretched and strained for the benefit of mascots, so it is stretched and strained to the detriment of targets.

Business and the Professions

No part of the law has been stretched and strained beyond recognition more often than the laws allowing businesses and the medical profession to be sued. It has always been possible to sue people for damages caused by their negligence. What happened after the vision of the anointed swept through the courts during the 1960s was that people could now be sued successfully whether they were negligent or not—and in some cases, without even being proved to have anything to do with whatever harm had occurred. But this never happened to those in groups who were mascots of the anointed. It happened to those in groups who were targets.

In a California case during the Rose Bird era, an employee who was waiting for his employer to arrive and open for business used the time to work under the hood of his own car on a public street and was injured by a passing motorist—and was then declared to be entitled to workman's compensation.[90] In a federal case, the purchaser of a farm machine from International Harvester specifically requested that the safety device which came with it be removed before delivery, apparently to make the machine easier to get in and out of a barn. Yet, when his employee was killed as a result of the safety device being missing, it was International Harvester who was held to be legally liable for the death. The fact that the purchaser made the decision to remove the safety device, and that the employee made the decision to operate it without the safety device, meant nothing. Neither did the fact that the employee died as a result of taking a chance by standing up on a machine part to try to see what was happening nearby, slipping and then falling under another machine part that crushed him. His "exercise of prudence or care" was ruled by the court to be "irrelevant."[91] Apparently mascots can do no wrong and targets can do no right.

In another federal case, the producer of a herbicide was held responsible for the death of a worker who paid no attention to the warning label, even though that label said exactly what federal rules said that it should say. Despite the fact that the company had no legal choice except to word the label precisely as prescribed by the Environmental Protection Agency, the court ruled that "the duty to provide an adequate warning of the danger was not met"[92] because its warnings about fatal consequences did not include the particular fatal consequence from which this individual died. Compliance with both federal laws prescribing the exact wording of the warning and state laws requiring more extensive warning "cannot be said to be impossible," according to the court, which reasoned:

> Chevron can continue to use the EPA-approved label and can at the same time pay damages to successful tort plaintiffs such as Mr. Ferebee; alternatively, Chevron can petition to EPA to allow the label to be made more comprehensive.[93]

Another helpful suggestion was that Chevron could simply stop selling this chemical in this state.[94] That this one-sided way of looking at things violated centuries of legal tradition was brushed aside:

> We live in an organizational society in which traditional common-law limitations on an actor's duty must give way to the realities of society.[95]

In numerous other situations, people in businesses and professions began to be held legally liable who would never have been held liable in the past—and this not due to changed statutory law but because of new judicial interpretations. For example, when the manager of an apartment complex raped a tenant, the owners were sued.[96] Consumers who ignored warnings and disclaimers on the products they bought were nevertheless allowed to sue the manufacturers for damages when things went wrong.[97] Judges became so ingenious in circumventing warnings and contractual disclaimers, in order to allow manufacturers to be sued, that one wit suggested that torts be renamed *contorts.*

In many cases, it was no longer necessary to prove that a particular product caused a particular harm, or that a particular manufacturer produced that product if it did. When no one knew which firm in a given industry had produced the particular product that harmed particular individuals, courts sometimes let victims sue all those who were manufacturing that product, splitting up the damages to be paid according to the firms' respective shares of the market.[98] In other cases, juries were free to speculate as to whether they thought the product might have been responsible, even if the product met every safety standard prescribed by law and even if the preponderance of scientific opinion was that the product in question did not produce the harm in question.[99]

In many cases, what was crucial was whether cases were allowed to go to trial, not what the outcome of the trial was. The vast penumbra of uncertainty around tort liability trials in the wake of the judicial revolution of the 1960s and 1970s, which jettisoned centuries-old laws and principles, leaving judges and juries to roam free and indulge their own inclinations, made it prudent for defendants to settle out of court, even if they had done nothing wrong. The uncertainty of outcomes was epitomized in two cases in which crane operators drove into high-tension electric power lines, leading to lawsuits against the manufacturer of the crane for failure to warn them—a claim dismissed without a trial in one state, on grounds that the danger was too obvious to require warning, and yet in another state leading to a damage award of more than $12 million against the manufacturer.[100] In other words, there was no longer *law* in the real sense of the word, but only unpredictable edicts emanating from courtrooms.

Nothing could so plainly show the role of the consumer as mascot and the producer as target as cases in which the user's own dangerous behavior was the obvious cause of the harm for which he was being allowed to sue. Someone who sprayed a plainly marked flammable liquid into a candle was nevertheless allowed to sue the manufacturer for the burns which resulted.[101] A woman who cradled a cup of coffee between her legs while seated in a moving car was allowed to sue McDonald's, who sold her the coffee, when the coffee spilled and scalded her. She was awarded $2.9 million in damages.[102]

Virtually all aspects of medicine became targets for escalating lawsuits. By 1985, one-fourth of all obstetricians-gynecologists in the country had been sued.[103] Psychiatrists were sued for things their patients did, months after their last visit.[104] Pharmaceutical companies were sued for the side effects of drugs which had been approved by the Food and Drug Administration and which no one even alleged that the companies had produced or distributed in any wrongful way.[105] With pharmaceutical companies as with manufacturers of automobiles, tools, and equipment, when no negligence could be found, the product's "design" was blamed—as if there were any way to design anything without negative side effects or a potential for negative consequences if misused.

In treating businesses and professions as targets, the courts were often also exhibiting another aspect of the vision of the anointed—presupposing far more knowledge and control than anyone ever possessed. In holding defendants responsible for harmful consequences which they did not cause, courts often relied on the new legal doctrine that these defendants could and should prevent "reasonably foreseeable" harm, even if that harm resulted from someone else's reckless or irresponsible use of the product or service. In short, the targets had vast responsibilities placed on them, while the mascots need not exercise even common sense. Moreover, the sheer luck of life—"the thousand natural shocks that flesh is heir to," as Hamlet said—disappeared as a factor. If something went wrong, someone was to blame, preferably someone with a "deep pocket" from which to pay damages. Often these deep pockets were nothing more than an aggregation of much shallower pockets, whether of taxpayers or of stockholders.

This presumption of available "solutions" was particularly devastating in medical fields where only painful and inescapable trade-offs have been common as regards vaccines, medicines, and medical procedures in general. Yet courts have permitted hundreds of lawsuits against whooping cough vaccine manufacturers, for example, leading some pharmaceutical houses to stop producing it.

Families

The family is inherently an obstacle to schemes for central control of social processes. Therefore the anointed necessarily find themselves repeatedly on a collision course with the family. It is not a matter of any subjective animus on their part against families. The anointed may in fact be willing to shower government largess upon families, as they do on other social entities. But the preservation of the family as an *autonomous decision-making unit* is incompatible with the third-party decision making that is at the heart of the vision of the anointed.

The very existence of families and the viability of marriage are both grossly understated through misused statistics, as noted in Chapter 3. Similarly, the incidence of various problems in families is overstated by artful definitions and half-truths. For example, alarmist stories in the media about domestic violence often lump together husbands and boyfriends as "partners" who batter women, when in fact a woman who heads her own household is nearly three times as likely to be beaten as a wife is. Separated, divorced, and never-married women are all more likely to be beaten than a wife is.[106] In other words, the traditional family is the safest setting for a woman—though that is, of course, not the message which the anointed seek to convey.

Because neither the traditional family nor any other setting is *perfectly* safe, there will always be examples of "battered wives," just as there are battered husbands, battered bachelors, and battered women in lesbian relations, among others. But the rate of violence among lesbians living together—about the same as in heterosexual relationships[107]—is of no interest to those seeking to depict male-female relationships as violence-prone. In fact, men tend to assault one another more often than they assault women. The rate of victimization by assault has generally been higher for men than for women, and the rate of victimization by aggravated assault usually at least twice as high for men as for women. The total number of women assaulted tends to be somewhat greater, but the total number of assaults suffered is greater for men.[108] Put differently, the target of a given assault is far more likely to be a man than a woman. Given that all categories of human beings are both victims and perpetrators of violence, the question is not whether anyone can be absolutely safe from assault but who is more likely or less likely to be victimized. The least likely of all victims is a wife. Men and single women are assaulted more often. Yet the impression spread by those with the vision of the anointed is just the opposite. Some of the claims made are internally contradictory. The *Christian Science Monitor,* for example, said:

> Domestic violence affects an estimated 4–5 million women a year. Every 15 seconds, an American woman is abused by her partner.[109]

Quite aside from the "partner" problem, the arithmetic is wrong. Five million women would mean an incident every 6.3 seconds.[110] This botching of simple arithmetic may be indicative of how anxious zealots have been to proclaim a conclusion in keeping with the vision of the anointed—and how gullibly many highly regarded newspapers, such as the *Washington Post,* the *Chicago Tribune* and the *New York Times,* in addition to the *Christian Science Monitor,* have repeated these claims, without even bothering to check for internal consistency with a pocket calculator.[111] As if this mathematical inconsistency were not enough, the estimate itself is also unreliable. Empirical studies which distinguish serious violence from merely grabbing or pushing come up with figures less than a tenth of those widely quoted in the media.[112] Not only is the total amount of family violence exaggerated, its sources and incidents are

falsely attributed to the least violent social setting, the traditional
family. It is the setting of unmarried sex partners—the "nontradi-
tional family," as the anointed put it—that is especially violent. A
study of men charged with domestic violence found that the offender
was typically young, unmarried, and either unemployed or working
in a blue-collar job. Other studies indicate that alcohol and drugs
are involved in most cases.[113] Ozzie and Harriet are not the problem, though what they represent is a target of the anointed, who seek
to undermine the autonomy of families, in order to promote the
moral surrogacy which is at the heart of their vision.

Among the family decisions which various political crusades are
attempting to transfer to third parties are:

1. At what age, in what manner, and with what moral principles
   sex is to be taught to children.
2. What general moral and social philosophy shall be taught to
   children.
3. Whether adoption should include a pledge of confidentiality
   to the biological mother who gave up the child for adoption.
4. Whether a child of another race may be adopted.
5. Whether a child shall have an abortion.
6. Whether an agreement can be made for surrogate motherhood.
7. Whether couples who did not choose to take on the obligations
   of marriage shall have those obligations retrospectively imposed
   on one of them via "palimony" suits by the other after the disso-
   lution of the relationship.

The notion that third parties can make such personal decisions is
not a peculiarity of our times or of American society. Friedrich
Engels' first draft of the *Communist Manifesto* included a deliberate
undermining of family bonds as part of the Marxian political
agenda,[114] though Marx himself was politically astute enough to
leave that out of the final version. Nor has this war against the autonomy of the family been confined to extremists. The modern Swedish
welfare state has made it illegal for parents to spank their own children and various so-called "children's advocates" in the United

States have urged third-party intervention in families under the rubric of "children's rights"[115]—obviously to be enforced by adults, and more particularly by adult lawyers for such organizations as the Children's Defense Fund, National Child Rights Alliance, and the like. This is not about neglect and abuse—which are already illegal—but about giving third parties a say in family decisions. In New Zealand, a whole campaign of scare advertisements during the 1980s promoted the claim that one out of eight fathers sexually abused their own daughters, when in fact research showed that not even one out of a hundred did so.[116]

The pervasive preference of the anointed for collective and third-party decision making ("solutions" by "society") takes the form of promotion of "day care" for children. Enabling families to take care of their own children at home by allowing the income tax exemption to keep pace with inflation and the real cost of raising children has no such support among the anointed. Indeed, this is an idea often pushed—in vain—by conservatives. While the anointed are often ready to spend vast amounts of government money on families, especially in ways which allow outsiders to intrude into family decisions, they are by no means equally willing to let families keep money that they have earned and make their own independent decisions. In family matters, as in other matters, power and preemption are the touchstones of the vision of the anointed, however much that vision is described in terms of the beneficent goals it is seeking.

Despite the faith of the anointed in "expertise" and "professionals" in the raising of children, the facts paint a grim picture of the actual results of transferring children from individual home care to collective day care. A study in the *Journal of the American Medical Association* found that preschool children were from 4 to more than 12 times as likely to contract meningitis if they attended a day-care center than if they were cared for at home.[117] The incidence of other diseases also rose with the growth of day care.[118] Studies have indicated that psychological problems are also more prevalent among children in day-care centers.[119]

The mind-set of those who view traditional families as failed institutions needing the superior wisdom of the anointed permeates laws

and policies on child abuse. Children may be removed from the
parental home on the basis of anonymous accusations alone—even
when both the children and the parents deny the accusations. Moreover, the protections afforded criminals are not afforded parents:

> Somewhere between 2 million and 3 million allegations of child
> abuse and neglect tie up the nation's hot lines every year. Of that
> number, 60 percent are deemed false and dropped. Of the remaining
> 40 percent that lead to investigations, about half (involving nearly
> 700,000 families) eventually are dismissed, but not before children
> have been strip-searched, interrogated by a stream of social workers,
> police officers and prosecutors, psychologically tested and sometimes
> placed in foster care. Such actions usually occur without search war-
> rants, parental consent, court hearings or official charges—and often
> solely on the basis of the anonymous telephone call.[120]

A Virginia couple, for example, came home one Friday afternoon
to find their 10-year-old son missing and a note ordering them to
appear in court the next Monday morning. Fearing that their son had
been kidnapped, they phoned the police, only to be told that he had
been taken into custody by the Department of Social Services. The
son himself spent the weekend in a foster home, forbidden to phone
his parents. All this was triggered by a phone call by a neighbor who
did not think that a 10-year-old boy should have been left alone at
home during the day while his parents worked.[121] The problem, however, was not the busybody neighbor but the fact that the law was
armed with extraordinary powers—far beyond what could be exercised against criminals, who are mascots of the anointed, while families are targets.

Within the general framework of such extraordinary powers,
zealots ready to believe the worst of fathers can plant ideas in young
children's minds, with disastrous consequences. When an 8-year-old
girl in San Diego was sexually assaulted and stated that it was done
by a man who climbed into her bedroom window, the social workers
dismissed her story, named her father as the primary suspect, and
removed the child from her home. After more than a year in foster

custody and in therapy, the girl changed her story and named her father as the attacker. Yet the DNA evidence indicated that it could not possibly have been her father and in fact the DNA matched that of a convicted child molester who entered the bedroom window of another child in the same neighborhood within days of the assault on this girl. But once the authorities had committed themselves to a different scenario, and had taken drastic action in response to their belief, admitting to being wrong was virtually out of the question. Only after a grand jury investigation was the child returned to her parents—after more than a year away and after the father had paid out more than a quarter of a million dollars in attorney's fees during the legal struggle to regain custody of his daughter. Moreover, the grand jury noted in its report that this was *not* an isolated situation, either in San Diego or in the country at large, that social workers in such situations had "nearly unlimited power" and that the social welfare agency involved seemed "incapable of policing itself."[122] Studies on the suggestibility of small children indicate that they can be induced to change their stories, even in a laboratory setting,[123] much less after they find themselves inexplicably snatched from their homes, helpless in the hands of strangers, and held incommunicado from their parents for months while various authorities obviously want them to make accusations.

Some have defended the unusual powers granted to police and social welfare agencies in child abuse cases by saying that if just one child's life is saved, it is worth it. However, many of the anointed take no such position when an animal on the endangered species list kills a child. On the contrary, the first response is usually to denounce public "hysteria" over the killing and to oppose letting people shoot dangerous animals on that list when they enter human communities. Even when there is proven child abuse, the response is often to send the child back into the same home if the family agrees to psychological counseling and visits by social workers—even though neither of these things guarantees the safety of the child. In short, it is only the *independent* and autonomous families that are sacrificed when they refuse to "admit" to what the anointed presuppose.

Religion

Some of the most adventurous interpretations of the Constitution have grown out of the simple words of the First Amendment: "Congress shall make no law respecting an establishment of religion, or prohibiting the free exercise thereof." Basing itself ostensibly on those words, the Supreme Court has banned prayer in public schools and repeatedly engaged in hand-wringing over nativity scenes in public places at Christmastime. Yet none of these things was meant by the phrase "an establishment of religion," which was not some esoteric expression from a philosophy seminar but something very ordinary and personally experienced by those who wrote the Constitution. The Church of England was "established" as the official church of the country, a church supported by taxes collected even from those who belonged to other churches, and a church whose members had legal privileges denied to members of other churches. The First Amendment forbad Congress to create any such institution in the United States.

Just as plain and straightforward laws have been stretched and twisted for the benefit of various mascots, so this plain and straightforward provision of the Constitution has been stretched and twisted to target religion. Such phrases as a "wall of separation" between church and state and government "neutrality" toward religion have become staples of constitutional interpretation by the Supreme Court, though neither phrase appears anywhere in the Constitution. In a 1988 case, for example, Justice Harry Blackmun's majority opinion declared, "the Constitution mandates that the government remain secular, rather than affiliate itself with religious beliefs or institutions"[124]—all this because both a nativity scene contributed by local Catholics and a menorah contributed by a local Jewish group were displayed during the Christmas holidays on public property in Pittsburgh.

Since the Allegheny County government could hardly be committing itself to being both Catholic and Jewish at the same time, the argument was that these displays violated the concept of a "secular state."[125] Although this secular state was another concept found nowhere in the Constitution, Justice Blackmun spoke of "the constitutional command of secular government,"[126] so that the "simultaneous endorsement of Judaism and Christianity is no less constitutionally infirm than the endorsement of Christianity alone."[127] The question before the Court was not whether these religious displays were a good idea in a society where many people were not religious, but whether they were forbidden by the Constitution. Unable to find anything in the Constitution itself to support such a strained interpretation, Blackmun relied on a precedent set by another Supreme Court case where a war memorial containing both crosses and stars of David was declared unconstitutional.[128]

The American Civil Liberties Union has been prominent among those objecting to Christmas holiday displays on public property, leading to cases in which Christmas trees are deemed constitutional if there is not too much religious symbolism involved. Justice Blackmun, for example, argued that "government may celebrate Christmas as a secular holiday,"[129] so that "when the city's tree stands alone in front of the City-County Building, it is not considered an endorsement of Christian faith"[130] and when there is a menorah nearby the "city's overall display must be understood as conveying the city's secular recognition of different traditions for celebrating the winter-holiday season."[131] However reminiscent of Medieval casuistry these and other fine-spun distinctions made about Christmas displays may be, they have nothing to do with the Constitution's prohibition against creating an establishment of religion. They have everything to do with imposing the vision of the anointed under cover of words about something very different.

It is not merely in the legal arena but also in education and the media that words are strained and twisted in discussions of religious issues. As public schools have increasingly become militant dispensers of indoctrination with fashionable avant-garde attitudes,[132] various religious individuals and groups have objected. These objections are then declared to be attempts by "the religious right" to "force their beliefs on other people." For example, when a group of fundamentalist parents in Tennessee objected to having their children required to read certain assignments which they considered to be undermining their religion, the media billed the resulting legal case as "Scopes II," likening this to the famous trial where schoolteacher John Scopes was prosecuted for teaching evolution. They were undeterred by the trial judge's clear explanation of the distinction:

> It is important to note at the outset that the plaintiffs are not requesting that the Holt series be banned from the classroom, nor are they seeking to expunge the theory of evolution from the public school curriculum. Despite considerable fanfare in the press billing this action as "Scopes II," it bears little relation to the famous "monkey trial" of 1925. These plaintiffs simply claim that they should not be forced to choose between reading books that offend their religious beliefs and foregoing a free public education.[133]

Whatever the merits or demerits of the fundamentalist parents' objections to these readings, they were seeking an exemption for their own children. And whatever the merits or demerits of the public school officials' granting or refusing that exemption, it had nothing to do with indoctrinating other children with fundamentalism. Yet, after a decision favorable to the parents was announced, the liberal organization "People for the American Way" declared that this was "an attempt to force one intolerant version of 'God's law' on everyone." Newspaper editorials decried the decision as "absurd" and "outrageous" and even conservative columnists George Will and James J. Kilpatrick attacked the decision—as it had been reported in the media.[134]

This was one of the rare legal victories won by religious people attempting to retain the right to raise their own children by their own values. The more general mind-set of contemporary judicial application of the First Amendment was illustrated in a case involving a group of handicapped children going to a public school in a small village inhabited by Hasidic Jews in New York State. Religion was not taught in this school. For that the Hasidim had their own private schools. What the public school did was to allow deaf, retarded, or otherwise handicapped children of this sect to receive the same fed-

eral benefits as other handicapped children, without having to subject themselves to the shock and ridicule of going to school among
other children to whom their unusual appearance, beliefs, and
behavior were sure to attract unwelcome attention. By passing a law
to allow this particular village to have its own school district, the
state legislature tried to spare these children that fate. But the U.S.
Supreme Court declared the law unconstitutional.

While conceding that the "curriculum and the environment of the
services were entirely secular" in the public school attended by the
handicapped Hasidic children,[135] and that they received "special
education programs like those available to all handicapped children,
religious or not,"[136] Justice David Souter's majority opinion nevertheless declared the legislation creating this school district in a village
inhabited solely by Hasidic Jews unconstitutional because it "singles
out a particular religious group for favorable treatment."[137] In a number of other special situations, the state legislature had also created
special school districts to accommodate other particular groups of
citizens for various other reasons,[138] but to do the same for a religious
community was considered a "threat to neutrality" among religions
because "we have no assurance that the next similarly situated group
seeking a school district of its own will receive one."[139]

This remarkable criterion would invalidate virtually every law or
government policy as unconstitutional, since there can be no prior
assurance that any law or policy will be applied without discrimination in the future. As Justice Antonin Scalia said in dissent: "I never
heard of such a principle, nor has anyone else, nor will it ever be
heard of again."[140] In other words, it was another ad hoc, disingenu-
ous excuse for imposing the vision of the anointed as "the law of the
land" under the guise of interpreting the Constitution.

Another remarkable principle emerged in Justice John Paul
Stevens' opinion concurring with that of the majority that this village
school district was unconstitutional:

> The isolation of these children, while it may protect them from
> "panic, fear and trauma," also unquestionably increased the likeli-
> hood that they would remain within the fold, faithful adherents of

their parents' religious faith. By specifically creating a school district that is specifically intended to shield children from contact with others who have "different ways," the State provided official support to cement the attachment of young adherents to a particular faith.[141]

In other words, the collateral benefit to the religious community from having its children spared being the butt of ridicule in school was enough to make this law a violation of the First Amendment. Again, this was the vision of the anointed, not the mandate of the Constitution. Also symptomatic of that vision was Justice Stevens' casual assumption of an alternative government solution, in this case that New York State could take "steps to alleviate the children's fear by teaching their schoolmates to be tolerant and respectful" of the Hasidic customs.[142] Miracles on demand!

In response to Justice Scalia's ridicule of the notion that a little village of Hasidic Jews was "an 'establishment' of the Empire State,"[143] Justice Souter said, "the First Amendment reaches more than classic, 18th century establishments."[144] In other words, the Constitution no longer means what it meant when it was written but what successive stretchings and strainings now cause it to mean. Since it will be stretched and strained in different directions for those who are mascots than for those who are targets, the motto on the facade of the Supreme Court likewise no longer means what it seems to mean: "Equal Justice Under Law."

CHAPTER 7

THE VOCABULARY OF THE ANOINTED

*Men have an all but incurable propensity to try to
prejudge all the great questions which interest them
by stamping their prejudices upon their language.*

—James Fitzjames Stephen[1]

In light of the underlying assumptions of the prevailing vision, it may
be easier to see why the particular vocabulary used by the anointed
is what it is. The swirl of their buzzwords—"access," "stigma," "progressive," "diversity," "crisis," etc.—shows a discernible pattern.
What these innumerable buzzwords have in common is that they
either (1) preempt issues rather than debate them, (2) set the
anointed and the benighted on different moral and intellectual
planes, or (3) evade the issue of personal responsibility.

VERBAL PREEMPTION

The word "crisis," for example, is a preemptive word used for its
prospective political effect, rather than for its contemporary or retrospective accuracy. As noted in Chapter 2, all sorts of situations have
been called a "crisis," even when they have in fact been getting better for years. When the anointed say that there is a crisis this means
that something must be done—and it must be done simply because
the anointed want it done. This word becomes one of many substitutes for evidence or logic. So do words like "genuine need"[2] (as

determined by third parties) or self-contradictory phrases like people living "below subsistence."

Phrases like "the peace movement," used to describe disarmament advocates, preempt the whole momentous question as to whether peace is more likely to be achieved through disarmament or through military deterrence. With untold millions of lives depending on the answer to that question, something more substantive than a presumption that some people like peace more than others might be expected. But here, as elsewhere, all sorts of factual and analytical issues are reduced to psychological propensities.

One of the never-ending crusades of the anointed is for more "public service." Like so many of the special buzzwords of the anointed, this phrase does not mean what the straightforward sense of the words seems to say. Not every service to the public is a "public service" in this Newspeak. For example, those who deliver tons of life-sustaining food to supermarkets are not engaged in "public service," as the anointed use the term. Neither are those who build a roof over people's heads or produce the clothes on people's backs. Those who perform these vital services are activated by the incentives of the marketplace, perhaps even by "greed," another fashionable buzzword that puts the anointed and the benighted on different moral planes.

The call for more "public service" is then a call for more people to work in jobs *not* representing the preferences of the public, as revealed through the marketplace, but the preferences of third parties enforced through government and paid for by the power of taxation. Sometimes work for foundations and other nonprofit organizations is also included in "public service." What is crucial is that public service not be service defined by the public itself through its choices of how to spend its own money in market transactions, but defined for them by third-party elites. Otherwise the most valuable and even life-saving activities are not worthy of the benediction "public service," while making oneself a nuisance to other people with door-to-door solicitations is an activity worthy of that verbal aura, when it is in a cause favored by the anointed. Forcing the public to pay for art calculatingly insulting to the public's sensibilities is also a "public service," as the anointed define the term—and a failure to pay is "censorship" in this same lexicon, regardless of how free those artists remain to produce and sell their products to those willing to pay their own money.

What is crucial about the concept of "public service" as used by the anointed is that it must be defined by third parties, not by the public itself.

In this context, it is not hard to understand why repeated attempts to create a "national service" corps of some sort can always count on the hearty support of the anointed, as it seeks to direct young people, especially, not by what other people want them to do enough to pay for it with their own money, but by what the anointed want and pay for with money extracted through taxation. Thus *New York Times* columnist Bob Herbert hailed the federal government's creation of an agency called "Americorp"—a sort of "domestic Peace Corps"—as a "noble effort" regarded as a relief from the previous Reagan-Bush era "poisoned by greed."[3] In other words, when people choose their occupations according to what the public wants and is willing to pay for, that is "greed," but when the public is forced to pay for what the anointed want done, that is "public service."

The word "greed" itself preempts all sorts of issues. If greed is defined by making money, then any era of prosperity is an era of greed, by definition, and any especially prosperous classes of people are especially greedy. But surely, in the ordinary sense of the word, someone who murders a store owner for the small amount of money in his cash register is greedy—perhaps more greedy than someone who makes millions in legitimate work. The sums of money involved cannot be the touchstone of greed. What is remarkable, however, is how utterly undefined this widely used term remains—and yet how fervently asserted. If the term has any concrete meaning, then there might be some way to test empirically, for example, whether or not the 1980s were indeed a "decade of greed" as so often claimed by the anointed.

Once we abandon the notion that the sums of money earned are a measure of "greed," then perhaps the disposition of that money might offer a clue. The 1980s in fact saw a rise of philanthropy to unprecedented levels, not only absolutely but as a percentage of income.[4] Much of this philanthropy was directed toward academia, one of the severest critics of "greed"—and perhaps a candidate for the title itself, as both tuition and professors' salaries rose faster than the rate of inflation nine years in a row during that decade.[5] Moreover, not all of this was due to the operations of a free market, as a Justice Department investigation found that organized collusion among the Ivy League colleges, MIT, and more than two dozen other elite institutions collectively fixed prices that students and their parents would have to pay.[6]

Among the many other questions raised by the nebulous concept of "greed" is why it is a term applied almost exclusively to those who want to earn more money or to keep what they have already earned— never to those wanting to take other people's money in taxes or to those wishing to live on the largess dispensed from such taxation. No amount of taxation is ever described by the anointed as "greed" on the part of government or the clientele of government. Moreover, money is not the only thing for which one might be greedy, nor necessarily the most harmful to society. Greed for material things can be satisfied simultaneously throughout a prospering society, so that even the "poor" of today have amenities that were rare among the elites of earlier times. (The installation of a bathtub with plumbing in the White House was controversial in the nineteenth century because it was felt to be a needless luxury.) Widespread greed for power cannot be satisfied simultaneously, however, since power is by its very nature relative.

These inconsistencies in the use of the word are not random. Those things which serve the purposes of the anointed are exempt from the term and those which go counter to the vision of the anointed are prime candidates. Just as those activities which are responses to what the benighted masses want, as transmitted through the systemic processes of the marketplace, are not going to be considered "public services," so income received as a result of satisfying the benighted is far more likely to be regarded as representing "greed" than monies received or power exercised by those carrying out the vision of the anointed. Families who wish to be independent financially and to make their own decisions about their lives are of little interest or use to those who are seeking to impose their superior wisdom and virtue on other people. Earning their own money makes these families unlikely candidates for third-party direction and wishing to retain what they have earned threatens to deprive the anointed of the money needed to distribute as largess to others who would thus become subject to their direction. In these circumstances, it is understandable why the desire to increase and retain one's own earnings should be characterized negatively as "greed," while wishing to live at the expense of others is not.

In all of this, the vocabulary of the anointed requires no clear definitions, logical arguments, or empirical verifications. Its role is precisely to be a substitute for all these things.

DISDAINING THE BENIGHTED

The vocabulary of the anointed also serves to put the anointed and the benighted on different planes. A concern that is important to the anointed is called "a matter of principle," while a concern that is important to the benighted is called "an emotional issue." Apparently other people don't have reasons or principles; all they have are emotions. Often, when the media formally present both sides of an issue, the reasons given by the anointed are "balanced" by the emotions expressed by the benighted. Even when "both sides" are presented in the media, seldom are the *reasons* for each side presented.

The beliefs of the benighted are depicted as being at best "perceptions," more often "stereotypes," and more bluntly "false consciousness." Such words—and many others to the same effect—express not only a disdain for the firsthand experiences of millions of other people, but also a disregard of the systemic processes which create incentives to be right and winnow out those who are wrong too often. For example, the oft-repeated claim that women receive only about 60 percent of what men receive for doing the same work ignores the competitive economic pressures which are constantly winnowing out businesses. To say that women are paid 60 percent of what men receive for doing the same work is to say that employers can afford to pay two male workers more than they pay three female workers—the women producing 50 percent more output—and still survive economically in a system so competitive that most businesses go under inside of a decade.

It may be in keeping with the vision of the anointed to imagine that the benighted would engage in such economic insanity, but only ignoring the rigors of economic competition could lead anyone to expect employers to survive with such vastly inflated costs of hiring men. As already noted in Chapter 3, women's skills are often not the same as men's, even when efforts are made to match them by education. Women also tend to work part-time more often than men, to average fewer hours of work per year, to interrupt their careers for the sake of their children, to choose occupations which are compatible with their domestic responsibilities even when more remunerative work might be available, and to leave their own jobs to move where their husbands find new jobs—all of which tend to reduce their average earnings, though not for the same work. Before there were laws or government policies on pay differentials, single women who worked continuously and full-time earned slightly more than single men who worked continuously and full-time.[7]

Much discussion of the decisions of businessmen in general by intellectuals proceeds as if employers, landlords, and others operating under the systemic pressures of the marketplace are free to make arbitrary and capricious decisions based on prejudice and misinformation—as if they were intellectuals sitting around a seminar table—and pay no price for being mistaken. Banks and savings-and-loan associations, for example, are treated as if they lose nothing by refusing to lend to minority mortgage loan applicants who have the "same" qualifications as others—and this in an industry where financial institutions have been going bankrupt on a large scale, with others teetering on the brink. Even if most bankers were so completely blinded by prejudice as to risk financial suicide, those whose prejudices were less or whose sense of self-interest was greater would have an enormous advantage in the competition for survival. What matters in a systemic process is not what the initial mixture was like but what the surviving entities are like. Differential survival rates are the whole point of a systemic competition, whether among trees on a mountainside, animals evolving in the wild, or businesses in a competitive market.

The fact that a closer look at the statistical data in Chapter 3 suggests that mortgage lenders are a lot closer to the facts about repayment prospects than the anointed who criticized them is almost incidental. What is crucial is that the very possibility that the benighted may be closer to the truth, even in a given area, is simply not taken seriously by the anointed. Verbal preemption makes it unnecessary for those with the prevailing vision to have to face such a possibility.

FEASIBILITY

Another common characteristic of the vocabulary of the anointed is that it puts off-limits the question as to whether what is proposed is in fact achievable: Result A may be preferable to result B, but the latter may be a better objective if result A cannot be reached. While those with the tragic vision may see social issues in terms of making the best choice among limited and often unpalatable alternatives, those with the vision of the anointed tend to see these same issues in terms of what should be done to make things right in the cosmic scheme of things.

Paradoxically, while feasibility is seldom addressed when proposing public policy, severe limitations on what is feasible by others are often assumed by those with the vision of the anointed and pushed to the point of determinism, with a corresponding denial of personal responsibility. Since the bottom line of the prevailing vision is that the anointed are moral surrogates to make decisions for other people, those other people must be seen as incapable of making the right decisions for themselves. The concept of personal responsibility is thus anathema to this vision and the vocabulary of the anointed reflects this. For example, a story on the front page of the *Los Angeles Times* was headlined "A Deck Stacked Against the Young" even though the specifics of this supposedly stacked deck included:

Skills: Dubious.
Education: Over, without a diploma.
Job prospects: Nil, save for minimum wage.[8]

In other words, this "stacked deck" consisted of the fact that some youths had not chosen to learn in school or to acquire skills at work, and thought that they should be paid according to the needs of their egos rather than the productivity of their labor.

Another feature of the prevailing vision is that the anointed must try to change the fundamental character of their fellow human beings, to make them more like themselves. Thus phrases about "raising the consciousness" of others, making them "aware," or hoping that they will "grow." In other words, the anointed must not only design a different social world from that which exists, they must people that world with different creatures, custom-made for the purpose.

Here the contrast with the tragic vision is particularly sharp. Those with the tragic vision are seeking to maintain or promote social arrangements which they deem suitable to the kind of people they are familiar with, whether from personal experience or from historical or other sources, and tend to regard schemes that would require people to be fundamentally different as schemes likely to fail. But, to those with the vision of the anointed, to say that a particular plan or policy is contrary to human nature as we know it is only to say that human nature must be changed. Thus the vocabulary of the anointed is replete with such terms as "sensitizing," "enlightening," or "reeducating" other people.

Given the assumption of a vast intellectual and moral gulf between the anointed and the benighted, the role of "thinking people" in general and "experts" in particular is decisive. This requires many decisions to be collectivized and those collectivized decisions to be made by surrogates. All sorts of collective "planning," from a national energy policy to imposed school busing, national "public service" requirements for young people, environmental regulations, and outright socialism fit this pattern. All have been viewed sympathetically by those with the vision of the anointed.

Stated baldly in terms of process characteristics—collectivized decisions made by third parties—these schemes have little appeal. But they are almost invariably stated instead in terms of the goals they propose to achieve—for example, rational "planning" to avoid "chaos," racial "integration," or more sweeping goals such as "social justice" today or "liberty, equality, fraternity" in an earlier era. One of the verbal contrasts between the tragic vision and the vision of the anointed is that the former tends to describe its goals in terms of the processes involved—"free markets," "judicial restraint," or "traditional values," for example—which seldom have the emotional impact of statements about ideals and goals.

There is nothing obviously or intrinsically desirable about most of the things espoused by those with the tragic vision. It is only after understanding the reasoning which causes those particular processes to be favored over others that the merits and demerits of these systemic processes can be meaningfully discussed. But anyone can be in favor of "social justice" without further ado. In short, the ideas of so-called "thinking people" often require much less thinking. Indeed, the less thinking there is about definitions, means, and consequences, the more attractive "social justice" seems.

Advocacy in terms of goals rather than processes is only one of the verbal advantages of those with the vision of the anointed. Another is adoption of a cosmic viewpoint from which to discuss moral issues—a viewpoint which spawns a whole galaxy of buzzwords. Finally, there is simple verbal inflation, as useful as monetary inflation for defrauding people without their being fully aware of what is going on.

THE COSMIC VIEWPOINT

Many of the ideas and approaches of the anointed make sense only when looking at the world through the eyes of God or from the viewpoint of the cosmos. When Judge David L. Bazelon spoke of a social imperative to "provide every family with the means to create the kind of home all human beings need,"[9] it was with no reservations as to whether anyone, anywhere, had ever possessed either the knowledge or the power to externally impose all the values, skills, discipline, and habits—much less love and dedication—required for such a home.

Similarly, when Chief Justice Earl Warren responded to indignant outcries against criminals by calling the people who made such outcries "self-righteous,"[10] he was making a statement whose validity depended on adopting the cosmic viewpoint. From such a viewpoint, particular individuals might turn out to be either criminals or law-abiding citizens as a result of innumerable influences resulting from the accidental circumstances into which they were born and which they chanced to encounter as they grew up: *There but for the grace of God go I*. However, if one is nowhere close to being either God or the cosmos, the question becomes: Now that criminals are what they are, for whatever reasons, how are we to deal with them and protect all the other people? If it were oneself who was the criminal, the policy issue would be the same. The constrained options of the tragic vision permit no policies based on indulgences in cosmic questions—or cosmic dogmatism as to causation. After all, people born to great privilege have often done hideous things throughout history, for reasons beyond our ken today—and perhaps beyond our ken tomorrow and a thousand years thereafter. What we would do if we were omniscient, or could turn back the clock, is irrelevant to choices confronting us within the unyielding constraints of the present and our constrained present knowledge of the past and future.

We shoot mad dogs not only because they are dangerous but also because we do not know how to capture them safely and render them harmless. Surely it would be unconscionable to shoot them if we did. But we shoot them because of our own limitations, as much as because of their dangerousness. Such are the constrained options of the tragic vision. To assume the more sweeping options of the vision of the anointed is more humane only in intention, risking in practice the needless sacrifice of more human lives if our presumptions prove to be unfounded.

The cosmic viewpoint affects all sorts of issues involving "fairness." Attorney General Ramsey Clark, for example, said that "elemental fairness" required that those arrested for crimes be advised of their right to remain silent because experienced criminals, gang members, and mafiosi already knew that.[11] This emphasis on fairness as between criminals ignores the larger fairness as between criminals and their victims. It also assumes that someone has the omniscience to equalize preexisting advantages—and that making such adjustments of the cosmos is an activity to be imposed on an already overburdened and faltering legal system, unable to carry out its more modest function of protecting law-abiding citizens from criminals. Again, this was not the idiosyncracy of one man. The Supreme Court in its landmark *Miranda* decision likewise argued that to fail to give everyone the same information already possessed by the more sophisticated would be to "take advantage of the poor, the ignorant, and the distracted."[12] Note what this *taking advantage* consists of: a failure to provide greater means of escaping punishment for crimes committed by criminals who fall below the state of the art in criminal evasions of the law.

Once launched on this line of thinking, however, there is no real reason why the courts should not equalize other preexisting advantages, such as the fact that some criminals can run faster than others, think quicker, or possess other talents to help them evade capture or punishment. All of these things are equally unfair from a cosmic perspective. But for the law to be engaged in equalizing criminals' ability to escape the law is to abandon the reason for criminal sanctions in the first place and substitute a cosmic crusade.

The cosmic viewpoint takes many forms, whether in the law or elsewhere. One is the desire to equalize "life chances" among individuals born into different classes, races, sexes, and other groups. Yet the full sweep of the range of things that go into "life chances" is as much beyond our ken and control as all the things that go into crime. Those factors which are already known to affect economic and other outcomes are both numerous and in many cases beyond the control of programs and institutions, including even totalitarian institutions. Unless we adopt the arbitrary doctrine that any degree of equalization, however small, is worth any sacrifice, however large, differences in life chances are among the many imperfections of life whose remedy is not even conceivable, short of the cosmic viewpoint.

At a minimum, public policy to equalize life chances would have to either divorce reward from performance or create equality of performance by early and comprehensive intervention in the raising of children, for all practical purposes destroying the family as a decision-making unit. How long parents would continue to regard children who are creatures of the state as being their own is another question. Even so, it is problematical how far the state could eliminate the influence of parents on their children's life chances, short of removing children from their homes.

As long as the values, habits, and mind-sets of parents remain an influence, these are certain to be *different* values, habits, and mind-sets—not only randomly from one set of parents to another, but systematically from parents from one social group to another. It is hard even to imagine how the state could offset these differences short of, for example, having someone stationed in the home to turn off the television set until all the children from noneducationally inclined groups had done as much reading and homework as the children from groups whose commitment to education goes back generations or even centuries. Alternatively, they could station someone in the homes of the latter children to take away their books and computers, and force them to watch as much television as the other children watch. And yet, even if all this were done, and done successfully, only *one* source of differences in life chances would have been eliminated. An enormous amount of personal and social disruption might be necessary to accomplish a rather modest change in those life chances.

An oft-quoted statement by President Lyndon Johnson on racial policy, espousing a need to go beyond formal equality before the law, likewise illustrates the cosmic viewpoint:

> You do not take a man who, for years, has been hobbled by chains, liberate him, and bring him to the starting line of a race, saying, "You are free to compete with all others," and still justly believe you have been completely fair.[13]

This reasoning presupposes that there is some identifiable group of decision makers—"you"—who have such cosmic control that this question can be meaningfully addressed to them. This whole approach is like the personification of "society" that is so much a part of the vocabulary of the anointed. Nor is this issue limited to racial questions. It is of course unfair from a cosmic viewpoint that any group should compete without all the advantages enjoyed by other groups—and those with the tragic vision readily concede it. The incidence of the "benefits and burdens" of the world "would in many instances have to be regarded as very unjust *if* it were the result of a deliberate allocation to particular people," according to Friedrich Hayek.[14] But the outcomes of a systemic process, or "spontaneous order" in Hayek's terms, "cannot be just or unjust."[15]

Returning to the issue of differences in criminals' knowledge of how to evade the law, from a cosmic viewpoint such a difference is of course not fair. But the relevant question is whether anyone has the omniscience or omnipotence to make policy from a cosmic viewpoint—and at the cost of undermining law and the reliance of millions of human beings on law. If law has any value in itself, then even the beneficiaries of a deviation from law lose something as members of the general society. Nor is it certain that they will gain more from the exceptions than they lose by losing the rule of law. In the case of American blacks, where life itself has often been lost as a general deterioration of law enforcement was accompanied by an escalating murder rate, it is particularly uncertain whether bending the law produced net benefits.

Although cosmic notions of justice are often invoked in racial issues, the issue is much broader. Every individual inherits a particular culture or subculture which evolved over a period of generations and centuries before he was born—and there is little or nothing that "we," "you," or "society" can do about this plain fact of history. Adopting a cosmic viewpoint only adds lofty presumptions and reckless gambles to the underlying futility.

The notion that it is somehow "self-righteous" to insist on social standards and rules that are easier for some people to conform to than for others is another expression of the cosmic viewpoint. People who complain about the ravages of teenage pregnancy and demand a return to traditional family values have been denounced by the anointed for being "self-righteous" and for "lecturing" the less fortunate. Here again, from a cosmic perspective, many girls who grew up living by traditional values, and who waited for responsible motherhood in tandem with a responsible father, might have taken the condemned path if a number of other influences had been different. But the observation *There but for the grace of God go I* does not imply that the grace of God must be destroyed, or its consequences neutralized, in the name of equality. These are, after all, not zero-sum games. The community as a whole is better off or worse off according to whether or not the next generation is raised under circumstances that are more likely to produce productive citizens rather than parasites and criminals. Indeed, the less fortunate are the hardest hit by the consequences when social standards are compromised or jettisoned for the sake of cosmic concepts of equality.

Those among the anointed who are not prepared to assume the cosmic role personally may nevertheless attribute or recommend it to "society"—and society often means some designated group of elite decision makers armed with governmental power. But third-party decision making by surrogates for "society" offers no *a priori* reason to expect a closer approximation to omniscience. On the contrary, such surrogates not only lack the detailed and direct knowledge of the innumerable circumstances surrounding each of the millions of individuals whose decisions they are preempting, they lack the incentives of direct gain and loss from being right or wrong, and they have every incentive to persist in mistaken policies (from which they suffer little), rather than admit to being wrong (from which they could suffer much).

Sometimes the blatancy of elite preemption of other people's decision making is mitigated by the notion of mass "participation" in collective decision making. If carried out as ideally presented, such general participation would then reduce the issue to one of individual decision making versus collective decision making. For example: Do you wish to raise your own child according to your own best judgment or to have one vote among millions as to how children in general should be raised? If the latter, then disproportionate influence is likely to fall to the articulate, the politically sophisticated, and the morally fervent—in other words, to the anointed.

Another way of verbally masking elite preemption of other people's decisions is to use the word "ask"—as in "We are just asking everyone to pay their fair share." But of course governments do not ask, they *tell*. The Internal Revenue Service does not "ask" for contributions. It takes. It can confiscate bank accounts and other assets and it can put people behind bars for not paying. Yet the word "ask" is used in all sorts of public policy contexts where elite preemption via governmental power is involved. For example, when some parents objected to having their children put at risk by attending public schools with other children stricken with AIDS, *New York Times* columnist Anna Quindlen said that we should "ask some parents to put their children at some risk, however small, for the sake of principle and fairness."[16] But these parents were not being *asked* anything. They were being told that it was none of their business to know who or where there were AIDS carriers amidst their children. The anointed had already decided how much risk other people's children should be exposed to—and official secrecy meant that those other people had nothing to say about it.

Whether this combination of characteristics makes for substantively better decision making, and to an extent sufficient to justify collective preemption, is another question. But it is easy to see why the cosmic viewpoint has such appeal to those with the vision of the anointed. It magnifies their influence and flatters their egos. While the anointed may assume that articulation, political activism, and moral fervor are sufficient, those with the tragic vision believe otherwise. As James Fitzjames Stephen said:

> The one talent which is worth all other talents put together in all
> human affairs is the talent of judging right upon imperfect materials,
> the talent if you please of guessing right. It is a talent which no rules
> will ever teach and which even experience does not always give. It
> often coexists with a good deal of slowness and dulness and with a
> very slight power of expression.[17]

Systemic processes tend to reward people for making decisions that turn out to be right—creating great resentments among the anointed, who feel themselves entitled to rewards for being articulate, politically active, and morally fervent.

Personal Responsibility

Many of the words and phrases used in the media and among academics suggest that things simply *happen* to people, rather than being caused by their own choices or behavior. Thus there is said to be an "epidemic" of teenage pregnancy, or of drug usage, as if these things were like the flu that people catch just by being in the wrong place at the wrong time. In a similar vein, Chief Judge David Bazelon spoke of "forces that drive people to commit crimes."[18] In the economy as well, both parents are often said to be "forced" to work, in order to "make ends meet," even if the family owns luxury cars, a vacation home, designer clothes, and a swimming pool. Parents, of course, have every right to make whatever choices they wish, but suggesting that people had no choice is precisely what the vocabulary of the anointed does repeatedly, on the most disparate issues— which it reduces to nonissues with deterministic assertions.

People are often said to lack "access" to various jobs, educational institutions, or credit, when in fact they may not have behaved or performed in a way that would enable them to meet the same standards that others meet. "Access" is just one of a number of *ex ante* expressions—"opportunity," "bias," and "glass ceiling," for example—used to describe *ex post* results in such a way as to preempt the whole question as to why those results turned out the way they did. If a job ceiling is glass, for example, that says that it is invisible—that the assertion must be accepted without evidence. Implicit in much of this verbiage is the notion that the rules were rigged for or against some individual or group. But whether, or to what extent, this is true is precisely the issue that should be argued—not circumvented by verbal sleight-of-hand.

People who do not choose to spend their money on health insurance, but on other things, are not denied "access" to health care by "society." On the contrary, they are often given medical treatment at other people's expense, whether under specific social programs or in various other ways, such as using hospital emergency rooms for things that are not emergencies at all, or which have become emergencies only because nothing was done until a medical problem grew too large to ignore. How often people have chosen to spend their money on things other than health insurance—especially when they are young and healthy—and how often they lack health insurance due to circumstances beyond their control is the crucial question that is sidestepped verbally by speaking of "access." Millions of individuals from families with incomes of $50,000 and up lack health insurance[19]—clearly not because they lack "access" but because they have chosen to spend their money on other things. Choice, like behavior and performance, is often circumvented by the vocabulary of the anointed.

Performance standards are often depicted as mere subjective barriers reflecting the biases of those who create them. Thus Professor Stanley Fish of Duke University charges "insincerity" to opponents of affirmative action who want everyone to compete by the same rules by saying that "the playing field is already tilted" in favor of the majority because "the skills that make for success are nurtured by institutions and cultural practices from which the disadvantaged minority has been systematically excluded."[20] With the word "excluded" being used in very elastic senses today, it is hard to know how this statement differs from saying that people from different cultural backgrounds have the prerequisites for various activities to varying extents. In a similar vein, former Harvard president Derek Bok said that to apply the same admissions standards to minority students as to everyone else would be to "exclude them from the university."[21] Among other things, this ignores the fact that blacks were receiving both college and postgraduate degrees from Harvard in the nineteenth century, when it was very unlikely that they were being admitted under lower standards. The more fundamental fallacy, however, is in using *ex ante* words like "exclude" to describe *ex post* results.

Widespread personification of "society" is another verbal tactic that evades issues of individual responsibility. Such use of the term "society" is a more sophisticated version of the notion that "the devil made me do it." Like much of the rest of the special vocabulary of the anointed, it is used as a magic word to make choice, behavior, and performance vanish into thin air. With these three inconvenient complications out of the picture, results after the fact can then be equated with conditions existing before the fact. Success thus becomes "privilege" and failure "disadvantage"—by definition.

Even inanimate things like classics of literature are called "privileged" writings, rather than writings which have achieved appreciation from many successive generations. Such concepts as achievement are precisely what the new vocabulary seeks to displace. By all-or-nothing reasoning, it is of course possible to show that not every individual or group has had the same favorable or unfavorable conditions. Indeed, it is hard to imagine how anything short of omniscience and omnipotence could have made such blanket equality possible. But that is still radically different from saying that outcomes *ex post* are simply results of circumstances *ex ante*. For example, voluminous evidence from countries around the world repeatedly shows particular immigrant groups beginning their lives destitute in a new country, taking low-level jobs disdained by the native population, and yet ultimately rising above the economic level of those around them.

The "overseas Chinese" have done this throughout Southeast Asia and in several Western Hemisphere nations. Jews have done the same in numerous countries. The history of the United States has seen this achievement repeated by a number of European immigrant groups and by the Japanese and the Cubans, among others. Such evidence is suggestive, rather than decisive. There is room for debate, but substantive debate is wholly different from verbal preemption, the weapon of choice among the anointed.

In the vision of the anointed, not only must other people be either intellectually or morally incapable of making the right decisions for themselves individually, the traditions they use to supplement their own thinking, and the systemic processes which coordinate their competing desires and complementary inputs—the marketplace, for example—must also be depicted as inadequate to the task, without the benign intervention of the anointed. Surrogate decision making is the common thread in the highly disparate crusades which have captured the imagination and sparked the fervor of the anointed at various times, whether this moral surrogacy was in the form of the eugenics movement, Keynesian economics, or environmentalism. All urgently require the superior wisdom of the anointed to be imposed on the benighted masses, in order to avert disaster.

Merit versus Performance

Underlying much social criticism is the notion that individual merit cannot explain all differences in individual or group results. Professor Stanley Fish of Duke University, for example, condemns the Scholastic Aptitude Test because it does not measure merit.[22] Others condemn the incomes earned in the marketplace for the same reason. Whatever weight such considerations as merit might have if we were God on Judgment Day, making a retrospective assessment, the situation is radically different when we are attempting to establish *prospective* rules or policies in a society of human beings with necessarily limited knowledge and limited ability to monitor what is in anyone else's heart of hearts.

The requirements for judging "merit" vastly exceed the requirements for judging behavior or performance. We do not know how much innate ability anyone has, and therefore cannot assess how much of the observed performance was simply a windfall gain from nature, rather than being a result of exhausting, disciplined, or otherwise meritorious efforts. Moreover, individual behavior and performance depend on factors reaching well beyond the individual— including the surrounding general culture or special subculture, the particular family, and the complementary performances of others. Had Einstein been born into a family of illiterate peasants in a Third World country, neither he nor the world would have gained the benefits of his potential. But that is still light-years away from saying that observers can look at Third World peasants and decide which ones would have been Einsteins in a wholly different setting, or that anyone knows how to transform the cultural universe of the Third World, or any other world. Still less can anyone grandly wave aside as "irrelevant" the inherent prerequisites for civilization and progress.

Even at a more mundane level, nothing seems to be more of a purely individual feat than a baseball player hitting a home run, and yet the number of home runs hit depends on factors that reach

beyond the individual player. Ted Williams, for example, hit home
runs with greater frequency, in proportion to his times at bat, than
either Roger Maris or Hank Aaron[23]—and yet Williams never came
close to Babe Ruth's home-run records that Maris and Aaron broke.
The difference is that Williams was walked far more often than either
Maris or Aaron—in fact, about as often as the two of them put
together[24]—and that in turn was due to who was batting after each of
these players.

To walk Ted Williams was to drastically reduce the danger of a
home run, but to walk Maris or Aaron was only to bring to bat Mickey
Mantle or Eddie Matthews, each of them top-rank home-run hitters
in his own right, leading the league in that department four years
each. Individual batters must of course hit their own home runs, but
the man on deck has a lot to do with how the man in the batter's box
will be pitched to—or whether he will be pitched to at all.

In short, performance cannot be due solely to individual merit
where the influence of other individuals and circumstances is at
work. The case for rewarding performance is that we can do it, not
that it is the same as rewarding merit. Likewise, holding individuals
personally responsible for the consequences of their own actions is a
social expedient for prospective control, not a cosmic retrospective
moral judgment.

The hubris of imagining that one can judge merit, as distinguished
from judging behavior and performance, can be seen in attempts of
educators to grade students according to how well they used their
own ability, rather than how well they performed relative to some
fixed standard or to other students. This hubris is consonant with the
vision of the anointed and with the vocabulary in which that vision is
expressed. Conversely, the *inability* of ordinary people to make valid
assessments, even of observable behavior and performance, is likewise part of the vision of the anointed and finds expressions in such
words as "stereotypes," "bias," and "prejudice"—all widely used
without any corroborating evidence being asked or given.

One of the uses of the concept of merit is to claim that various
rewards produced by the economic forces of the marketplace are
unmerited. Again, this implicitly assumes that it is possible for a

human being to determine merit—otherwise, all conceivable economic systems and policies will produce rewards whose merit is unsubstantiated. Moreover, applying the impossible standard of merit forfeits benefits attainable under the feasible standard of performance in satisfying consumer desires more fully. If, for example, a new product is introduced by five different producers—each in a somewhat different version—then it is possible that none of the five fully understands just exactly what the consumer wants, nor need any of the five be any wiser or more prescient than the others. Yet if one of these products happens to be far closer to the consumers' desires than the others, its producer may become wealthy as his sales skyrocket, while some of his less fortunate competitors cannot sell enough to avoid bankruptcy. The unmerited gain of the lucky producer, however, serves the larger social purpose of enabling the consumers to receive the product nearest to their desires and stops the economy's resources from being wasted on the production of other versions that are less satisfactory.

Often, it is precisely the lure of a chance to hit the jackpot which causes all the producers to gamble on untried ventures, out of which some prove to be beneficial to the public. To insist on a closer approximation to merit would reduce the incentives and the benefits to society that flow from these incentives. And is it not equally an injustice to deprive innocent consumers of benefits they could have had, for the sake of an abstract notion important only to a relative handful of the intelligentsia—and little analyzed, even by them?

The vision of the anointed is one in which such ills as poverty, irresponsible sex, and crime derive primarily from "society," rather than from individual choices and behavior. To believe in personal responsibility would be to destroy the whole special role of the anointed, whose vision casts them in the role of rescuers of people treated unfairly by "society." Since no society has ever treated everyone fairly, there will always be real examples of what the anointed envision. The fatal step is to make those examples universal explanations of social ills—and to remain oblivious to evidence to the contrary.

The Certainty of the Anointed

What is at stake for the anointed in their discussions of public policy issues is their whole image of themselves as people whose knowledge and wisdom are essential to the diagnosis of social ills and the prescription of "solutions." To believe that their knowledge and understanding are grossly inadequate for what they are attempting—even if everyone else's knowledge is also grossly inadequate for such ambitious social engineering—would be to bring their whole world crashing down around them. *They must believe that they know—and that they know better than others.*

Utter certainty has long been the hallmark of the anointed. When John Maynard Keynes predicted dire economic problems resulting from *under*population in Western society—on the eve of sharp increases in population growth—he said that we know "much more securely than we know almost any other social or economic factor relating to the future" that we were facing a "stationary or declining" population level.[25] Similarly, when Lyndon Johnson spoke of the "conditions that breed despair and violence," he added: "All of us know what those conditions are" and proceeded to list the explanations that were part of the prevailing social vision.[26] His policies followed the logic of that vision, and the failure of such policies to achieve their goals, either in his time or later, calls into question that underlying vision itself. Whatever its failures as social policy, that vision has a logical structure of coherent beliefs and assumptions, as well as a history going back for centuries.

Specialization

Since specialization is a way of coping with the inadequacies of the human mind, it should hardly be surprising that those with the vision of the anointed often view specialization negatively, or that their vocabulary often reflects that. Cosmic decisions require minds with cosmic scope—and to say that there are no such minds, that the human experience must be broken down into manageable-sized pieces, is to deny the vision of the anointed. Meanwhile, those with the tragic vision have often proclaimed the virtues of specialization. Adam Smith attributed much of economic progress to the "division of labor,"[27] Edmund Burke said that he "revered" the specialist within his specialty,[28] and Oliver Wendell Holmes said that specialists were more needed than generalists, whose presumptions he derided.[29] But such views are the opposite of the views among the anointed.

One symptom of the disdain for specialization among the anointed is their widespread use of the term "microcosm." Thus a college, for example, may be said to be a microcosm of society—even though its very reason for existence is its specialized activity—that is, its difference from the rest of society. The eye is not a microcosm of the body, although it engages in many of the same general biological processes as other organs (such as using nutrients and expelling wastes), because its whole significance is that it does something that no other part of the body does.

"Interdisciplinary" is another popular buzzword among the anointed, reflecting their aversion to, or lack of appreciation of, specialization. This is understandable, given their underlying assumptions about the scope of the human mind, at least as it exists in themselves and like-minded colleagues. But academic disciplines exist precisely because the human mind is inadequate to grasp things whole and spontaneously, or to judge "the whole person." Thus mathematics must be separated out for special study, even though it is an ingredient in a vast spectrum of other activities. To the anointed, it seems merely arbitrary to make such separations, and they are forever explaining—as if it were a great discovery of theirs—that all these various disciplines interact in the real world. But specialists are not solipsists. They are simply aware of the limitations of the human mind, and of the implications of those limitations, as the anointed so often are not.

Much of what is called "interdisciplinary" by those with the vision of the anointed is not interdisciplinary at all. It is *nondisciplinary,* in that it simply ignores boundaries between disciplines. Physical chemistry is truly interdisciplinary in that it requires prior mastery of two different disciplines—physics and chemistry—but many ethnic, gender, and other "studies" do not require prior mastery of any discipline. They are nondisciplinary.

No matter how many disciplines may be mastered by a given individual, that does not make these disciplines any less separate, just as the fact that a particular quarterback can play the violin does not mean that the distinction between football and music is any less sharp. While those with the vision of the anointed often lament the "artificial barriers" between fields, as Supreme Court Justice William J. Brennan did,[30] or assert "the organic connection between education and personal experience," as John Dewey did,[31] those with the tragic vision who urge that more than one field be studied do so without ever suggesting that the barriers between these fields be erased. Justice Holmes urged legal practitioners to learn economics[32]—but not to blur the distinction between law and economics. By contrast, Ronald Dworkin has urged a "fusion" of law and moral theory,[33] much more in keeping with the unconstrained vistas envisioned by the anointed. When Justice William O. Douglas called for "fresh air blowing from other disciplines" to "ventilate the law,"[34] he was likewise reflecting the assumptions underlying his whole vision of the world.

One of the ramifications of the notion that specialization is arbitrary is the application of concepts appropriate to one field to another field where they are not only out of place but counterproductive. Accusations that corporations are "undemocratic" presuppose that the norms of the political order will be beneficial when applied in a very different institutional setting, established for wholly different purposes. Similarly, the imposition of "due process" requirements by courts on institutions such as schools arbitrarily assumes that what is beneficial in one kind of specialized institution is beneficial in a very different institution pursuing very different purposes.

NAMING NAMES

Numerous issues are preempted, and numerous gaps in logic papered over, simply by the names that are given to various things—"capitalism," "the left," "the right," "human rights," etc. A few examples may be suggestive as to how easily the need for either logic or evidence can be circumvented by a simple repetition of names that dulls people's awareness so that they literally do not know what they are talking about.

Capitalism

Since capitalism was named by its enemies, it is perhaps not surprising that the name is completely misleading. Despite the name, capitalism is not an "ism." It is not a philosophy but an economy. Ultimately it is nothing more and nothing less than an economy not run by political authorities. There are no capitalist institutions; any number of institutional ways of carrying out economic activities may flourish under "capitalism"—that is, in the absence of control from above. You may get food from a restaurant, or by buying it from the supermarket and cooking it yourself, or by growing the food on your own land and processing it all the way through to the dinner table. Each of these is just as much "capitalism" as the others. At any given time, caravans, supermarkets, or computerized shopping methods may be used, but none of these is anything more than a modality of the moment. They do not define capitalism but are simply one of the innumerable ways of doing things when choices are unconstrained by authorities.

Many have argued that capitalism does not offer a satisfactory moral message. But that is like saying that calculus does not contain carbohydrates, amino acids, or other essential nutrients. Everything fails by irrelevant standards. Yet no one regards this as making calculus invalid or illegitimate. Once again, the selective application of arbitrary standards is invoked only when it promotes the vision of the anointed.

The Political "Left" and "Right"

Among the many thoughtless labels which have gained currency, the dichotomy between the political left and the political right is one of the most striking, not only for its wide acceptance but also for its utter lack of definition—or even an attempt at definition. Only the left is defined—initially by the kinds of ideas held by those who sat on the left side of the French national assembly in the eighteenth century. But while the left is defined, at least in this general sense, the *dichotomy itself* remains undefined because "the right" remains undefined. Those who oppose the left are said to be on the right— and when they are strongly opposed, or opposed across a broad spectrum of issues, they are said to be on the "far right." But this is a somewhat Ptolemaic view of the political universe, with the political left being in the center of that universe and all who differ—in any direction—being called "the right."

Whether free-market libertarians or statists ranging from those with monarchist to fascist views, opponents of the left are called "the right." In the United States, especially, the related term "conservative" is routinely used to encompass people who have no desire to preserve the status quo or to return to some status quo ante. Friedrich Hayek, for more than half a century a prime opponent of leftist policies on the international stage, was thus considered a conservative, if not part of "the far right." Yet Hayek himself wrote an article entitled, "Why I Am Not a Conservative."[35] Milton Friedman has likewise repudiated the "conservative" label[36] and wrote a book entitled *The Tyranny of the Status Quo.* Yet he is regarded as the leading "conservative" intellectual of his age, though many of the things he advocates have never existed in any society, or—like school vouchers—did not exist when he first advocated them. Among so-called "black conservatives," it is virtually impossible to find anyone who wants to go back to anything, this group being opposed to both the racial discrimination policies of the past and the racial preference policies that came after them.

Although the free market is clearly the antithesis of state control of the economy, such as fascists advocate, the left-right dichotomy makes it seem as if fascists are just more extreme versions of "conservatives," in the same sense in which socialism is a more extreme version of the welfare state. But this vision of a symmetrical political spectrum corresponds to no empirical reality. Those who advocate the free market typically do so as just one aspect of a more general vision in which government's role in the lives of individuals is to be minimized, within limits set by a need to avoid anarchy and a need to maintain military defense against other nations. In no sense is fascism a further extension of that idea. It is in fact the antithesis of that whole line of thinking. Yet much talk in terms of left and right suggests that there is a political spectrum which proceeds from the center to conservatives to "far right" neo-fascism to fascism itself.

The only logic to such a conception is that it allows disparate opponents of the vision of the anointed to be lumped together and dismissed through guilt by association.

THE CATEGORICAL VERSUS THE INCREMENTAL

The vocabulary of the anointed is filled with words reflecting their rejection of incremental trade-offs and advocacy of categorical "solutions." This is most clear in the law and in writings among the legal intelligentsia, where individual and social trade-offs are transformed into categorical legal "rights." Ronald Dworkin perhaps best expressed this view when he said: "Individual rights are political trumps held by individuals."[37] Just as the smallest trump beats the highest card in any other suit, so these "rights" take precedence over the weightiest other considerations which are not in the form of rights. Thus the "rights" of criminals take precedence over crime control, the "right" to various social "entitlements" takes precedence over the interests of taxpayers, the "rights" of those entitled to compensation for past injustices take precedence over the interests of displaced contemporaries who complain of "reverse discrimination," and so on. Rights trump interests in this vision.

At its worst, this line of argument arbitrarily singles out some particular kind of individual or group to be made sacred and leaves others to be sacrificed on the altar to this sacredness. The particular beneficiaries chosen may range from racial or ethnic minorities to people with AIDS or endangered species of animals. Alternatively, the categorical priorities may be established and defined by particular benefits rather than particular people or species—food being more important than music, medical care being more important than transportation, etc. But, however reasonable the order of precedence may seem, making that order *categorical* is the fatal step. Surely everyone would agree that life itself is more important than photography. But would anyone wipe out the entire photographic industry, in order that one person could live 30 seconds longer than otherwise? Life is indeed more important than photography, in the general and elliptical senses in which we usually speak—but not in the categorical senses used in intellectual models or legal proscriptions. It is precisely in relying on intellectual models and legal proscriptions for categorical decisions that we risk absurd and disastrous consequences.

Among many objections to categorical thinking is that it is incompatible with a world of diminishing returns. Where an individual or a society has available any two benefits, to say that benefit X is a "right" and benefit Y is not is to say that the most trivial incremental advantage from a further extension of benefit X is worth the most devastating losses from a further reduction of benefit Y. Since even the most essential things—food, for example, as noted in Chapter 5—reach the point where further increments are of diminishing value, and may even become negative in value, a rule making anything categorically more important than other benefits risks reaching the point of making huge sacrifices of one thing for trivial benefits from another—or no benefits at all from another. Virtually no one would advocate such a thing in plain, straightforward language. It is only in the lofty and roundabout language of "rights," "priorities," "entitlements," and the like that the same kind of categorical results are advocated in different words.

The vision of categorical precedence is central to John Rawls's celebrated book, *A Theory of Justice,* where it was asserted that "the rights secured by justice" are not subject to "the calculus of social interests."[38] In short, let justice be done even if the skies must fall—regardless of what this does to those on whom the skies fall. Rawls was quite clear as to the categorical priorities being established in what he called a "lexical order":

> This is an order which requires us to satisfy the first principle in the ordering before we can move on to the second, the second before we consider the third, and so on. A principle does not come into play

until those previous to it are either fully met or do not apply. A serial ordering avoids, then, having to balance principles at all; those earlier in the sequence have an absolute weight, so to speak, with respect to later ones, and hold without exception.[39]

According to Rawls, "The principles of justice are to be ranked in lexical order and therefore liberty can be restricted only for the sake of liberty."[40] The principle of "fair equality of opportunity"—meaning "equal life prospects in all sectors of society for those similarly endowed and motivated"[41]—cannot be allowed to be infringed for the sake of a greater sum of benefits available to society as a whole by alternative social arrangements.[42] In short, there are not to be incremental trade-offs but categorical priorities in which one thing "trumps" another.

There is little danger that anyone would voluntarily adopt such rigidities, if plainly and openly presented. The danger is that lofty words and obscure terms may lead many through the murky and meandering marshlands of abstract theory toward the same disastrous result.

INCOME "DISTRIBUTION"

Despite a voluminous and often fervent literature on "income distribution," the cold fact is that most income is *not* distributed: It is *earned*. People paying each other for goods and services generate income. While many people's entire income comes from a salary paid to them by a given employer, many others collect individual fees for everything from shoe shines to surgery, and it is the sum total of these innumerable fees which constitutes their income. Other income is distributed from a central point as social security checks, welfare payments, unemployment compensation, and the like. But that is not how most people get most income.

To say that "wealth is so unfairly distributed in America," as Ronald Dworkin does,[43] is grossly misleading when most wealth in the United States is not distributed *at all*. People create it, earn it, save it, and spend it.

If one believes that income and wealth should not originate as they do now, but should instead be distributed as largess from some central point, then that argument should be made openly, plainly, and honestly. But to talk as if we currently have a certain distribution result *A* which should be changed to distribution result *B* is to misstate the issue and disguise a radical institutional change as a simple adjustment of preferences. The word "distribution" can of course be used in more than one sense. In a purely statistical sense, we can speak of the "distribution" of heights in the population, without believing that someone in Washington decides how tall we should all be and then mails out these heights to different individuals. What we cannot do, either logically or morally, is to shift back and forth between these two very different conceptions of distribution. Newspapers are distributed in one sense—they are sent out from a printing plant to scattered sites to be sold to readers—but heights are distributed only in the other sense.

Those who criticize the existing "distribution" of income in the United States are criticizing the statistical results of systemic processes. They are usually not even discussing the economic fate of actual flesh-and-blood human beings, for the economic positions of given individuals vary greatly within a relatively few years. What is really being said is that *numbers don't look right to the anointed*— and that this is what matters, that all the myriad purposes of the millions of human beings who are transacting with one another in the marketplace must be subordinated to the goal of presenting a certain statistical tableau to anointed observers.

To question the "fairness" or other index of validity of the existing statistics growing out of voluntary economic transactions is to question whether those who spent their own money to buy what they wanted from other people have a right to do so. To say that a shoe shine boy earns "too little" or a surgeon "too much" is to say that third parties should have the right to preempt the decisions of those who elected to spend their money on shoe shines or surgery. To say that "society" should decide how much it values various goods and services is to say that individual decisions on these matters should be superseded by collective decisions made by political surrogates.

But to say this openly would require some persuasive reasons why collective decisions are better than individual decisions and why third parties are better judges than those who are making their own trade-offs at their own expense.

Again, no one would seriously entertain such an arrogant and presumptuous goal, if presented openly, plainly, and honestly. They may, however, be led in that direction if the anointed are able to slip undetected back and forth between one definition of "distribution" and another, as the exigencies of the argument require.

DEFINITIONAL BENEDICTIONS AND CURSES

A whole family of self-flattering words serves as benedictions for the vision of the anointed. "Progress" and "progressive" are prominent examples. But *everyone* is for "progress," by definition. They differ only on specifics, though these differences may be extreme and even violent. Words like "progress" or "progressive" preempt these specific issues by arbitrarily assuming the differential desirability of one's own preferred changes, without having to debate substance—or even acknowledge its relevance.

Conversely, others' beliefs or behavior can be verbally put under a cloud by arbitrary labels that substitute for substance. Anyone who has examined and rejected some particular proposition favored by the anointed is often said to have "dismissed" this proposition. No matter how much time, meticulous attention, voluminous evidence, or detailed analysis went into the conclusion reached, it becomes a "dismissal" if it ends up rejecting part of the vision of the anointed. Thus anyone who concludes that racial discrimination, for example, explains less of the intergroup differences in income among racial or ethnic groups than is commonly supposed will be said to have "dismissed" discrimination as a factor, no matter how extensive the data or history examined before reaching that conclusion. This usage of the word "dismiss" is very common in book reviews,[44] for example, and serves as a substitute for confronting the arguments in books which challenge some aspect of the vision of the anointed. It preempts the very possibility that there is anything to argue about.

Science and "Experts"

One of the most common benedictions of the anointed is the use of the word "science" to describe notions which are consonant with their vision, but which have neither the certainty nor the intellectual rigor of science. Thus the speculations of sociologists, psychologists, and psychiatrists became part of the criminal justice system under the guise of "science." In the landmark *Durham* case of 1954, which expanded the insanity defense for criminals, Chief Judge Bazelon spoke of "the science of psychiatry,"[45] of "relevant scientific disciplines" in general,[46] and of "scientific knowledge" which supposedly vitiated the previous test of whether the criminal was sane enough to tell right from wrong.[47] Justice William J. Brennan likewise spoke of "experts in the behavioral sciences" and of opening "the doors of the nation's courts to the insights of the social sciences."[48] He also applied the medical concept of "etiology" to crime—to be revealed by anthropologists, social workers, and the like.[49] To allow such people to deflect punishment from criminals with theories was equated by Judge Bazelon with opening "the legal process to the widest possible array of information."[50]

The notion of judging criminals after seeking "information from any and all sources about their lives"[51] ignores or disregards the obvious fact that only those with mitigating or exculpatory testimony have any real incentives to present such "information." Relatives, friends, and criminal associates have such incentives. But why should those neighbors, teachers, or others with firsthand knowledge contradicting such "information" be expected to step forward and needlessly subject themselves to the prospect of retaliation? Nor is the "expert" testimony of "social scientists" any less likely to be asymmetrical. Numerous studies of the ideological leanings of intellectuals show them clearly in the camp of those with the vision of the anointed, in which punishment is decried. Why should the speculations of those with the vision of the anointed supersede the penalties prescribed by laws passed by elected officials? That question is evaded by calling those speculations "science."

The most important characteristic of science—empirical verification—is often omitted entirely by those with the vision of the anointed. Indeed, much of their verbal dexterity goes into evading empirical evidence. The crowning irony is that no empirical data are collected or sought as to how often these "scientists" are wrong. A psychiatrist or psychologist whose testimony has freed a hundred criminals, who have committed dozens of violent crimes after being released, will be listened to the one hundred and first time with no record available as to how much havoc he has already contributed to. Nothing could be less scientific.

One of the incidental examples of "scientific" puffery is widespread use of the term "parameters" to mean boundaries, rather than its actual meaning in mathematical equations. What are usually called "parameters" in discussions of social policies could more accurately be called perimeters. But of course that would not foster the illusion of "science."

VERBAL INFLATION

In addition to particular words and phrases which betray the mindset of those with the prevailing vision, there is a more general tendency toward verbal inflation among the anointed. Thus the ordinary vicissitudes of life become "traumas." Any situation which they wish to change becomes a "crisis," regardless of whether it is any worse than usual or is already getting better on its own.

Verbal inflation, like monetary inflation, would have no effect if everyone understood what was happening and could adjust to it immediately. A ten-fold increase in the price level would mean nothing if everyone were free to add a zero to the sums in all contracts, laws, cash on hand, etc., and did so immediately. Inflation has an economic effect precisely because there is no such instantaneous and total flexibility. In the real world of lagging adjustments, borrowers pay back less than they owe, workers are paid less than they were promised, and the government cheats its way out of part of the national debt by paying it off in dollars that are worth less than the dollars that were borrowed. Verbal inflation likewise enables some people to cheat others. When "harassment," "discrimination," or

even "rape" are redefined to include things going far beyond the
original meanings of these words, there would be no real change if
everyone understood what the inflated words now mean and neither
social stigmas nor the penalties of the laws applied to the vast range
of new things encompassed by these new meanings.

In both cases, runaway inflation is not just a zero-sum game. Monetary inflation not only redistributes benefits but can also reduce the
sum total of those benefits, by undermining the credibility of the
monetary unit and with it undermining the predictability of the whole
system of which it is part, causing the economy to be less productive
as people restrict what they do and plan, in order to avoid vastly
increased risks. For similar reasons, human relations suffer when the
verbal common currency of social interaction loses its meaning and
predictability, so that people now protect themselves from new risks
by various ways of withdrawing from one another and reducing
their cooperation. For example, where mere statistics are enough
to enmesh an employer in costly litigation over an inflated meaning of "discrimination," locations some distance from concentra-
tions of minority workers become more attractive as sites for facto-
ries and offices. This works to the detriment of the very minority
workers for whom this inflated meaning was created. It also works to
the detriment of the economy as a whole, as resources are no longer
used where they would be most productive in the absence of the vast
new uncertainties created by inflated words. Some other inflated
words—"homophobia," "violence," and "hopelessness"—are worth
a closer look.

"Homophobia"

Writers who have written for years, or even decades, without ever
mentioning homosexuals have been denounced for "homophobia"
because they began to write about the subject after the AIDS epidemic appeared—and did not take the "politically correct" position
on the issues. How can someone have a "phobia" about something he
has scarcely noticed? Many people never knew or cared what homosexuals were doing, until it became a danger to them as a result of

the AIDS epidemic. Whether those people's reactions were right or wrong is something that can be debated. But attributing their position to a "phobia" is circular reasoning, when there is no evidence of any such phobia other than the position itself. Like so much in the vocabulary of the anointed, it is a way of avoiding substantive debate.

Among the writers who took non–"politically correct" positions on AIDS was the late Randy Shilts, whose best-selling book *And the Band Played On*[52] is a chilling exploration of the political irresponsibility, based on fears of offending the organized gay lobby, that led to thousands of unnecessary deaths before the most elementary public health measures were taken to reduce the spread of AIDS. No doubt he too would have been called "homophobic" if he were not himself an avowed homosexual who later died of AIDS.

"Violence"

One of the fashionable inflationary words of our times is "violence"—used to describe whatever social circumstances or political policies one disagrees with, however peaceful such circumstances or policies may be in the ordinary usage of words. Thus any "power that oppresses" is violence, according to some,[53] which opens up boundless vistas, based only on what one chooses to call oppression.

Jesse Jackson refers to "economic violence,"[54] Ralph Nader refers to "violence" done to the environment by corporations and government,[55] and Jonathan Kozol refers to "savage inequalities" in public school financing.[56] Similarly, Professor Kenneth B. Clark responded to public concerns about muggings by referring to "pervasive social muggings" such as "the crimes of deteriorating neighborhoods, job discrimination and criminally inferior education." Thus Professor Clark could speak of "mugged communities," "mugged neighborhoods," and "mugged schools which spawn urban 'muggers.'"[57]

For some, figurative "violence" serves as an explicit justification of real violence or "counterviolence" as it is called.[58] For others, the justification is only implicit. Still others are just practicing the politics of verbal inflation.

"Hopelessness"

One of the inflated words that plays a key role in promoting the vision of the anointed and the social policies based on it is "hopelessness." Unhappy social circumstances are almost automatically described in this way, with neither evidence nor a demand for evidence, nor even a sign of awareness that evidence might be relevant. Political rhetoric abounds with many empirically unverifiable assertions that "hopelessness" exists among the poor—or would, in the absence of government social programs. Media figure Hodding Carter III used such "hopelessness" as a justification for the "war on poverty" programs of the Johnson administration in which he served.[59] *New York Times* columnist Tom Wicker likewise claimed that "Americans were given hope" by the Johnson administration programs.[60]

In the absence of any evidence that such widespread hopelessness existed outside the vision of the anointed, it may be useful to look at history. Tens of millions of immigrants came to the United States, often beginning in destitution and rising up the socioeconomic ladder, in the process creating and celebrating "the American dream." Far from being hopeless, such immigrants, with their enthusiastic letters back to their relatives and friends in Europe, kept more millions crossing the Atlantic in their wake.[61] More recently, as already noted, both poverty and dependency were declining for years prior to the Johnson administration's "war on poverty." Black income was rising, not only absolutely but relative to rising white income.[62] In the five years prior to passage of the Civil Rights Act of 1964, blacks were rising into professional and other high-level positions at a rate greater than in the five years following passage of the Act.[63] Nationwide, Scholastic Aptitude Test scores were rising, venereal diseases were declining sharply, and the murder rate was at an all-time low. This was the "hopelessness" from which the anointed came to rescue us.

CHAPTER 8

COURTING DISASTER

Law has lost its soul and become jungle.

—Bertrand de Jouvenel[1]

Law is more than the sum of all the statutes, regulations, constitutional provisions, and judicial interpretations currently in force. What gives them all coherence, and the public support without which they could not be enforced, is that they are expressions of an underlying notion that we live by rules rather than by either arbitrary edicts or anarchy. The ideal is "a government of laws and not of men," and while neither this ideal nor any other has ever been realized 100 percent, such an all-or-nothing standard would trivialize out of existence virtually everything that matters in life.

There is a fundamental difference between a society where a ruler can seize the wealth or the wife of any subject and one in which the poorest citizen can refuse to allow the highest official of the land inside his home. There is a fundamental difference between a time when the great English jurist Coke cringed as King James threatened to beat him physically with his own hands—resistance being treason, punishable by death—and a world in which the Supreme Court of the United States could order President Nixon to turn over evidence to a special prosecutor. No clever trivializing can erase these differences. Centuries of struggle, sacrifice, and bloodshed went into creating the ideal of a government of laws superior to any ruler or political organ.

Law in this sense is more than any given ensemble of particular edicts and rulings—such edicts and rulings being common to all sorts of societies, from the freest to the most totalitarian. But law in the full sense cannot exist under totalitarianism, as the totalitarians themselves acknowledge. The point was well made by a Soviet writer who said, "communism means not the victory of socialist law, but the victory of socialism over any law."[2] There was likewise no law restraining Hitler, any more than any law or any concept of law limited what Stalin could do. Similarly, a sultan of the Ottoman Empire could order any person executed on the spot at any time for any reason, or for no reason.

By "the rule of law" is not meant simply that edicts are enforced but that only laws set forth in advance can be used to punish and that only legal enactments conforming to some accepted principles—set forth in a written constitution in some countries—will be enforceable. Every society has its rules but not every society has the rule of law. When Bertrand de Jouvenel said that law had lost its soul, he meant that the grand concept of law was being eroded away, or prostituted, until it became nothing more than an ensemble of rules and rulings, changeable without notice, and reflecting little more than an arbitrary exercise of power—the very antithesis of law. This is the direction in which American law has been driven by those with the vision of the anointed.

The rule of law and the vision of the anointed are inherently at loggerheads. The judge who carries out the law as written is the agent of others, and the law that emerges from the political process in a democratic country reflects the values and experiences of the benighted, not the anointed. That judges with the elite vision should find such a situation unduly constricting, if not intolerable, is consistent with the premises of their vision. Only by going beyond the law as written can they impose their superior wisdom and virtue, and in the process preempt the decisions of others. Creative and adventurous "interpretations" of the Constitution, statutes, and contracts give judges that power. While those with the tragic vision decry the presumptions of judges who circumvent the systemic processes of society—as expressed in economic transactions, social practices, and legal traditions, for example—those who assume a more sweeping capability are little deterred by any fear of inadvertently deranging these systemic processes.

Perhaps the classic expression of the objection to the rule of law was by socialist writer Anatole France, when he said sarcastically: "The Law, in its majestic equality, forbids rich and poor alike to sleep under bridges, beg in the streets or steal bread."[3] The differential impact of the same laws on people in different social circumstances has long been a key reason given for departing from the ideal of law and government as a set of impartial processes, and instead making law and government instruments of a set of policies directed toward prescribed social results. Moreover, these prescribed results are often conceived within a framework of a cosmic perspective on justice, in which it is not sufficient to treat everyone the same after they enter the legal system, if they entered with preexisting inequalities that must be compensated for, in order to achieve "real" justice. Such are the ambitious goals—the vision of the anointed—behind the stretching and bending of the law that has become known as "judicial activism."

It is in seeking cosmic justice that the law has become less and less law and more and more a series of ad hoc pronouncements which the judicial activists call "evolving standards" or "a living constitution."

COSMIC JUSTICE

Seeking a range of justice reaching beyond the narrow confines of the traditional legal system, or the Constitution as historically written, takes many forms. For example, the Constitution's plain and simple statement that no person "shall be compelled in any criminal case to be a witness against himself" has been stretched in legal theory to cover the following situation:

The police arrested Eugene Frazier for the robbery of Mike's Carry Out. After they advised him of his rights and let him read a copy of the *Miranda* warnings, Frazier signed a "Consent to Speak" form and told an officer that he understood his rights and did not want a lawyer. When an officer began questioning him about Mike's Carry Out, Frazier interrupted and admitted to robbing High's Market. The policeman started to transcribe Frazier's remarks, but the defendant stopped him, saying, "Don't write anything down. I will tell you about this but I don't want you to write anything down."

The officer put down the pad and continued listening in silence as Frazier went on about the High's robbery. After about five minutes of this, Frazier confessed to the robbery of the Meridian Market. Two hours or so later Frazier ended the questioning, stating, "That's it; that's all I am going to tell you." When the police asked the defendant to write out his confession or to sign a typed summary, Frazier refused. "No, I'm not going to sign anything," he said.[4]

When Frazier's conviction for the robberies he confessed to was appealed to the District of Columbia Circuit Court of Appeals, according to Chief Judge David Bazelon, "we were troubled" by the robber's apparent misconception that his confession did not count if it were not written down. Therefore the burden of proof was on the government to show that Frazier "intelligently and knowingly" waived his constitutional right—and the case was sent back to the trial court. When the case came back up again and a majority on the Circuit Court of Appeals voted to uphold the conviction, Judge Bazelon dissented on grounds that using the confession "denied people like Frazier genuinely equal treatment before the law" because *Miranda* warnings ought to be made "so clear that no one possessing even minimal intelligence could possibly misunderstand them."[5]

Although Judge Bazelon did not ultimately prevail in this particular case, it is revealing for the kind of reasoning which caused the Court of Appeals to send the case back to the trial court in the first place. At no point was the robber "compelled to be a witness against himself," in the words of the Fifth Amendment. This whole issue arose because judges went beyond the Fifth Amendment, in pursuit of a more cosmic view of justice. Judge Bazelon stated the issue as so many others with the vision of the anointed have stated it: "Educated, respectable suspects ordinarily know of their rights to be silent and to retain a lawyer."[6] In short, the task of the courts was conceived to be not simply to treat everyone equally within the confines of the legal system but to *offset preexisting inequalities.* They were to pursue cosmic justice.

The cosmic perspective of course extends beyond the law. But, in whatever field it appears, its adherents are quick to say that people did not really have a "free choice" in what they did. Thus to Noam Chomsky "freedom is illusion and mockery when conditions for the exercise of free choice do not exist"—and those conditions do not exist for "the person compelled to sell his labor power to survive,"[7] i.e., for anyone who works for a living. Any circumstantial constraints or potential consequences hanging over people's decisions makes their choices not "really" free. But this conception of a free choice requires an unconstrained universe. Only God could have a free choice—and only on the first day of creation, since He would be confronted on the second day by what He had already done on the first.

Constitutional right after constitutional right has been stretched far beyond anything encompassed by those rights when they were written—but only when the rights in question were consonant with the vision of the anointed. Where a constitutional right goes counter to, or inhibits, some aspect of that vision, that constitutional right is far more likely to be reduced or ignored. For example, the Fifth Amendment's prohibition against anyone's being "twice put in jeopardy" for "the same offense" has been judicially interpreted out of existence in the case of policemen acquitted in state court of criminally mistreating arrested suspects such as Rodney King and then retried in federal court for the same acts as civil offenses. Likewise, the Fifth Amendment's protections of property rights have been routinely overridden by other considerations—almost any other consideration—in numerous cases.[8] The selective indignation of the anointed is reflected in legal theory that is selectively cosmic.

Even if cosmic justice were sought equally and consistently for all, however, it would still conflict disastrously with the law of diminishing returns. The proliferation of new technicalities in the criminal law, each designed to eliminate various residual biases and uncertainties surrounding arrest and trial, beyond some point risks far greater dangers to the public from criminals out on bail awaiting trial when there is an overcrowded court system taking longer and longer

time to complete each trial, due to these new technicalities. A few
years after the criminal justice revolution of the 1960s, a California
appellate judge said:

> It is with almost melancholy nostalgia that we recall how only five
> years ago it was possible to sustain a judgment of conviction entered
> in such a clear case of unquestionable guilt and to accomplish it with-
> out undue strain.[9]

Judicially expanded "rights" to appeal state court decisions to the
federal courts led to an increase in such appeals for habeas corpus
from fewer than a hundred in 1940 to more than 12,000 by 1970.
Commenting on this explosive growth, a federal appeals court judge
in New York noted the effects of this expanded role of the federal
judiciary in second-guessing state appellate court decisions:

> For all our work on thousands of state prisoner cases I have yet to
> hear of one where an innocent man had been convicted. The net
> result of our fruitless meddling in search of the non-existent needle in
> the ever-larger haystack has been a serious detriment to the adminis-
> tration of criminal justice by the states.[10]

This is not to say that there are literally no innocent men ever convicted in a country with a quarter of a billion people. It is simply to
raise the question whether extended federal second-guessing of state
appellate courts will turn up many or any—and at what cost, not only
in terms of money, but in terms of the increased number of innocent
people sacrificed as victims of violent criminals walking the streets
longer and longer, while legal processes grind on slowly and at seem-
ingly interminable length. In short, while saving some innocent individuals from a false conviction is important, the question is whether
it is *more* important than sparing other equally innocent individuals
from violence and death at the hands of criminals. Is saving one
innocent defendant per decade worth sacrificing ten innocent murder
victims? A hundred? A thousand? Once we recognize that there are
no solutions, but only trade-offs, we can no longer pursue cosmic jus-

tice, but must make our choices among alternatives actually available—and these alternatives do not include guaranteeing that no harm can possibly befall any innocent individual. The only way to make sure that no innocent individual is ever falsely convicted is to do away with the criminal justice system and accept the horrors of anarchy. No one would advocate such a situation. That is simply the direction in which the legal system has drifted in pursuit of cosmic justice. Nowhere is the maxim that "the best is the enemy of the good" more painfully demonstrated than when violent felonies have to be plea-bargained down to misdemeanors because of the prohibitive cost of trying more cases in a system bogged down in proliferating technicalities growing out of a quixotic quest for cosmic justice. This is part of what Judge Macklin Fleming has aptly called, in the title of his book, *The Price of Perfect Justice.*[11]

Nothing is more of a search for cosmic justice than attempts to redress the wrongs of history, not simply for particular individuals wrongly convicted or victimized in some other way, but for whole categories of people whose ancestors' misfortunes are to be redressed in the present generation. Given the innumerable factors influencing the current well-being or misfortunes of individuals and groups, the presumption of being able to disentangle all these factors and determine how much is due to the injustices of history is truly staggering. We have already seen in Chapter 4 how easy it is to confuse what is and is not a "legacy of slavery." But the principle applies far more broadly. What would the people of Spain be like today if they had not been conquered by the Moors and then spent centuries of struggle to get free of Moorish rule? What would Egyptians be like if there were no Nile? Southern Asians if there were no monsoons? It would be difficult enough to reach an assessment that was defensible as intellectual speculation, much less a compelling conclusion by the standards of a court of law. Yet judges pursuing cosmic justice make sweeping assumptions about equally complex historical questions.

An ever more lengthy and complex jury-selection process likewise proceeds in defiance of the law of diminishing returns. Detailed questionnaires for jurors to answer—including highly personal questions which they are compelled to answer, in disregard of "privacy" rights which count for so much in other contexts—and the use of expensive consultants specializing in the selection of jurors are just some of the costs of this attempt to achieve a closer approximation to cosmic justice. But, even aside from the immediate delays and other costs, this complex process opens up the whole trial, verdict, and sentence to further challenges in the appellate courts, even when there is not the slightest doubt about the guilt of the defendant and when even his own attorneys no longer make any claim of innocence. All this is part of the cost of the quest for cosmic justice.

JUDICIAL ACTIVISM

The general process of stretching and twisting the written law—and especially the Constitution—to reach results desired by judges has been called "judicial activism." It is not only an example of the vision of the anointed in action, it is also a crucial mechanism by which other aspects of that vision—the cosmic justice being sought through affirmative action, for example—has been imposed as "the law of the land" when elected legislators would be reluctant to go as far as unelected judges. Like most phrases, like all of language in fact, the term "judicial activism" is itself a subject to varying interpretations and distortions. In the pattern of these interpretations and distortions, there is once more visible the vision of the anointed, not only in the way some litigants are treated as mascots or as targets, but also in the more general way that the exercise of power is shifted from the benighted to the anointed.

Definitions and Distortions

Activity, as such, is not the touchstone of judicial activism. There is nothing to prevent a judicial activist from being lazy or his opposite, the practitioner of "judicial restraint," from being a dynamo of energy. Judicial activism cannot be quantified according to how many laws or lower court decisions are overturned, since it is the *grounds* on which they are overturned that defines judicial activism or judicial restraint. As with so much language, the phrase "judicial activism" is just an elliptical way of indicating a particular thing—but what that thing is does not depend on what can be extracted from isolated words. It depends on what concrete meaning those words have in the particular context in which they are used. This is nothing unusual. The word "shortstop" has a very different meaning in a photographic laboratory than it does on a baseball field and "closing" means something very different in real estate than it does in horse racing. Because evasion by trivialization has been as common a pattern among the anointed in discussions of judicial activism and judicial restraint as in other areas, it will be necessary to define these terms carefully before looking at the phenomena they represent.

Words like "due process," "freedom of speech," and other phrases from the Constitution might be interpreted in a sweeping variety of ways, if one simply relied on the dictionary meanings of those words and applied them according to one's own sense of what that meant in practice. But these phrases existed and had a long history in the laws of England, even before the Constitution of the United States was written. Therefore the *historical* meanings of such terms, in the legal context in which they were used, were much more limited than all the conceivable meanings that one might derive from a dictionary and apply according to one's own vision. Those who wrote the American Constitution were of course familiar with such terms as "due process," "freedom of speech," etc., from English law and indicated no intention of giving them different meanings from what those terms already had.

Those who today advocate "judicial restraint" define it as judges interpreting laws, including the Constitution, according to the meanings that the words in those laws had when they were written. Judge Robert H. Bork, for example, has said that judges should render decisions "according to the historical Constitution."[12] More broadly, Judge Richard Posner has written of the self-disciplined judge as "the honest agent of others until the will of the principals can no longer be discerned."[13] Justice Oliver Wendell Holmes saw that his job was "to see that the game is played according to the rules whether I like them or not."[14] According to Holmes: "When we know what the source of the law has said that it shall be, our authority is at an end."[15] In one of his Supreme Court decisions, Holmes said, "I am not at liberty to discuss the justice of the Act."[16] That was a cosmic question and he had no commission from the cosmos.

Those who argue for this view of the judge's role—for "judicial restraint"—often say that judges should follow the "original intent" of laws in general and the Constitution in particular. Yet, ironically, this very phrase itself has been seized upon by opponents and given meanings far removed from that of those who use it. Professor Ronald Dworkin, for example, argues against original intent on grounds that "mental events" in the minds of legislators or writers of the Constitution are difficult or impossible to discern.[17] But, of course, *nobody voted on what was in the back of somebody else's mind.* What was enacted into law were the meanings of those words to others—in short, the public meaning of words. As Justice Holmes put it, the relevant question was "not what this man meant, but what those words would mean in the mouth of a normal speaker of English, using them in the circumstances in which they were used."[18] Those who have urged judicial restraint have been very explicit that they did *not* mean to delve into the psyches of lawmakers but to begin with the *public meaning* of the words that lawmakers used, as of the time they used them. For Holmes, legal interpretation of what someone said did not mean trying to "get into his mind."[19] What was needed was the *public meaning* of his words, not the subjective intentions or personal psychology of whoever used them. Holmes said: "We do not inquire what the legislature meant; we ask only what the statute meant."[20]

In a very similar vein, Judge Bork wrote:

. . . what the ratifiers understood themselves to be enacting must be taken to be what the public of that time would have understood the words to mean. It is important to be clear about this. The search is not for a subjective intention. If someone found a letter from George Washington to Martha telling her that what he meant by the power to lay taxes was not what other people meant, that would not change our reading of the Constitution in the slightest.[21]

Despite these clear and unmistakable statements, from the time of Holmes to the time of Bork, gross distortions of this view have remained the rule rather than the exception among those with the vision of the anointed. Justice William J. Brennan, for example, said that judges following original intent would have to "discern exactly what the Framers thought,"[22] and of course he found that impossible. Professor Stephen Macedo of Harvard objected to Bork's views on original intent because "public statements often do not reflect actual intentions"[23]—as if this were either a revelation or relevant. Professor Jack Rakove of Stanford took a similarly condescending view of Attorney General Edwin Meese's advocacy of judicial restraint by going into the subjective intentions of the writers of the Constitution—the fact that James Madison "approached the Convention in the grip of a great intellectual passion," that he had "fear" of certain policies regarding property and religion, and that he "privately described" constitutional amendments in a certain way.[24]

Far more is involved here than a mere misunderstanding. Power is at the heart of the dispute. Although *New York Times* columnist Anthony Lewis wrote of the Constitution's "expansive phrases that would be given contemporary meaning by each generation,"[25] generations do not vote on the constitutionality of laws. Judges do. Thus the current generation's decisions are not replacing those of a previous generation; judges' decisions are replacing those of the current generation by imposing their own revision of what a past generation has said. The replacement of historical meanings by "contemporary meanings" is a major transfer of power to judges, not only from other branches of government, but from the people. It is an erosion of self-government and an imposition of the social vision of judges in its place. That the anointed should favor this is hardly surprising.

A constitution was created for a purpose, to prescribe and restrict what power could be wielded, by whom, and within what limits. Unlike the Constitution of England, which exists not as a tangible document but as a collection of traditions, the Constitution of the United States was written down to fix the limits of government power—not forever, but until an authorized change was made in an authorized way. The imperative words of the Constitution—"Con-

gress shall make no law"—were clearly intended to convey a substantive meaning rather than simply to provide a "text" for judges to
"deconstruct" and reassemble to mean whatever they wanted it to
mean.

Judicial activists and the legal theorists who promote judicial
activism seek to free judges' decisions from the constraints of the
Constitution as written and the limitations of legislation as passed.
They seek judicial decisions which reach beyond these confines to
encompass more sweeping moral principles. Ronald Dworkin, for
example, rejects a "strict interpretation" of the words in the Constitution because that would limit constitutional rights "to those recognized by a limited group of people at a fixed date in history."[26] In
other words, judges are to be free to seek cosmic justice. According to
Justice William J. Brennan, "the genius of the Constitution rests not
in any static meaning it might have had in a world that is dead and
gone, but in the adaptability of its great principles to cope with current problems and current needs."[27] To Chief Justice Earl Warren as
well, the idea of a strict construction of the words of the Constitution
was "ludicrous" and "a spurious issue" because of "ever-changing
circumstances," including circumstances "far beyond the vision of
even the wisest of the Founding Fathers."[28]

Similar statements abound throughout a large literature on legal
theory. The stress placed on changing circumstances and on the need
for legal changes to deal with them is a central part of the verbal fanfare over something that is not even at issue—for absolutely no one
denies that there have been major changes since the eighteenth century. This verbal fanfare serves only to distract attention from what is
in fact crucially at issue: *Who* is to make those legal changes and *by
what authority?* Power is the issue—and the usurpation of power.
The Constitution itself clearly contemplates legal changes—otherwise, why create a Congress to pass laws or a president charged with
enforcing them, much less spell out a whole legal procedure for
amending the Constitution's own provisions?

The issue as regards judicial activism is not whether there shall
be "change"—since no one is against generic "change"—but who
shall wield the enormous power of prescribing the particular nature

and direction of change *and by whose authorization?* More specifically, shall it be done openly by officials assigned this task by the Constitution and responsible to the voters, or shall it be done furtively by unelected judges using verbal sleight-of-hand to attribute to the Constitution things that the Constitution never said? The issue is preemption of power, not "change."

What the rule of law means, among other things, is that certain questions have been settled, at least as far as the law is concerned. Therefore the citizens of the country can rely on "the law of the land" in their plans and actions, until such time as that law is explicitly changed by new statutes or constitutional amendments. The occasions of such change provide advance warning that we are all now living under different rules. Judicial activism makes all this radically different. Individuals and organizations discover only after the fact that they are violating "evolving standards"—such discoveries sometimes costing millions of dollars in damage awards. More important, loose interpretations of words in contracts, statutes, and the Constitution itself empower judges to reopen questions that were settled when these contracts, statutes, and the Constitution were written— imposing judges' notions of what should have been done on what the parties concerned had decided to do. Far from defining the boundaries of governmental power and contractual obligations, judicial activism allows judges to second-guess the decisions made within those boundaries—and to call the decisions they dislike "unconstitutional."

Much criticism of judicial activists' decisions has centered on the merits or demerits of the particular policies imposed by such decisions. But, however much those policies may deserve criticism, the most fundamental damage done is not in these particular policies but in undermining the very concept and purpose of law itself. Freewheeling judges make the whole framework of law unreliable. One obvious consequence is that this facilitates legalized extortion when those with "deep pockets"—which are often only an accumulation from much shallower pockets of individual taxpayers or stockholders—are afraid to go into court to defend themselves against even the most frivolous or far-fetched claims for damages, for fear of what some judge or jury's arbitrary notions or emotions might be on a given day. But forfeiting the benefits of "a government of laws and not of men" goes far beyond that. It goes to the heart of a free, self-governing society, which is being superseded by *ex post facto* laws deriving not from legislation but from judicial fiats. That the particular policy decisions imposed by judges may often be counterproductive is secondary.

Those who seek to have judges go beyond the document authorizing judicial power, and beyond the principles agreed to in that document, are seeking essentially cosmic justice. However much better cosmic justice might be, judges have no authorization from the cosmos, nor do human beings have cosmic capacities, even when they have cosmic presumptions.

One of the more remarkable defenses of judicial activism is that courts were "forced" to act because Congress, the president, or other authorities and institutions "failed" to act. Only by arbitrarily presuming that policy X *must* be enacted can the fact that all institutions except one believed otherwise be taken as a mandate for that single institution to impose policy X anyway. Only where the policy is one favored by the anointed is any such non sequitur likely to pass muster. The whole constitutional system of checks and balances—designed precisely to prevent any given branch of government from acting as sovereign—is thus blithely tossed aside by those who see the courts as legislatures of last resort for policies that reflect the vision of the anointed, but which cannot become law otherwise.

Although the great changes that have occurred over the centuries since the Constitution was written provide talking points for those advocating judicial activism, the particular judicial rulings which have sparked the greatest controversies in recent decades have involved things common and well-known when the Constitution was written: abortion, prayer in schools, the arrest of criminals, the segregation of the races, differential weighting of votes, and executions.[29] Most of the great rhetorical flourishes about technological and other changes have no bearing on the particular controversies in which they are invoked. Nor is a long passage of time either necessary or sufficient to explain judicial activism. The Civil Rights Act of 1964 was passed during the lifetimes, and in some cases during their tenure on the Supreme Court, of those who voted with Justice William J. Brennan not to follow "a literal interpretation" of its words in the 1979 *Weber* case.[30] The Supreme Court majority's interpretation went so directly counter to the plain words of the Act that a dissenting justice likened the Court's evasion of those words to the great escapes of Houdini.[31]

The same Justice Brennan who claimed elsewhere that discerning the original intent of lawmakers was virtually impossible,[32] in this case saw lawmakers' intent so clearly—Congress' "primary concern" for "the plight of the Negro in our economy"[33]—that he disregarded the plain words of the Civil Rights Act, which forbade *any* racial discrimination in apprenticeship training programs, such as that which excluded a white worker, Brian F. Weber, in order to include black workers with lower qualifications. Nor can it be claimed that Congress had not thought of such possibilities, for the legislative history of the Civil Rights Act abounds in discussions of the possibility of "reverse discrimination"—and abounds in repudiations of any such policies.[34]

Among the amazing rationales for compensatory preferences for selected minorities to be imposed by courts is that such preferences merely offset previous preferences for members of the majority population. According to *New York Times* columnist Tom Wicker, "American life never was 'even-handed, color-blind, non-preferential.' "[35] But this again raises the question which arises in so many other contexts: Is the law to attempt intertemporal cosmic justice or simply apply the same rules to all in the only temporal realm in which it has jurisdiction—the present and the future? Moreover, is the decision to opt for intertemporal cosmic justice one for which judges have any authorization, either from the Constitution or from statutes passed by elected officials? Such straightforward questions are often evaded by being redefined as "simplistic." A federal judge in Texas provided a typical example of this tactic:

> The plaintiffs have contended that any preferential treatment to a
> group based on race violates the Fourteenth Amendment and, there-

fore, is unconstitutional. However, such a simplistic application of the Fourteenth Amendment would ignore the long history of pervasive racial discrimination in our society that the Fourteenth Amendment was adopted to remedy and the complexities of achieving the societal goal of overcoming the past effects of that discrimination.[36]

As in so many other contexts, the word "simplistic" was not part of an argument but a substitute for an argument. To interpret the Fourteenth Amendment as meaning what it says—equal treatment for all—does not ignore the history which led to the passage of that Amendment. Faced with blatant discrimination against blacks, those who wrote the Fourteenth Amendment could have chosen any number of responses—compensatory treatment for blacks, equal treatment for blacks, equal treatment for all, etc. They made that choice when they wrote the Amendment, just as those who wrote the Civil Rights Act of 1964 made the same choice when they wrote that legislation. Nor is there any indication from public opinion polls or any other source of a "societal" goal of compensating for the past, however much that goal may be part of the vision of the anointed. In short, all this vague and lofty rhetoric reopens a decision that was already made and enacted into law—and never repealed or amended, except by judicial "interpretation."

A similar reliance on the vision of the anointed, in lieu of the written constitution or statutes passed by elected officials, occurred in the very different case of *Planned Parenthood v. Casey*, an abortion case. Once again, "evolving standards that mark the progress of a maturing society" were cited—this time by Justices Sandra Day O'Connor, David Souter, and William Kennedy[37]—as a basis for the decision reached.

The larger significance of the issue of judicial activism versus judicial restraint goes far beyond a question of particular theories of legal interpretation or the merits or demerits of the particular social policies involved in particular cases. Indeed, it goes to the foundations of a free and self-governing society. When those with the vision of the anointed line up solidly behind judicial activism, as they do, it is not because of a chance coincidence that they all happen to prefer one legal theory to another. Judicial activism is a mechanism through which that vision can be imposed on a public which does not support it, without having to go through elected officials who would not dare to vote for many of the features of that vision, including an expansion of criminals' rights, affirmative action quotas, and other controversial policies on which the public and the anointed are lined up on opposite sides.

Some of the statements in Supreme Court opinions themselves betray the extent to which judicial activism is responsive to the vision of the anointed, using that vision as a basis for rulings which lack a basis in the words of the Constitution or in any statute passed by legislators. For example, in overturning the death penalty in the case of a murderer who committed his crime at age 15, Justice John Paul Stevens cited "evolving standards of decency" which made the Eighth Amendment's "cruel and unusual punishment" prohibition applicable.[38] Although claiming that such an execution would be "abhorrent to the conscience of the community,"[39] Justice Stevens' specific references were to "views expressed by respected professional organizations," to "other nations that share our Anglo-Saxon heritage," and to "leading members of the Western European community"[40]—in short, to the anointed. Clearly, there would be no issue before the Supreme Court in the first place unless the *general* community in which this murder took place had not prescribed the death penalty, even for murderers 15 years of age. Similarly, in a later case, the Supreme Court referred to how its decision would be seen by "the thoughtful part of the Nation."[41]

Judicial activism in effect allows the vision of the anointed to veto the legally imposed decisions of the community, even when those decisions do not conflict with the written Constitution. Moreover, this veto is exercised in the name of the Constitution and even in the name of the community, meaning by the latter those who presume to consider themselves the "conscience" of the community.

Selective Activity

Courts whose decisions are based on the written law and the historical meanings of the Constitution are practicing judicial restraint, even if that leads them to much activity in issuing court orders or striking down legislation not consistent with the Constitution. Conversely, courts whose decisions allow other considerations to be decisive are practicing judicial activism, even if that leads them to passive acceptance of policies and legislation at variance with constitutional guarantees. In short, activity is not the hallmark of judicial activism. It is the nature and basis of that activity that matter.

A court which allows its own notions of "evolving standards" and "the conscience of the community," to supersede the written law and the historical Constitution is practicing judicial activism—even if that means *doing nothing* when property rights are violated by sit-ins or by legislation which ignores the protections of the Fifth Amendment against government seizures of property without due process or just compensation. A judge who would enforce the written law in these cases would be following "judicial restraint," even though he might be more active in issuing court orders or in declaring offending legislation unconstitutional. Historically, the judicial revolution that began with President Franklin D. Roosevelt's appointees to the Supreme Court initially took the form of a broader permissiveness toward legislation of the sort that had been struck down as unconstitutional by prior courts. Even a classic judicial activist like Justice William O. Douglas could use the language of judicial restraint—"We do not sit as a super-legislature,"[42] for example—in cases involving "economic and social programs,"[43] "the business-labor field,"[44] or "business and industrial conditions."[45]

Although in principle judicial activism may be expressed in inactivity, many of the judicial decisions which have attracted public attention and controversy in recent decades have been cases where the courts were active in overturning legislation and prior court decisions. This has confused the issue, rather than defined it. The clear line of consistency in judicially activist decisions— whether in expansive permissiveness toward legislation overriding private property rights or the constitutional right to make mutually agreeable contracts, on the one hand, or in striking down state abortion laws or prescribing local police procedures when making arrests, on the other—is that judges do not bind themselves to enforcing rules made by others, even when the historical meanings of those rules are quite clear, but feel free to evade such rules by "interpretations" based on broader social philosophies or a sense of cosmic justice.

Thus, for example, the fact that the "cruel and unusual punishment" prohibition of the Eighth Amendment clearly did not include the death penalty, which was permitted and regulated by other constitutional Amendments passed at the same time, has not prevented judicial activists from striking down death penalties on grounds having no basis either in the historical Constitution or in subsequent legislation. Moreover, the Supreme Court has even proclaimed as a general principle its emancipation from such historical constraints. For example:

> Neither the Bill of Rights nor the specific practices of States at the time of the adoption of the Fourteenth Amendment marks the outer limits of the substantive sphere of liberty which the Fourteenth Amendment protects.[46]

In short, the Supreme Court cut itself loose from historical moorings and historical meanings, relying instead on its own "reasoned judgment."[47] How such ad hoc judgment could be law, in the ultimate sense of rules known in advance to others, was left undisclosed.

Precedents versus the Constitution

Judicial restraint has traditionally involved not only a reluctance to go beyond the historical Constitution and the duly enacted statutes (where the latter do not violate the Constitution), but also a reluctance to overturn prior court decisions on which the public has relied in making its own decisions and plans. In short, it attempts to leave intact a framework of law known in advance by which citizens may guide their actions. However, a long period of judicial activism makes it difficult, if not impossible, for subsequent courts to adhere simultaneously to both principles of judicial restraint. To uphold the original meanings of the Constitution, or of statutory legislation, may require overturning precedents which violate those meanings.

As federal judges more inclined toward judicial restraint began to be appointed in the 1980s, after several decades in which activist judges had remade the legal landscape, the dilemma which these new judges confronted repeatedly was whether to uphold precedents set by activists or to uphold the historical meanings of the written law. For example, in dissenting from the view that current "reasoned judgment" was the criterion of constitutional interpretation in an abortion case, Justice William Rehnquist went back to the historical circumstances in which the Fourteenth Amendment was passed:

> At the time of the adoption of the Fourteenth Amendment, statutory prohibitions or restrictions on abortion were commonplace; in 1868, at least 28 of the then-37 States and 8 Territories had statutes banning or limiting abortion. . . . On this record, it can hardly be said that any deeply rooted tradition of relatively unrestricted abortion in our history supported the classification of the right to abortion as "fundamental" under the Due Process Clause of the Fourteenth Amendment.[48]

This approach does not even address the cosmic question as to whether a woman has "a right to do what she will with her own body," as it is often phrased. The question addressed was whether the Fourteenth Amendment's protection of existing liberties from state interference encompassed abortions. Chief Justice Rehnquist's conclusion was that "the Court was mistaken" in *Roe v. Wade* when it classified a woman's decision to terminate her pregnancy as a "fundamental right" *under the Fourteenth Amendment.*[49] Whether it was a fundamental right in some cosmic sense was not a question within the jurisdiction of a court set up to apply the Constitution and the statutes. As Justice Antonin Scalia put it: "It is difficult to maintain the illusion that we are interpreting a Constitution, rather than inventing one, when we amend its provisions so breezily."[50] The "freedom to abort her unborn child" is of course "a liberty of great importance to many women," he said, but the "issue is whether it is a liberty protected by the Constitution of the United States."[51]

Given this historical approach of judicial restraint, Chief Justice

Rehnquist and the other dissenters called for the 1973 *Roe* precedent to be overruled in 1992:

> Our constitutional watch does not cease merely because we have spoken on an issue; when it comes clear that a prior constitutional interpretation is unsound we are obliged to reexamine the question.[52]

Although judicial restraint did not prevail in this case, in some other cases previous adventurous interpretations of laws were scaled back. This overturning of precedents set off denunciations by media and academic intellectuals who had applauded the precedent-shattering judicial activism of the Warren Court era. A *New York Times* editorial was typical:

> Recklessly reversing precedents: That is not the role assigned to the Supreme Court. The nine justices are indeed supreme and often have the last word. But they are also a court, bound by restraints against willfulness and unfairness. That marble temple wasn't built so that the nine could meet to poll themselves on matters of public interest.[53]

No such complaint was made when the Warren Court overturned precedents that were more numerous and of longer duration. Yet the *Times* continued to berate the Rehnquist Court for "contempt for precedent"[54] and its columnist Tom Wicker accused the new justices of "hypocrisy" and expressed his own contempt for the presidents who appointed them and "prattled about judicial restraint."[55] Even on the Supreme Court itself, Justice Thurgood Marshall complained of "a far-reaching assault on this Court's precedents."[56] Nothing in all of this acknowledged that the new overrulings of precedents were necessitated by previous overrulings of precedents and disregard of the Constitution itself, all of which had been applauded by those now speaking of precedents as sacrosanct.

Despite such cries of alarm from the anointed, the Supreme Court remained divided on the issue of respecting precedents versus overturning precedents that did not accord with the language of statutes or of the Constitution. Justices Antonin Scalia and Clarence Thomas have clearly shown that they are ready to reverse precedents that have no basis in the Constitution or in the text of statutes. In the 1994 case of *Holder v. Hall,* for example, Justice Thomas rejected the Supreme Court's "disastrous misadventure in judicial policymaking" in its prior interpretations of the Voting Rights Act. Such judicial practices "should not continue," he said. "Not for another Term, not until the next case, not for another day."[57] However, the much-praised "centrists" on the Court—Justices Sandra Day O'Connor, William Kennedy, and David Souter—often try to find a middle way and judicious compromises. Among these "centrists," Sandra Day O'Connor has been perhaps the sharpest in seeing through the flimsy pretenses on which judicial policy-making has been based—and at the same time the most unwilling to overturn precedents. The lofty term "jurisprudence" has been invoked frequently by Justice O'Connor in a way which seems to boil down to saying: This may not be in the Constitution or the statutes, but judges have said it, so we've got to stick by it.

Precedents are not to be sniffed at. People and institutions can base major decisions on the law as it exists and constant disruptions could be costly or even disastrous. However, the net effect of Justice O'Connor's approach is to get the worst of both worlds: The recklessly or cynically set precedents of the past become sacrosanct while denying the citizens the security of known law—for the precedents upheld are typically not clear-cut statements of law but only a promise of ongoing judicial tinkering, as in the case of *Planned Parenthood v. Casey,* where state restrictions on abortion were permitted, so long as these restrictions did not place an "undue burden" on the women concerned. Such a standard is not law; it is a charter of endless judicial second-guessing, with legal results to be known only after the fact. Law had indeed lost its soul and become jungle.

CHAPTER 9

OPTIONAL REALITY

> *... ideology ... is an instrument of power; a defense mechanism against information; a pretext for eluding moral constraints in doing or approving evil with a clean conscience; and finally, a way of banning the criterion of experience, that is, of completely eliminating or indefinitely postponing the pragmatic criteria of success and failure.*

> —Jean-François Revel[1]

This chapter's recapitulation of our exploration of the vision of the anointed will begin with its greatest achievement and its greatest danger, which are one and the same: That vision has become self-contained and self-justifying—which is to say, independent of empirical evidence. That is what makes it dangerous, not because a particular set of policies may be flawed or counterproductive, but because insulation from evidence virtually guarantees a never-ending supply of policies and practices fatally independent of reality. This self-contained and self-justifying vision has become a badge of honor and a proclamation of identity: To affirm it is to be one of *us* and to oppose it is to be one of *them*. Moreover, the pervasiveness of the vision of the anointed at all levels of the American educational system ensures future supplies of people indoctrinated with this vision and also convinced that they should "make a difference"—that public policymaking is to be seen as ego gratification from imposing one's vision on other people through the power of government.

The central tenets of the prevailing vision can be summarized in five propositions:

1. Painful social situations ("problems") exist not because of inherent limits to knowledge or resources, or inadequacies inherent in human beings, but because other people lack the wisdom or virtue of the anointed.

2. Evolved beliefs represent only a "socially constructed" set of notions, not reflections of an underlying reality. Therefore the way by which "problems" can be "solved" is by applying the articulated rationality of the anointed, rather than by relying on evolved traditions or systemic processes growing out of the experiences of the masses.

3. Social causation is intentional, rather than systemic, so that condemnation is in order when various features of the human experience are either unhappy or appear anomalous to the anointed.

4. Great social or biological dangers can be averted only by the imposition of the vision of the anointed on less enlightened people by the government.

5. Opposition to the vision of the anointed is due not to a different reading of complex and inconclusive evidence, but exists because opponents are lacking, either intellectually or morally, or both.

Perhaps even more important than the specific tenets of this vision is that these propositions are not treated as hypotheses to be tested but as self-evident axioms. Evidence is seldom asked or given—and evidence to the contrary is often either ignored or answered only by a sneer.

Whether dealing with crime, foreign policy, the economy, the environment, or a thousand other issues, the first prerequisite is that these issues must be conceived in terms which flatter the egos of the anointed. The question is not how to reduce crime, but how to showcase the superiority of the anointed to the benighted on the crime issue, such as by talking about "root causes." In foreign policy, the issue is not how best to safeguard the lives and livelihoods of the American people but how to showcase the superior wisdom and virtue of the anointed, such as by promoting disinterested knight-errantry around the world, a vision that has turned cold-war doves into post-cold-war hawks from Bosnia to Haiti. Any conception, theory, or policy which fulfills the vital function of validating the anointed's sense of differential rectitude has the inside track for becoming part of their vision, even with little or no evidence—and in fact despite mounting evidence to the contrary.

Adopting as mascots all sorts of people who create high costs for their fellow human beings—whether through crime, disease, or parasitic behavior—clearly fulfills the requirement of flattering the anointed on their superior vision, which allows them to see social issues in terms of how "society" has mistreated its "victims," who are to be rescued by the anointed. This vision requires that the mascots' own behavior, choices, and performances be brushed aside as factors in unhappy outcomes, as is done by the preemptive phrase, "blaming the victim." Rejecting traditional morality likewise allows the anointed to believe that, all over the world, millions of people of every race, creed, and nationality have for thousands of years been hopelessly mistaken in thinking that moral codes are necessary for the survival of civilization—a mistake to be corrected by the newly minted wisdom of the zeitgeist.

Verbal dexterity plays a key role in insulating the vision of the anointed from the vicissitudes of mere facts. Through the magic of definitions, no one can ever catch AIDS by "casual contact" and no one will ever be murdered by a "homeless" person. Any newly discovered way by which someone catches AIDS will then be removed from the category of "casual contact" and any homeless person who commits murder will thereafter be referred to in the media as a "transient" or a "drifter"—but not "homeless."

Indeed, the very conception of testing beliefs against reality is attacked by such things as deconstruction, cultural relativism, and the practice of describing uncongenial conclusions as "perceptions" or "stereotypes" and attributing "false consciousness" to those who hold them. Through these and other such tactics, intractable three-dimensional realities are reduced to one-dimensional psychological propensities—male-female pay differentials, for example, being due to "uncaring institutions" and "exploitative employers," as Barbara

Ehrenreich put it.[2] Any unflattering information about any group treated as mascots by the anointed is attributed to malign intentions toward that group when that information comes from outsiders and to "self-hate" when it comes from insiders. As Hannah Arendt has pointed out, transforming questions of fact into questions of intent has been the great achievement of twentieth-century totalitarians. It is a dangerous achievement which has survived the collapse of both fascist and Communist empires and has become a hallmark of much of the Western intelligentsia.

Divorce from reality is so nearly complete that the question rarely, if ever, arises as to whether the world inside the mind of the anointed differs from the world outside. That there is a vision in the first place—a framework of assumptions, without which even their most heartfelt beliefs are groundless—is something noted from time to time by those with the tragic vision,[3] but seldom, if ever, by those with the vision of the anointed. To the anointed, their vision and reality are one and the same. Yet the world inside their mind has few of the harsh constraints of the world inhabited by millions of other human beings. The crucial role of a vision is that it enables a vast range of beliefs to be regarded as presumptively true until definitively disproved by unchallengeable evidence—something seldom encountered outside of science laboratories. Another way of saying the same thing is that this vision puts all burdens of proof on others.

THE WORLD OF THE ANOINTED

The world of the anointed is a very tidy place—or, put differently, every deviation of the real world from the tidiness of their vision is considered to be someone's fault. If employment or college admissions statistics do not match the preconceptions of the anointed, then that indicates discrimination. If someone falls victim to one of "the thousand natural shocks that flesh is heir to," then that is the fault of someone else who should have foreseen and prevented it. Both assumptions have led to soaring litigation and huge damage awards under wildly expanded definitions of discrimination and of tort liability. If a murderer did not have as happy a childhood as everyone else is presumed to have had, then that becomes a reason to reduce his sentence.

In this highly predictable and highly controllable world, where prescient politicians can "invest" tax dollars in "the industries of the future," where criminals can be "rehabilitated," irresponsible mothers taught "parenting skills," and where all sorts of other social problems can be "solved," there is obviously a very expansive role for government and for the anointed in prescribing what government should do. Unfulfilled yearnings or chafing inhibitions have no place in this tidy world of the anointed, where even an inadequate supply of group heroes and historic group achievements is someone else's fault, presumably the historians'. It is a world where reality itself is "socially constructed" and can therefore be "deconstructed" and then reassembled to one's heart's desire.

It is not hard to understand why anyone would prefer to live in this kind of world, rather than in a world of inherently constrained options, tragic choices, and variably incremental trade-offs, rather than categorical and emotionally satisfying "solutions." The only question is whether it is within our power to choose between these alternative worlds—ultimately, whether reality is optional.

The perennial desire to make particular things "affordable" through public policy or to have government provide an ever-expanding list of "basic needs" suggests that the economic realities conveyed by prices are seen as mere arbitrary social conventions, rather than expressions of inherent constraints and inescapable costs. Similarly, the desire to spare people "stigmas" for their behavior treats such stigmas as representing mere arbitrary narrowness by others, rather than social retaliation for very real costs created by those who are being stigmatized—and deterrence to others who might create more such costs in the absence of stigmas.

The vision of the anointed divorces effects from causes. The very possibility that many inequalities of result are due to inequalities of causes is often sweepingly dismissed by those with the vision of the anointed, so that statistics on unequal outcomes become automatic indictments of "society." There is much discussion of the haves and the have-nots, but very little discussion of the *doers* and the *do-nots*, those who contribute and those who merely take. Widespread use of the word "unacceptable" for social circumstances suggests that reality depends upon our acceptance of it.

This whole approach has the net effect of insulating people and policies from an awareness of how and why their own actions are bringing on unhappy consequences. By treating reality as highly malleable, and unpleasant experiences as readily preventable, this approach ignores the powerful forces behind the reality, including the dangerous, though natural, impulses of human beings. Instead of treating ourselves as inherently constrained by reality, it treats reality as constrained by our acceptance. Activist government feeds this illusion, because it can in fact make dramatic changes in particular circumstances—though always at a cost exacted elsewhere, however much such costs may be ignored, denied, or finally treated as bolts from the blue, newly arising "problems" to be "solved" by yet more programs. Thus those who have for decades supported policies whose side effects have included a massive destruction of low-income housing—urban renewal programs, rent control, and increasingly costly building codes and environmental restrictions, for example—are often among those most shocked and outraged by growing homelessness. Those who have most consistently undermined the police and other elements of law enforcement are among those most shocked by the escalation of crime and violence.

In the world of the anointed, human nature is readily changeable. To say that a particular policy requires the changing of other people's dispositions and values may to others suggest a daunting prospect but, to the anointed, it is a golden opportunity. Making other people "aware," raising their consciousness, or helping them "grow" are all very attractive ideas to those with the vision of the anointed. Similarly, while polarization is to others something to fear, to those with the vision of the anointed it is a confirmation of their own superiority to the benighted. Indeed, the very concept of polarization is usually applied only to the actions of the benighted in resisting the imposition of a new uniformity. Whether it is the mandatory busing of schoolchildren for racial balance or the imposition of new policies on gays in the military, these are not thought of by the anointed as polarization which they are creating. It is only those who object who are said to be creating polarization.

One of the ominous consequences of such attitudes is that there is no logical stopping place in creating polarizations that may tear a society apart or lead to a backlash that can sweep aside not only such policies but also the basic institutions of a free society. Fascistic "strong men" have historically emerged with public support from those disgusted or alarmed by the breakdown of law and order and of traditional values. There is nothing in the prevailing vision to make the anointed stop before things reach that point. On the contrary, the warning signs of such an impending catastrophe may be seen by the anointed as only welcome indications of their own moral superiority to the benighted.

This self-flattering and self-centered view of the world is also related to the constant seeking of "exciting" and "new" things, and a "liberation" from the constraints imposed by lesser beings. But once we drop the assumption of a wonderful specialness of the anointed—which is to say, once we acknowledge "a decent respect for the opinion of mankind," as the Declaration of Independence put it—the whole picture changes. In social life, the more fundamental a truth is, the more likely it is to have been discovered long ago—and to have been repeated in a thousand ways to the point of utter boredom. In this context, to make excitement and novelty the touchstones of an idea is to run grave risks of abandoning the truth for ideological trinkets.

If the truth is boring, civilization is irksome. The constraints inherent in civilized living are frustrating in innumerable ways. Yet those with the vision of the anointed often see these constraints as only arbitrary impositions, things from which they—and we all—can be "liberated." The social disintegration which has followed in the wake of such liberation has seldom provoked any serious reconsideration of the whole set of assumptions—the vision—which led to such disasters. That vision is too well insulated from feedback.

Insulation from Feedback

The charge is often made against the intelligentsia and other members of the anointed that their theories and the policies based on them lack common sense. But the very commonness of common sense makes it unlikely to have any appeal to the anointed. How can they be wiser and nobler than everyone else while agreeing with everyone else? In everything from avant-garde art, music, and drama to exotic animals and "radical chic" activities, the stress is on their own differentness, their specialness. A chorus of public outcry against what they are doing or advocating is not a reason to reconsider but music to their ears. To disdain "public clamor," as it is called when court decisions are protested, is a badge of distinction. All this, of course, contributes to the sealing off of the vision from feedback from reality.

Consistent with this pattern of seeking differentiation at virtually all cost has been the adoption of a variety of anti-social individuals and groups as special objects of solicitude—which is to say, special examples of the wider and loftier vision of the anointed. From multiple murderers to smelly vagrants, these anti-social elements have been adopted as mascots, much like exotic animals. The stigmas put on these mascots by the rest of society merely provide yet another occasion for the anointed to blame society itself for failing to "solve" these people's "problems." Again, having committed themselves to this disdainful view of the benighted masses, the anointed have cut off their own path of retreat when evidence begins to pile up that their mascots have both richly deserved the stigmas they have received and are unlikely to be magically transformed by any of the innumerable programs and projects that the anointed have created for their benefit. Another avenue to reality is sealed off.

One symptom of divorce from the constraints of reality is the tendency to treat numbers as if they had a life of their own—for example, to make extrapolations from statistics without any serious analysis of the actual processes from which these numbers were generated. This has been common, not only in "overpopulation" projections and exhaustion-of-resources projections, but even in the claim that it is wrong to criticize the courts for the soaring crime rates that followed the criminal law revolutions of the 1960s because of "the abnormally low base from which the crime of the 1960s and early '70s began."[4] In other words, these numbers were apparently due to go up anyway—not for any specific, discernible reason, anchored in reality, but simply because they were "abnormally low."

One could just as easily have said that the crime rate was abnormally high when the country was expanding, with a lawless frontier still being settled, and when its cities had an unprecedented growth of a crowded, polyglot population of immigrants—and that when these and other adverse influences faded over time, crime rates likewise subsided. But to say this would be to say that the numbers did not have a life of their own, but reflected actual social processes—and that in turn would suggest that the soaring crime rates which followed the judicial revolution in the criminal justice system were also a result of actual facts in the real world. But the reluctance to say that people are responsible for the consequences of their action—even in a causal sense, much less in a moral sense—is here extended to judges.

Such an approach is part of a more general pattern among those with the vision of the anointed, a pattern exemplified by the use of the word "epidemic" to describe chosen behavior, including drug use and such consequences of sexual behavior as pregnancy and AIDS. Without a sense of the tragedy of the human condition, and of the painful trade-offs implied by inherent constraints, the anointed are free to believe that the unhappiness they observe and the anomalies they encounter are due to the public's not being as wise or as virtuous as themselves. Both their conceptions of social issues and the vocabulary in which they discuss them are pervaded by notions of "protecting" this group and "liberating" that one—in both cases, obviously from the benighted or malign actions of other people. It is a world of victims, villains, and rescuers, with the anointed cast in the last and most heroic of these roles. Thus, in this vision, the Third World is poor because the more prosperous nations have made them so, and problems within the black community are caused by the white community, women are less represented in given occupations because men keep them out—and so on and on. Alternative explanations of all these phenomena are neither lacking nor without evidence, but alternatives to the vision of the anointed are sweepingly and sneeringly dismissed.

Those with the vision of the anointed are especially reluctant to see human nature as a source of the evils they wish to eradicate. Instead, they seek *special* causes of particular evils. Nothing so exemplifies this approach as the perennial attempts to get at the causes—the "root causes," as it is phrased—of crime. There seems to be no awareness that people commit crimes because they are human beings. That is, people's natural impulses are to favor themselves over others and to disregard the harm they create in trying to satisfy their own desires in the easiest way. If most people do not behave this way with complete shamelessness in most things, it is because they have been through a long process of becoming civilized—and because this process is buttressed by law enforcement. Civilization has been aptly called, "a thin crust over a volcano."[5] The anointed are constantly picking at that crust.

The dangers in a vision come not simply from the answers it gives, but from the very way it frames the questions. The concept of "income distribution," for example, causes statistics to be looked at with certain preconceptions, so that the transient positions of individuals are seen as the enduring relationships between classes. The habit of looking at policy issues in terms of the goals they proclaim and the values they represent, not to mention the unconstrained options they assume, leads in a wholly different direction from an analysis of the incentives being created, within the constraints that exist, and the probable outcome of such incentives and constraints.

It is the intertwining of the intellect and the ego which is so dangerous in making the vision highly resistant to any facts that threaten the existing framework of beliefs and assumptions. Cultural wars are so desperate because they are not simply about the merits or demerits of particular policies. They are about the anointed's whole conception of themselves—about whether they are in the heady role of a vanguard or in the pathetic role of pretentious and self-infatuated people.

"Solutions" and Preemptions

In the light of an intertwining of the ego and the vision, it is understandable that those with the vision of the anointed so often seek some imposed "solution" instead of allowing incremental trade-offs to be made through systemic social processes by those directly involved. A "solution" represents a claim to superior wisdom or virtue, while mere variable trade-offs reflect nothing more than varying scales of preferences and circumstances among millions of individuals. The language of "problems" and "solutions" often not only ignores the reality of trade-offs but also conceals the imposition of the anointed's values on others. For example, imagine a society which has a choice between situation 1 and situation 2, as shown in the table below. For simplicity, we assume that there are three beneficial things whose quantities can differ according to which government policy is followed.

SITUATION 1	SITUATION 2
10,000 units of A	5,000 units of A
10,000 units of B	10,000 units of B
10,000 units of C	15,000 units of C

To those who prefer 5,000 incremental units of C to 5,000 incremental units of A, situation 1 is a "problem" and situation 2 is a "solution." But, of course, to those whose preferences are the reverse, it is situation 2 which is a problem and situation 1 which is a solution. Only by imposing one group's set of preferences on others can a solution even be defined, much less achieved. But this is no obstacle to those with the vision of the anointed, for the superiority of their preferences is so taken for granted that its imposition on others is scarcely noticed. Critics and evidence receive even less attention.

The Struggle to Control Memory

Desperate evasions of discordant evidence, and the denigration and even demonizing of those presenting such evidence, are indicative of the high stakes in contemporary cultural wars, which are not about alternative policies but alternative worlds and of alternative roles of the anointed in these worlds. Because differential rectitude is pivotal to the vision of the anointed, opponents must be shown to be not merely mistaken but morally lacking. As Jean-François Revel has aptly put it, this approach "replaces the intellectual discussion of arguments by the moral extermination of persons."[6] This denigration or demonizing of those opposed to their views not only has the desired effect of discrediting the opposition but also has the unintended effect of cutting off the path of retreat from positions which become progressively less tenable with the passage of time and the accumulation of discordant evidence. The very thought that those dismissed as simplistic or malign might have been right—even if only on a single issue—is at best galling and potentially devastating. The desperate expedients and heated rhetoric of the anointed, when confronted with results completely counter to what they expected, are symptomatic of the impossible situation in which they find themselves—or rather, in which they have placed themselves. Their last refuge in this situation are their good intentions.

For the anointed, it is desperately important to win, not simply because they believe that one policy or set of beliefs and values is better for society, but because their whole sense of themselves is at stake. Given the high stakes, it is not hard to understand the all-out attacks of the anointed on those who differ from them and their attempts to stifle alternative sources of values and beliefs, with campus speech codes and "political correctness" being prime examples of a spreading pattern of taboos. Here they are not content to squelch contemporary voices, they must also silence history and traditions—the national memory—as well. This too is a larger danger than the dangers flowing from particular policies.

Memory is what makes us who we are. If we lost all our memory whenever we fell asleep at night, it would be the same as if we died and a new person woke up in our body the next morning. History is the memory of a nation—and that memory is being erased by historians enthralled by the vision of the anointed. Open disdain for mere facts has been accompanied by adventurous reinterpretations known as "revisionist" history, which reads contemporary ideological preoccupations back into the past. This erasing of the national memory, and the recording of a preferred vision over it, is yet another expression of the notion that reality is optional.

A very similar development in the law treats the Constitution as meaning not what those who wrote it meant, but what one small segment of the public today wants it to mean. This is the "living constitution" of "evolving standards," reflecting what "thinking people" believe. Such sweeping dismissals of the past are more than a passing fashion or a personal vanity. They are a dangerous destruction of the hard-earned experience of millions of human beings, living through centuries of struggle with the tragedy of the human condition, and the replacement of this rich legacy with unsubstantiated theories and self-flattering fancies.

On the strength of such reasoning, murderers have been turned loose in our midst and whole industries have been crippled and livelihoods destroyed so that the anointed could "make a statement" about their own superior "concern" about some obscure subspecies or some other symbolic issue demonstrating their superiority to "society." Law itself has been prostituted to the service of ideological crusades, and the ability of society to defend itself against everything from criminals to the AIDS virus has been crippled in the name of special newly created "rights" for individuals to inflict costs and harm on others with impunity. The social cohesion that makes civilized life possible has been loosened by the systematic undermining of families and of commonly shared values and a common culture.

DECISION-MAKING PROCESSES

Among the innumerable, varied, and never-ending ideological crusades of the anointed a common pattern is discernible. Typically, a crusade begins when some substantial discrepancy is found between the world as they envision it and the world as it exists. To the anointed, it seems to follow, as the night follows the day, that reality must be brought into line with their vision. Logically, one might just as readily conclude that it is the theory which needs to be brought into line with reality. But that possibility is seldom given much consideration. The fact that reality has survived the test of time and experience, while the viability of their vision has yet to be proven in practice, is likewise seldom given much attention. Moreover, the process by which a society is to move from the existing situation to the situation desired by the anointed is seldom analyzed for *its characteristics as a process*. Some process may indeed be specified—a "war on poverty," criminal "rehabilitation" programs, "sex education" in the schools—but a critical evaluation of the characteristics of such processes is seldom forthcoming. The discussion tends to be in terms of goals rather than incentives, and assumptions rather than evidence.

That so many grandiose social schemes which sound plausible to the intellectual elites not only fail, but prove to be disastrously counterproductive, is by no means surprising when these schemes are analyzed in terms of the characteristics of the processes by which they operate, rather than the goals they seek or the visions to which they conform. At the heart of many of these schemes is third-party decision making. Third parties typically know less, even when convinced that they know more, in addition to lacking the incentives of those who directly benefit from being right and suffer from being wrong.

The knowledge brought to bear in even "ordinary" processes—the manufacturing of a pencil, for example—usually exists as a sum of many small, overlapping circles of individual information and skills which altogether add up to a vast expanse of information, experience, and understanding. As was pointed out in a celebrated essay years ago, no given human being knows enough to make even a simple lead pencil.[7] No single person knows how to mine the graphite, process the wood, produce the rubber, manufacture the paint, and make all the investment, marketing, inventory, and distribution decisions required to put a pencil in the hands of the ultimate consumer. This is clearly even more true of the manufacture of an automobile or a computer, much less the enormously more complex social processes which enable a civilization to function.

Even if the individual circles of knowledge possessed by members of the anointed are in fact larger than the average circle of knowledge possessed by those around them, these larger-than-average circles are still likely to be only a tiny fraction of the vast total. To allow the anointed to preempt the decisions of millions of other people is to confine the knowledge that is brought to bear on decisions to what exists within the circles of the anointed—in effect, shrinking the knowledge that can be used to a fraction of what is available. It can hardly be surprising that poorer decisions often emerge from this process. Indeed, dangerous decisions are often the consequence.

When one considers how small a defect in reasoning can utterly destroy a whole elaborate analysis, it is truly staggering to expect intellectuals to construct social policies which will compare with what emerges from the systemic interactions of millions of other human beings, continuously adjusting to consequences reflecting the revealed preferences of others and the changing opportunities and constraints of technology. The complex and highly sophisticated structure of Marx's *Capital,* for example, rests ultimately on crude and even bungling assumptions about the special role of labor in the economic process.[8] Sweeping assumptions about knowing the "root causes" of crime, mindless extrapolations that produce hysteria about "overpopulation" and "resource exhaustion," and shallow confusions of tax rates and tax revenues dominating discussions of the federal budget deficit, are just some of the fatally flawed intellectual output which seeks to displace systemic interactions with imposed "solutions."

One of the implications of the common observation that "hindsight is 20/20" is that people who judge results, as in economic transactions in the marketplace, have a far less daunting task than people who project social plans which require them to be correct simultaneously on innumerable assumptions, flawless in the logic with which the complex implications of these assumptions are derived, and at the same time prescient about an ever-changing reality within which events are unfolding.

Add to this the fact that publicly admitting fundamental mistakes can be fatal to a whole political career and the differences between the two decision-making processes become even wider when the need to admit and reverse mistakes is taken into account. Nothing worse than a momentary private embarrassment—if that—befalls the consumer who changes his or her accustomed patterns of purchases to adjust to changing prices or a changing availability of new products or services, or to other unexpected events. But one need only imagine the response if a political leader admitted to initiating or supporting policies which destroyed the livelihoods of thousands of people in a particular industry or sector of the economy, much less admitted to getting thousands of American soldiers killed in a war that was unnecessary or whose conditions were misconceived.

Given the severe prerequisites for reaching correct conclusions by rationalistically planning the activities of an economy, or engaging in successful social engineering, it can hardly be surprising that making such decisions through political processes so often turns out to be unsuccessful. The more comprehensive such collectivized decisions and centralized control, the more comprehensive the failure— the economic debacle of Eastern Europe under Communism being the classic example. Conversely, merely making a substantial reduction in the amount of political control over the economy has produced dramatic increases in prosperity in a relatively short time, in such disparate settings as post–World War II Germany, Sri Lanka in the 1970s, or the United States during the 1980s. One of the reasons why such experience does not become part of the social memory used to guide subsequent political decision making is that experience is so often filtered through the media, and the nature of that filtering process itself has built-in biases, quite aside from the biases of those who operate the media.

VISIONS, POLITICS, AND THE MEDIA

Practical politics, of course, has many dimensions besides visions. However, some kinds of visions are more congenial to the political world. The prevailing vision of the anointed is particularly well adapted to politics and the tragic vision particularly ill-suited. Anyone can see a "problem" before one's eyes and wish to "solve" it, or see an "unmet need" and wish to supply it. What is more difficult is to understand the implications of systemic causation within constrained options. The easier and more emotionally satisfying vision is clearly the vision of the anointed. Politicians can more readily reduce it to slogans and images, and the media can more readily dramatize it. This is a bias inherent in the media, irrespective of the personal philosophies of print or broadcast journalists.

Over the years, studies have repeatedly shown people in the mass media to be overwhelmingly of the political left but this kind of media bias may not be as important as a bias inherent in the way both broadcast and print media operate. Radio, television, and motion pictures can readily dramatize an individual situation, in a way in which the larger relationships and the implicit assumptions behind that situation cannot be dramatized. For example, the media cannot identify, much less dramatize, all those individuals who would have come down with some deadly disease if it were not for their being vaccinated. But nothing is easier to dramatize than the rare individual who caught the disease from the vaccine itself and is now devastated by illness, physically or mentally crippled, or dying. When the government creates some new program, nothing is easier than to show whatever benefits that program produces. Indeed, those who run the program will be more than cooperative in bringing those benefits to the attention of the media. But it is virtually impossible to trace the taxes that paid for the program back to their sources and to show the alternative uses of that same money that could have been far more beneficial.

In short, the built-in bias of the media is to show what happens right under our noses, with little or no regard to what that has cost elsewhere. A California farmer can always show the television audience the abundant crop he has been able to grow because of federal water projects. But no one can videotape the crops that would have been grown elsewhere, at less cost to the economy, if there were no federal subsidies to encourage the use of water delivered at great cost into the California desert instead of water delivered free from the clouds elsewhere. There is likewise no way the television camera can show which unemployed people would have had jobs, if the minimum wage laws had not made them too expensive to hire at their current levels of skill and experience—and thereby cut them off from acquiring the additional skills and experience they need. There is no way to identify and interview those people who would be living comfortably in New York City apartment buildings that are currently abandoned and boarded-up because rent-control laws have made them economically unviable. Regardless of the ideological bias of people in the media, there is no way for the camera to show all the businesses that would exist in the absence of government red tape and mandated costs.

Deceptive appearances have been with us long before the rise of the modern mass media. But never before have those appearances been able to reach so many people, with so much immediacy and so much seeming reality.

What makes the built-in bias of the mass media so dangerous is that it adds leverage to a similar bias in political decision making toward doing good right under our noses, without regard to wider and longer-run implications. Conversely, visible harm sustained immediately is easier to dramatize than the long-run benefits for which it is endured. Could slavery have been ended by the Civil War if television cameras had shown daily scenes of the horrors of Sherman's march through Georgia or the appalling sufferings of civilians in besieged Vicksburg? The televised sufferings of the war in Indo-China helped bring it to an end—leading to even more suffering and even more deaths after the Communists took over that region, but these sufferings (including the killing fields of Kampuchea) were not televised. Not being able to televise the horrors under totalitarian regimes is another built-in bias of the media, which can only show suffering in a free society—thereby making such societies easier to undermine.

The media can even build up sympathy for murderers by interviewing their mothers or wives, who proclaim their innocence, or fellow criminals who give them an alibi by saying that they were somewhere else when the crime was committed. Just the sight of a forlorn man on death row can be touching. The media cannot show that same man when he was exulting in the savagery of the crime that brought him there, cannot show his sadistic joy when he was raping and torturing a little girl who was tearfully pleading for her life. If they could show that on television, many of those people who gather outside prison to protest his execution might instead be inside volunteering to pull the switch.

The dangerous dramatizing of half-truths is the fatal talent of the television or movie camera. Even with honest and balanced people, that danger would be ever present, and would need to be constantly guarded against. With the media being overwhelmingly of one ideological bent, human bias and media bias only reinforce one another.

Add to this the philosophy of advocacy journalism and the result can be what has been called "lying for justice"[9]—which is to say, preempting other people's decisions by telling them only what leads to the conclusion desired. By sheer repetition of images of ordinary families who have been rendered homeless by unforeseeable misfortunes, the media can create a wholly distorted picture of the homeless population, in which such people are a very small fraction. By sheer repetition of certain kinds of dramatized experiences, such as "battered wives," the media can create the impression that one of the least assaulted groups in the society is one of the most assaulted, even when hard data show that a higher proportion of both men and single women are assaulted than are married women. This goes beyond the bias inherent in the media to the deliberate creation of a situation which has been aptly characterized by Paul Weaver:

> The media are less a window on reality than a stage on which officials and journalists perform self-scripted, self-serving fictions.[10]

The ease with which the media can choose what images to contrive and spread across the land feeds the dangerous illusion that reality is optional.

PAST CONSEQUENCES AND FUTURE DANGERS

After the vision of the anointed was given increasing scope in the education and public policy of the United States and other Western societies during the decades beginning with the 1960s, the social degeneration became palpable, documented beyond issue, and immense across a wide spectrum of social phenomena—declining educational standards, rising crime rates, broken homes, soaring rates of teenage pregnancy, growing drug usage, and unprecedented levels of suicide among adolescents. This social devastation was not due to poverty, for the material standard of living was rising substantially during this time. It was not due to repression, for an unprecedented variety of new "rights" emerged from the courts and legislatures to liberate people from the constraints of the law while they were being liberated from social constraints by the spread of "nonjudgmental" attitudes. Neither was this social degeneration due to the disruptions of war or natural catastrophes, for it was an unusually long period of peace, and science conquered many diseases that had plagued the human race for centuries, as well as providing better ways of protecting people from earthquakes and other destructive acts of nature. It was instead an era of self-inflicted wounds.

The full dangers of the vision of the anointed cannot reveal themselves immediately. Even the anointed themselves are currently under at least the residual influence of traditional philosophical, religious, and moral inhibitions. To the extent that their vision prevails and endures, however, successive generations of the anointed will be less and less under the influence of these eroding traditional constraints, and the pure logic of their vision can operate more fully. Conversely, among those not convinced of this vision's virtues, the spirit of resistance may well erode and the sense of outrage at its consequences become dulled by the accumulation of precedents for policies and actions that might once have been considered intolerable.

In the anointed we find a whole class of supposedly "thinking people" who do remarkably little thinking about substance and a great deal of verbal expression. In order that this relatively small group of people can believe themselves wiser and nobler than the common herd, we have adopted policies which impose heavy costs on millions of other human beings, not only in taxes but also in lost jobs, social disintegration, and a loss of personal safety. Seldom have so few cost so much to so many.

NOTES

EPIGRAPHS

Stigler quote is from George J. Stigler, *The Citizen and the State: Essays on Regulation* (Chicago: University of Chicago Press, 1975), p. 10.

Fearing quote is from Kenneth Fearing, "Conclusion," *Collected Poems of Kenneth Fearing* (New York: Random House, 1940), p. 35.

CHAPTER 1: FLATTERING UNCTION

1. See, for example, Carlo M. Cipolla, "Editor's Introduction," *The Economic Decline of Empires* (London: Methuen, 1970), p. 15; Bernard Lewis, "Some Reflections on the Decline of the Ottoman Empire," ibid., p. 227; Bernard Lewis, *Islam in History*, second edition (Chicago: Open Court, 1993), pp. 211–212.
2. See Thomas Sowell, *A Conflict of Visions* (New York: Morrow, 1987).
3. Ibid., pp. 227–228.
4. Edmund Burke, *The Correspondence of Edmund Burke*, edited by R. B. McDowell (Chicago: University of Chicago Press, 1969), Vol. VIII, p. 138.
5. Thomas Robert Malthus, *Population: The First Essay* (Ann Arbor: University of Michigan Press, 1959), p. 3.
6. William Godwin, *Of Population* (London: Longman, Hurst, Rees, Orme, and Brown, 1820), pp. 520, 550, 554.
7. F. A. Hayek, *The Road to Serfdom* (Chicago: University of Chicago Press, 1944), pp. 55, 185.

8. Myron Magnet, *The Dream and the Nightmare: The Sixties Legacy to the Underclass* (New York: Morrow, 1993), p. 23.

9. Ibid., p. 25.

10. Andrew Hacker, *Two Nations: Black and White, Separate, Hostile, Unequal* (New York: Charles Scribner's Sons, 1992), p. 51.

11. Jean-François Revel, *The Flight from Truth: The Reign of Deceit in the Age of Information* (New York: Random House, 1991), p. 192.

12. Joseph Epstein, "True Virtue," *New York Times Magazine*, November 24, 1985, p. 95.

CHAPTER 2: THE PATTERN

1. Joseph A. Schumpeter, review of Keynes's General Theory, *Journal of the American Statistical Association*, December 1936, p. 795.

2. "Public Welfare Program—Message from the President of the United States (H. Doc. No. 325)," *Congressional Record—House*, February 1, 1962, p. 1405.

3. Ibid., p. 1406.

4. Ibid., p. 1405.

5. "Relief Is No Solution," *New York Times*, February 2, 1962, p. 28.

6. *Congressional Quarterly*, February 2, 1962, p. 140.

7. Marjorie Hunter, "Johnson Signs Bill to Fight Poverty; Pledges New Era," *New York Times*, August 21, 1964, p. 1.

8. Ibid.

9. "Excerpts from President Lyndon B. Johnson's Address to the Nation on Civil Disorders, July 27, 1967," *Report of the National Advisory Commission on Civil Disorders*, March 1, 1968, p. 297; "Transcript of Johnson's TV Address on the Riots," *New York Times*, July 28, 1967, p. A11.

10. Report of the National Advisory Commission on Civil Disorders, March 1, 1968, p. 91.

11. Robert B. Semple, Jr., "Dr. King Scores Poverty Budget," *New York Times*, December 16, 1966, p. A33; Robert B. Semple, Jr., "2 More Score U.S. on Help for Poor," *New York Times*, December 7, 1966, p. A32.

12. See, for example, Daniel Patrick Moynihan, *Maximum Feasible Misunderstanding: Community Action in the War on Poverty* (New York: Free Press, 1969), pp. xxvi–xxvii.

13. Charles Mohr, " 'Viva Goldwater' Greets Senator," *New York Times*, February 16, 1964, p. 47.

14. "Goldwater Sees Johnson Retreat," *New York Times*, January 19, 1964, p. 49.

15. James T. Patterson, *America's Struggle Against Poverty: 1900–1980* (Cambridge, Mass.: Harvard University Press, 1981), pp. 145, 146, 149, 152.

16. Henry Hazlitt, "The War on Poverty," *Newsweek*, April 6, 1964, p. 74.

17. Charles Murray, *Losing Ground: American Social Policy, 1950–1960* (New York: Basic Books, 1984), p. 57.

18. Ibid., p. 64.

19. James T. Patterson, *America's Struggle Against Poverty*, p. 132.

20. Ibid., pp. 64–65.

21. U.S. Bureau of the Census, *Current Population Reports*, Series P60-185 (Washington, D.C.: U.S. Government Printing Office, 1993), p. ix. The poverty rate as a percentage of the total population was not yet as high as in 1964 but the absolute number of people in poverty was. This rise in the absolute number of people in poverty began in the late 1970s. U.S. Bureau of the Census, *Current Population Reports*, Series P-23, No. 173 (Washington, D.C.: U.S. Government Printing Office, 1991), p. 18.

22. Charles Murray, *Losing Ground*, pp. 49, 67.

23. James T. Patterson, *America's Struggle Against Poverty*, p. 170.

24. Ibid., pp. 164–165.

25. James T. Patterson, *America's Struggle Against Poverty*, p. 164.

26. Daniel Patrick Moynihan, *Maximum Feasible Misunderstanding*, pp. liii, 150, 156.

27. Hodding Carter III, "'Disarmament' Spells Defeat in War on Poverty," *Wall Street Journal*, August 11, 1983, p. 21.

28. "How Great Was the Great Society?" in *The Great Society: A Twenty Year Critique* (Austin, Tex.: Lyndon Baines Johnson Library, 1986), p. 125.

29. Hodding Carter III, "'Disarmament' Spells Defeat in War on Poverty," *Wall Street Journal*, August 11, 1983, p. 21.

30. Harry J. Middleton, "Welcome," *The Great Society: A Twenty Year Critique*, p. 1.

31. Mrs. Lyndon B. Johnson, "Welcome," ibid., p. 2.

32. Lucia Mount, "U.S. War on Poverty: No Sweeping Victory, But Some Battles May Have Been Won," *Christian Science Monitor*, September 19, 1984, pp. 3–4.

33. United States Senate, Ninetieth Congress, first session, *Hearings Before the Subcommittee on Employment, Manpower, and Poverty of the Committee on Labor and Public Welfare*, Part 7 (Washington, D.C.: U.S. Government Printing Office, 1967), pp. 2170–2171.

34. Aida Tores, Jacqueline Darroch Forrest, and Susan Eisman, "Family Planning Services in the United States, 1978–79," *Family Planning Perspectives*, Vol. 13, No. 3 (May/June 1981), pp. 139, 141.

35. Patricia Schiller, "Sex Education That Makes Sense," *NEA Journal*, February 1968, p. 19.

36. Theodore Ooms, *Teenage Pregnancy in a Family Context* (Philadelphia: Temple University Press, 1981), p. 26.

37. Alan Guttmacher Institute, *Informing Public Change* (New York: Alan Guttmacher Institute, 1980), p. 7.

38. Cheryl D. Hayes, editor, *Risking the Future: Adolescent Sexuality, Pregnancy, and Childbearing* (Washington. D.C.: National Academy Press, 1987), p. 160.

39. Theodore Ooms, *Teenage Pregnancy in a Family Context*, pp. 39–40.

40. H. S. Hoyman, "Should We Teach About Birth Control in High School Sex Education?" *Education Digest*, February 1969, p. 22.

41. United States Senate, Eighty-ninth Congress, second session, *Family Planning Program: Hearing Before the Subcommittee on Employment, Manpower and Poverty of the Committee on Labor and Public Welfare* (Washington, D.C.: U.S. Government Printing Office, 1966), p. 84.

42. Joanne Zazzaro, "Critics or No Critics, Most Americans Still Firmly Support Sex Education in Schools," *American School Board Journal*, September 1969, p. 31.

43. Robert P. Hildrup, "Why Sex Education Belongs in the Schools," *PTA Magazine*, February 1974, p. 13.

44. Jacqueline Kasun, *The War Against Population* (San Francisco: Ignatius Press, 1988), p. 144.

45. Today's VD Control Problem: Joint Statement by American Public Health Association, American Social Health Association, American Venereal Disease Association, Association of State and Territorial Health Officers in Co-operation with the American Medical Association, February 1966, p. 20.

46. Lester A. Kirkendall, "Sex Education: A Reappraisal," *The Humanist*, Spring 1965, p. 82.

47. "Three's a Crowd," *New York Times*, March 17, 1972, p. 40.

48. Fred M. Hechinger, "Introduction," *Sex Education and the Schools*, edited by Virginia Hilu (New York: Harper & Row, 1967), p. xiv.

49. John Kobler, "Sex Invades the Schoolhouse," *Saturday Evening Post*, June 29, 1968, p. 26.

50. Jacqueline Kasun, *The War Against Population*, pp. 142, 144.

51. Cheryl D. Hayes, editor, *Risking the Future: Adolescent Sexuality, Pregnancy, and Childbearing* (Washington, D.C.: National Academy Press, 1987), p. 66.

52. Ibid., p. 58.

53. Alan Guttmacher Institute, *Informing Public Change*, p. 30.

54. Hearings before the Select Committee on Population, Ninety-fifth Congress, second session, *Fertility and Contraception in America: Adolescent and Pre-Adolescent Pregnancy* (Washington, D.C.: U.S. Government Printing Office, 1978), Vol. II, p. 253.

55. Ibid., p. 625.

56. Les Picker, "Human Sexuality Education Implications for Biology Teaching," *American Biology Teacher*, Vol. 46, No. 2 (February 1984), p. 92.

57. Hearings before the Select Committee on Population, Ninety-fifth Congress, second session, *Fertility and Contraception in America: Adolescent*

and Pre-Adolescent Pregnancy (Washington, D.C.: U.S. Government Printing Office, 1978), Vol. II, p. 1.

58. Paul A. Reichelt and Harriet H. Werley, "Contraception, Abortion and Venereal Disease: Teenagers' Knowledge and the Effect of Education," *Family Planning Perspectives,* March/April 1975, p. 83.

59. Ibid., p. 88.

60. Peter Scales, "The New Opposition to Sex Education: A Powerful Threat to a Democratic Society," *Journal of School Health,* April 1981, p. 303.

61. *Fertility and Contraception in the United States: Report Prepared by the Select Committee on Population* (Washington, D.C.: U.S. Government Printing Office, 1978), p. 5.

62. Sylvia S. Hacker, "It Isn't Sex Education Unless. . . " *Journal of School Health,* April 1981, p. 208.

63. See, for example, Thomas Sowell, *Inside American Education* (New York: Free Press, 1992), Chapter 3.

64. Suzanne Fields, " 'War' Pits Parents vs. Public Policy," *Chicago Sun-Times,* October 17, 1992, p. 19.

65. Ibid.

66. See, for example, Thomas Sowell, *Inside American Education,* pp. 51–53, 255.

67. On the denigration of parents within the classroom, see ibid., pp. 48–53.

68. James Hottois and Neal A. Milner, *The Sex Education Controversy: A Study of Politics, Education, and Morality* (Lexington, Mass.: D. C. Heath and Co., 1975), p. 6.

69. David L. Bazelon, "The Imperative to Punish," *Atlantic Monthly,* July 1960, p. 41.

70. U.S. Bureau of the Census, *Historical Statistics of the United States: Colonial Times to 1970* (Washington, D.C.: U.S. Government Printing Office, 1975), p. 414.

71. Ibid.

72. David L. Bazelon, "The Imperative to Punish," p. 41.

73. Ibid., p. 42.

74. Ibid., p. 43.

75. Ibid.

76. Ibid.

77. Ibid.

78. Ibid.

79. Ibid., p. 47.

80. William J. Brennan, "Foreword," David L. Bazelon, *Questioning Authority: Justice and Criminal Law* (New York: Knopf, 1988), pp. ix–xii.

81. Ibid., pp. xi, xii.

82. William O. Douglas, *The Court Years: The Autobiography of William O. Douglas* (New York: Random House, 1980), p. 84.

83. Ramsey Clark, *Crime in America: Observations on Its Nature, Causes, Prevention and Control* (New York: Simon & Schuster, 1970), p. 220.

84. Ibid., p. 202.

85. Tom Wicker, "Introduction," ibid., pp. 11, 14.

86. "Pick of the Paperbacks," *Saturday Review*, November 27, 1971, p. 48.

87. Robert Shnayerson, "Force and the Law," *Time*, November 30, 1970, pp. 83–84; Herbert Packer, "Causes of Crime," *New Republic*, November 7, 1970, pp. 28–30.

88. "The Liberals' Friend," *Times Literary Supplement*, November 26, 1971, p. 1467.

89. See, for example, Macklin Fleming, *The Price of Perfect Justice* (New York: Basic Books, 1974), Chapter 9.

90. James Q. Wilson, *Thinking About Crime* (New York: Basic Books, 1975), p. 173; Ernest van den Haag, *Punishing Criminals: Concerning a Very Old and Painful Question* (New York: Basic Books, 1975), p. 158; U.S. Department of Justice, *The Case for More Incarceration*, 1992, NCJ-139583 (Washington, D.C.: U.S. Department of Justice, 1992), pp. 1–5.

91. David L. Bazelon, "The Imperative to Punish," *Atlantic Monthly*, July 1960, p. 42.

92. Ibid., p. 46.

93. Max Frankel, "Johnson Derides Urban Reform Foes," *New York Times*, June 26, 1967, p. 45.

94. Thomas A. Johnson, "Muskie, in Jersey, Calls Wallace 'The Man We've Got to Defeat,'" *New York Times*, October 24, 1968, p. 42.

95. Fred P. Graham, "Dissenters Bitter: Four View Limitation on Confessions as Aid to Criminals," *New York Times*, June 17, 1966, pp. 1*ff.*

96. Sidney E. Zion, "Attack on Court Heard by Warren," *New York Times*, September 10, 1965, pp. 1*ff.*

97. James Q. Wilson and Richard J. Herrnstein, *Crime and Human Nature* (New York: Simon & Schuster, 1985), p. 409.

98. Charles H. Silberman, *Criminal Violence, Criminal Justice* (New York: Random House, 1978), p. 4.

99. U.S. Bureau of the Census, *Historical Statistics of the United States: Colonial Times to 1970*, p. 415.

100. Federal Bureau of Investigation, *Uniform Crime Reports: Crime in the United States, 1991* (Washington, D.C.: U.S. Government Printing Office, 1992), p. 280.

101. "No Shackles on the Law," *New York Times*, August 15, 1966, p. 26.

102. "There are striking examples of 'crime waves' which turned out to be nothing more than statistical reporting waves." Yale Kamisar, "Public Safety v. Individual Liberties: Some 'Facts' and 'Theories,'" *Journal of Criminal Law, Criminology and Police Science*, Vol. 63 (1962), p. 187. "They have made loud noises about the 'disastrous' and 'catastrophic' prices we are paying to effectuate constitutional liberties, but they have

yet to furnish convincing evidence that the price is even substantial."
Ibid., p. 193.

103. James Q. Wilson, *Thinking About Crime* (New York: Basic Books, 1975), p. 75.

104. Michael Stern, "Menninger Discounts Criminality in Nation," *New York Times,* October 30, 1968, p. 49.

105. Charles E. Silberman, *Criminal Violence, Criminal Justice* (New York: Random House, 1978), p. 261.

106. James Q. Wilson and Richard J. Herrnstein, *Crime and Human Nature,* pp. 424–425.

107. Ibid., p. 429.

108. U.S. Bureau of the Census, *Historical Statistics of the United States, Colonial Times to 1970* (Washington, D.C.: U.S. Government Printing Office, 1975), p. 414.

109. James Q. Wilson, *Thinking About Crime,* p. 17.

110. Federal Bureau of Investigation, *Uniform Crime Reports: Crime in the United States, 1991,* p. 13.

111. *Newsweek* called Silberman's book "one of the most thorough and provocative studies ever made of crime in America." Jerold K. Footlick, "White Fear, Black Crime," *Newsweek,* October 23, 1978, p. 134. Similar praise appeared in the *New Yorker,* the *New York Review of Books,* and other bastions of the anointed. See Naomi Bliven, "Crime and Punishment," *New Yorker,* March 26, 1979, pp. 3–4; "As American as Jesse James," *Time,* November 6, 1978, pp. 76, 78; Peter Gardner, review, *Psychology Today,* January 1979, p. 99.

112. Fred P. Graham, "Warren Says All Share Crime Onus," *New York Times,* August 2, 1968, pp. 1, 13.

113. Chief Justice Earl Warren, *The Memoirs of Earl Warren* (Garden City, N.Y.: Doubleday, 1977), p. 317.

CHAPTER 3: BY THE NUMBERS

1. Kenneth Fearing, "Andy and Jerry and Joe," *Collected Poems of Kenneth Fearing* (New York: Random House, 1940), p. 7.

2. National Center for Health Statistics, *Health, United States, 1990* (Hyattsville, Md.: U.S. Public Health Service, 1991), p. 41. The corresponding graphs are on pages 9 and 11.

3. "More Babies Are Dying," *New York Times,* August 9, 1990, p. A22.

4. "Infant Deaths," *Washington Post,* March 13, 1990, p. A24.

5. National Center for Health Statistics, *Health, United States, 1990,* p. 41.

6. Ibid.

7. Marian Wright Edelman, "The Status of Children and Our National Future," *Stanford Law Policy Review,* Fall 1989, p. 20. An essay on Marian Wright Edelman and the Children's Defense Fund in the *New Yorker*

magazine said: "C.D.F. was able to show that increasing health service to children actually led to decreased government costs in doctor and hospital bills further down the line—an economic argument that has proved persuasive with Congress." Calvin Tomkins, "A Sense of Urgency," *New Yorker*, March 27, 1989, p. 70. As in many other cases, "persuasive" does not necessarily mean accurate. For a more critical example of the Children's Defense Fund, see John Hood, "Children's Crusade," *Reason*, June 1992, pp. 32–35.

8. Jane Huntington and Frederick A. Connell, "For Every Dollar Spent— The Cost-Savings Argument for Prenatal Care," *New England Journal of Medicine*, Vol. 331, No. 19 (November 10, 1994), pp. 1303–1307.

9. Gina Kolata, "Reassessing Costs of Prenatal Care," *New York Times*, November 10, 1994, p. A10.

10. Joel Glenn Brenner, "A Pattern of Bias in Mortgage Loans," *Washington Post*, June 6, 1993, p. A1.

11. Jesse Jackson, "Racism Is the Bottom Line in Home Loans," *Los Angeles Times*, October 28, 1991, p. B5.

12. See, for example, Paulette Thomas, "Blacks Can Face a Host of Trying Conditions in Getting Mortgages," *Wall Street Journal*, November 30, 1992, p. A8.

13. Rochelle Sharpe, "Losing Ground: In Latest Recession, Only Blacks Suffered Net Employment Loss," *Wall Street Journal*, September 14, 1993, p. 14.

14. Vladimir G. Treml, *Alcohol in the USSR: A Statistical Study* (Durham, N.C.: Duke University Press, 1982), pp. 64, 71, 81; Andrew M. Greeley, *That Most Distressful Nation* (New York: Quadrangle Books, 1972), pp. 129, 132; Australian Government Commission into Poverty, *Welfare of Migrants* (Canberra: Australian Government Publishing Service, 1975), p. 108; Raphael Patai, *The Jewish Mind* (New York: Charles Scribner's Sons, 1977), pp. 441–443.

15. See, for example, Hélène Carrère d'Encausse, *Decline of an Empire: The Soviet Socialist Republics in Revolt* (New York: Harper & Row, 1981), pp. 68–69; Thomas Sowell, "Three Black Histories," *Essays and Data on American Ethnic Groups*, edited by Thomas Sowell and Lynn D. Collins (Washington, D.C.: The Urban Institute, 1978), pp. 41–42; "Part Two: Statistical Data on American Ethnic Groups," ibid., pp. 257–258, 273–277, 291–295, 309–313, 327–331, 357–361, 369–373, 393–397, 411–415. For differences in fertility rates between nations, see U.S. Bureau of the Census, *World Population Profile: 1991* (Washington, D.C.: U.S. Government Printing Office, 1991), pp. 18–20.

16. K. M. de Silva, "University Admissions and Ethnic Tension in Sri Lanka, 1977–1982," *From Independence to Statehood: Managing Ethnic Conflict in Five African and Asian States* (London: Frances Pinter, 1984), pp. 98–99, 103; James R. Flynn, *Asian Americans: Achievement Beyond IQ*

(Hillsdale, N.J.: Lawrence Erlbaum, 1991), pp. 95–98; Robert Klitgaard, *Elitism and Meritocracy in Developing Countries: Selection Policies for Higher Education* (Baltimore: Johns Hopkins University Press, 1986), p. 121; Mohamed Suffian bin Hashim, "Problems and Issues of Higher Education Development in Malaysia," *Development of Higher Education in Southeast Asia: Problems and Issues,* edited by Yat Hoong Yip (Singapore: Regional Institute of Higher Education, 1973), pp. 63–64; Padma Ramkrishna Velaskar, "Inequality in Higher Education: A Study of Scheduled Caste Students in Medical Colleges of Bombay," Ph.D. dissertation, Tata Institute of Social Sciences (Bombay), 1986, pp. 335–337; Leonard P. Ayres, *Laggards in Our Schools: A Study of Retardation and Elimination in Our City Schools* (New York: Russell Sage Foundation, 1909), passim.

17. "Lightning Hits More Men," *USA Today,* April 16, 1992, p. 1.

18. Vladimir G. Treml, *Alcohol in the USSR,* p. 73.

19. Mohamed Suffian bin Hashim, "Problems and Issues in Higher Education Development in Malaysia," *Development of Higher Education in Southeast Asia,* edited by Yat Hoong Yip, Table 8, pp. 63, 64.

20. Charles Assawi, "The Transformation of the Economic Position of the *Millets* in the Nineteenth Century," *Christians and Jews in the Ottoman Empire: The Functioning of a Plural Society,* edited by Benjamin Braude and Bernard Lewis, Vol. I: *The Central Lands* (New York: Holmes & Meier, 1982), pp. 261–285.

21. Donald L. Horowitz, *Ethnic Groups in Conflict* (Berkeley: University of California Press, 1985), pp. 448, 451.

22. Myron Weiner, *Sons of Soil: Migration and Ethnic Conflict in India* (Princeton, N.J.: Princeton University Press, 1978), pp. 91, 103–104.

23. Mavis Puthucheary, "Public Policies Relating Business and Land," *From Independence to Statehood: Managing Ethnic Conflict in Five African and Asian States,* edited by Robert B. Goldmann and A. Jeyaratnam Wilson (London: Frances Pinter, 1984), p. 158.

24. S. J. Tambiah, "Ethnic Representation in Ceylon's Higher Administrative Services, 1870–1964," *University of Ceylon Review,* Vol. 13 (1955), p. 130.

25. See Leonard Ramist and Solomon Arbeiter, *Profiles, College-Bound Seniors, 1985* (New York: College Entrance Examination Board, 1986), pp. 42, 82.

26. Ralph R. Premdas, "The Political Economy of Ethnic Strife in Fiji and Guyana," *Ethnic Studies Report* (International Centre for Ethnic Studies, Sri Lanka), July 1991, p. 36.

27. Ingeborg Fleischhauer, "The Germans' Role in Tsarist Russia: A Reappraisal," *The Soviet Germans: Past and Present,* edited by Edith Rogovin Frankel (New York: St. Martin's, 1986), pp. 17–18; Fred C. Koch, *The Volga Germans: In Rusia and the Americas, from 1763 to the Presents,* (University Park: Pennsylvania State University Press, 1977), p. 195.

28. James L. Tigner, "Japanese Immigration into Latin America," *Journal of Interamerican Studies and World Affairs*, November 1981, p. 476.

29. Carl Solberg, *Immigration and Nationalism: Argentina and Chile, 1890–1914* (Austin: University of Texas Press, 1970), p. 50.

30. Daniel J. Elazar, *Jewish Communities in Frontier Societies* (New York: Holmes & Meier, 1983), p. 243.

31. Carl Solberg, *Immigration and Nationalism*, p. 63.

32. See, Mohamed Suffian bin Hashim, "Problems and Issues of Higher Education Development in Malaysia," *Development of Higher Education in Southeast Asia: Problems and Issues* (Singapore: Regional Institute of Higher Education and Development, 1973), pp. 56–78; Sammy Smooha and Yochanan Peres, "The Dynamics of Ethnic Inequalities: The Case of Israel," *Studies of Israeli Society*, Vol. I: *Migration, Ethnicity and Community*, edited by Ernest Krausz (New Brunswick, N.J.: Transaction Books, 1980), p. 173; George H. Brown, Nan L. Rosen, and Susan T. Hill, *The Condition of Education for Hispanic Americans* (Washington, D.C.: National Center for Educational Statistics, 1980), p. 119; Thomas Sowell, "Ethnicity in a Changing America," *Daedalus*, Winter 1978, p. 214; Chandra Richard de Silva, "Sinhala-Tamil Relations in Sri Lanka: The University Admissions Issue—the First Phase, 1971–7," *From Independence to Statehood: Managing Ethnic Conflict in Five African and Asian States*, edited by R. B. Goldmann and A. J. Wilson (London: Frances Pinter, 1984), pp. 125–146; Paul Compton, "The Conflict in Northern Ireland: Demographic and Economic Considerations," *Economic Dimensions of Ethnic Conflict: International Perspectives*, edited by S. W. R. de A. Samarasinghe and Reed Coughlan (London: Pinter Publishers, 1991), p. 42.

33. Computed from statistics in *The Chronicle of Higher Education Almanac*, August 25, 1993, p. 17.

34. Ibid., p. 16.

35. See Thomas Sowell, *Civil Rights: Rhetoric or Reality?* (New York: Morrow, 1984), p. 58.

36. U.S. Bureau of the Census, Current Population Reports, Series P-23, No. 173, *Population Profile of the United States, 1991* (Washington, D.C.: U.S. Government Printing Office, 1991), p. 20.

37. Paulette Thomas, "Behind the Figures: Federal Reserve Detail Pervasive Racial Gap in Mortgage Lending," *Wall Street Journal*, March 31, 1992, p. A1.

38. Glenn B. Canner, "Expanded HMDA Data on Residential Lending: One Year Later," *Federal Reserve Bulletin*, November 1992, p. 801.

39. Alicia H. Munnell, *Mortgage Lending in Boston: Interpreting HMDA Data*, Working Paper No. 92–7, October 1992, Federal Reserve Bank of Boston, pp. 2, 24, 25.

40. Ibid., p. 25.

41. Ibid., p. 24.

42. Ibid., p. 2.

43. Ibid.

44. Peter Brimelow and Leslie Spencer, "The Hidden Clue," *Forbes*, January 4, 1993, p. 48.

45. Ibid.

46. Ibid.

47. Herbert Stein and Murray Foss, *An Illustrated Guide to the American Economy* (Washington, D.C.: AEI Press, 1992), p. 140.

48. *U.S. v. Syufy Enterprises*, 903 F.2d 659 (9th Cir. 1990) at 665.

49. See, for example, Greg J. Duncan, et al., *Years of Poverty, Years of Plenty: The Changing Economic Fortunes of American Workers and Families* (Ann Arbor: University of Michigan Press, 1984); *Income Mobility and Economic Opportunity*, report prepared for Representative Richard K. Armey, Ranking Republican, Joint Economic Committee, June 1992, p. 5.

50. *Income Mobility and Economic Opportunity*, p. 5.

51. Greg J. Duncan, et al., *Years of Poverty, Years of Plenty: The Changing Economic Fortunes of American Workers and Families* (Ann Arbor: University of Michigan, 1984), pp. 3, 13, 41.

52. Robert Rector, "Poverty in U.S. Is Exaggerated by Census," *Wall Street Journal*, September 25, 1990, p. A18.

53. Ibid.

54. Carolyn Lochhead, "How Hungry? How Many?" *Insight*, June 27, 1988, pp. 8–9.

55. Robert E. Rector, "Hunger and Malnutrition Among American Children," *Backgrounder*, No. 843 (August 2, 1991), The Heritage Foundation, p. 2.

56. "Media Eat Up Hunger Study," *Media Watch*, April 1991, p. 1.

57. Ibid.

58. Christina Hoff Sommers, *Who Stole Feminism: How Women Have Betrayed Women* (New York: Simon & Schuster, 1994), p. 196.

59. Anna Quindlen, "Game Time," *New York Times*, June 25, 1994, p. A15.

60. Christina Hoff Sommers, *Who Stole Feminism*, pp. 189–192.

61. U.S. Bureau of the Census, *Current Population Reports*, Series P-60, No. 177 (Washington, D.C.: U.S. Government Printing Office, 1991), p. 19.

62. U.S. Bureau of the Census, *Current Population Reports*, Series P-60, No. 184 (Washington, D.C.: U.S. Government Printing Office, 1993), p. 7.

63. U.S. Bureau of the Census, *Current Population Reports*, Series P-60, No. 179 (Washington, D.C.: U.S. Government Printing Office, 1992), p. 27.

64. U.S. Bureau of the Census, *Current Population Reports*, Series P-60, No. 184 (Washington, D.C.: U.S. Government Printing Office, 1993), p. 5.

65. Ibid.

66. Ibid., p. 49.

67. U.S. Bureau of the Census, *Current Population Reports*, Series P-60, No.
     181 (Washington, D.C.: U.S. Government Printing Office, 1992), p. 14;
     U.S. Bureau of the Census, *Current Population Reports*, Series P-20, No.
     477 (Washington, D.C.: U.S. Government Printing Office, 1993), p. A-1.

68. U.S. Bureau of the Census, *Current Population Reports*, Series P-60, No.
     181 (Washington, D.C.: U.S. Government Printing Office, 1992), p. 14;
     U.S. Bureau of the Census, *Current Population Reports*, Series P-20, No.
     477 (Washington, D.C.: U.S. Government Printing Office, 1993), p. A-1.

69. U.S. Bureau of the Census, *Current Population Reports*, Series P-60, No.
     184, p. xiv.

70. Ibid., pp. xvi, B-2; U.S. Bureau of the Census, *Current Population
     Reports*, Series P-60, No. 167, p. 68.

71. Compare U.S. Bureau of the Census, *Current Population Reports*, Series
     P-60, No. 167, pp. 9, 68.

72. Louis Uchitelle, "Trapped in the Impoverished Middle Class," *New York
     Times*, November 17, 1991, p. F1. See a similar refrain in Tom Wicker,
     "Let 'Em Eat Swiss Cheese," *New York Times*, September 2, 1968,
     p. A27.

73. Compare Tom Wicker, "LBJ's Great Society," *New York Times*, May 7,
     1990, p. A15; Tom Wicker, "Let 'Em Eat Cheese," *New York Times*, Sep-
     tember 2, 1988, p. A27.

74. U.S. Bureau of the Census, *Current Population Reports*, Series P-60, No.
     184, p. 7.

75. These statistical disparities would be even greater if we took into account
     the fact that people die, so that all these age brackets would not be the
     same in size, even at a constant birth rate. If people die before reaching
     their peak earnings years, that will tend to increase the inequalities in
     income and wealth. Inheritance would also tend to increase inequalities,
     if elderly people leave much of their wealth to their spouses in the same
     age brackets, with their children receiving the inheritance of both par-
     ents as those children are entering their own peak earnings years.

76. John Flinn, "Census Shows Stanford Among Area's Poorest," *San Fran-
     cisco Examiner*, June 21, 1992, p. B3.

77. "More Babies Are Dying," *New York Times*, August 9, 1990, p. A22;
     "Infant Deaths," *Washington Post*, March 13, 1990, p. A24.

78. Nicholas Eberstadt, "Parents and the District's Endangered Children,"
     Washington Times, February 23, 1994, p. A19.

79. Victor R. Fuchs and Diane M. Reklis,"America's Children: Economic
     Perspectives and Policy Options," *Science*, Vol. 255 (January 3, 1992),
     p. 45.

80. Calvin Tomkins, "A Sense of Urgency," *New Yorker*, March 27, 1989,
     p. 74.

81. Marian Wright Edelman, "The Status of Children and Our National
     Future," *Stanford Law and Policy Review*, Fall 1989, p. 26.

82. Richard B. Freeman, *Black Elite* (New York: McGraw-Hill, 1976), Chapter 4.

83. U.S. Bureau of the Census, *Current Population Reports*, Series P-23, No. 80 (Washington, D.C.: U.S. Government Printing Office, no date), p. 44.

84. U.S. Bureau of the Census, *Current Population Reports*, Series P-20, No. 366 (Washington, D.C.: U.S. Government Printing Office, 1981), pp. 182, 184.

85. U.S. Bureau of the Census, *Current Population Reports*, Series P-23, No. 181 (Washington, D.C.: U.S. Government Printing Office, 1992), p. 32.

86. Nicholas Eberstadt, "America's Infant Mortality Puzzle," *The Public Interest*, Fall 1991, p. 38.

87. "Reader's Digest Poll Reveals Family Gap—Powerful Hidden Force in Presidential Politics," news release, *Reader's Digest*, June 10, 1992, pp. 2–3. Fred Barnes, "The Family Gap," *Reader's Digest*, July 1992, p. 52.

88. Ann W. Richards, "Girls, Pull Your Freight," *New York Times*, June 25, 1994, p. A15.

89. Haynes Johnson, *Sleepwalking Through History: America in the Reagan Years* (New York: Anchor Books, 1992), p. 451; Ann Richards, "Girls, Pull Your Own Freight," p. A15; Barbara Ehrenreich, "Burt, Loni and Our Way of Life," *Time*, September 25, 1994, p. 92.

90. U.S. Bureau of the Census, "Marital Status and Living Arrangements," *Current Population Reports*, Series P-20, No. 468 (Washington, D.C.: U.S. Government Printing Office, 1992), p. vii.

91. Ibid., p. xvi.

92. Ibid., p. 1.

93. Ibid., p. vii.

94. Henry A. Walker, "Black-White Differences in Marriage and Family Patterns," *Feminism, Children and New Families*, edited by Sanford M. Dornbusch and Myra H. Strober (New York: Guilford Press, 1988), p. 92.

95. U.S. Bureau of the Census, "Marital Status and Living Arrangements: March 1992," *Current Population Reports*, Series P-20, No. 468, pp. 1, 2.

96. Ibid., p. 93.

97. Arlene Skolnick, "The American Family," *Focus on Children: The Beat of the Future*, Report of the 1992 Media Conference at the Columbia University Graduate School of Journalism (no publisher, no date), p. 60.

98. Ibid.

99. Ibid., p. xii.

100. Karl Marx and Friedrich Engels, *Collected Works* (New York: International Publishers), Vol. VI, p. 354.

101. See, for example, Hillary Rodham, "Children Under the Law, *Harvard Educational Review*, Vol. 43, No. 4 (November 1973), pp. 487–514; Larry Rohter, "11-Year-Old Seeks Right to 'Divorce Parents,'" *New York Times*, July 8, 1992, p. A10.

102. Emily Flynn, "Child Abuse: The Facts," *NZ Listener* (New Zealand), August 13, 1988, p. 17.

103. Clark E. Vincent, "Teen-Age Unwed Mothers in American Society," *Journal of Social Issues*, April 1966, p. 22.

104. Ibid., p. 25.

105. Ibid., p. 27.

106. Ibid., p. 23.

107. Ibid., p. 29.

108. Ibid., p. 32.

109. Quoted in Nicholas Eberstadt, "America's Infant Mortality Puzzle," *The Public Interest*, Fall 1991, p. 37.

110. Hillary Rodham, "Children Under the Law," *Harvard Educational Review*, Vol. 43, No. 4 (November 1973), p. 513.

CHAPTER 4: THE IRRELEVANCE OF EVIDENCE

1. *John Adams: A Biography in His Own Words*, edited by James Bishop Peabody (New York: Newsweek, 1973), pp. 121–122.

2. John Kenneth Galbraith, *The Affluent Society* (Cambridge, Mass.: Riverside Press, 1958), p. 82.

3. Ibid., p. 84.

4. Ibid., p. 85.

5. Ibid., pp. 84, 86.

6. Ibid., p. 97.

7. Ibid., p. 103.

8. John Kenneth Galbraith, *The New Industrial State* (Boston: Houghton Mifflin, 1967), p. 76.

9. Ibid., p. 58.

10. Ibid.

11. Robert L. Bartley, *The Seven Fat Years: And How to Do It Again* (New York: Free Press, 1992), p. 140.

12. Paul R. Ehrlich, *The Population Bomb* (revised) (Rivercity, Mass.: Rivercity Press, 1975), p. xi.

13. Ibid.

14. Ibid., pp. xi–xii.

15. "Appraisal of Current Trends in Business and Finance," *Wall Street Journal*, December 28, 1970, p. 1.

16. "The Population 'Explosion,'" *Wall Street Journal*, December 16, 1974, p. A14.

17. Roy J. Harris, Jr., "With Birth Rate Falling, Makers of Infant Goods Decide to Diversify," *Wall Street Journal*, January 4, 1972, p. 1.

18. "Maternity Ward Closings Free Hospital Staff for Other Duties," *Wall Street Journal*, April 23, 1974, p. 1.

19. Ibid., p. 6.

20. Calculation may be found in Thomas Sowell, *The Economics and Politics of Race* (New York: Morrow, 1982), p. 209.

21. U.S. Bureau of the Census, *World Population Profile: 1991* (Washington, D.C.: U.S. Government Printing Office, 1991), pp. A33, A34.

22. See, for example, Jean W. Sedlar, *East Central Europe in the Middle Ages, 1000–1500* (Seattle: University of Washington Press, 1994), pp. 90, 98, 99; Peter Gunst, "Agrarian Systems of Central and Eastern Europe," *The Origins of Backwardness in Eastern Europe: Economics and Politics from the Middle Ages Until the Early Twentieth Century*, edited by Daniel Chirot (Berkeley: University of California Press, 1989), pp. 53–54, 63–64.

23. John Stuart Mill, *Autobiography of John Stuart Mill* (New York: Columbia University Press, 1944), p. 102.

24. John Tierney, "Betting the Planet," *New York Times*, December 2, 1990, Section VI, pp. 74, 81.

25. American Petroleum Institute, *Basic Petroleum Data Book: Petroleum Industry Statistics*, Vol. XIII, No. 3 (Washington, D.C.: American Petroleum Institute, 1993), Section II, Tables 1, 1a.

26. Vance Packard, *The Waste Makers* (New York: David McKay, 1960), p. 200.

27. American Petroleum Institute, *Basic Petroleum Data Book: Petroleum Industry Statistics*, Vol. XIII, No. 3, Section II, Table 1.

28. Ralph Nader, "The Safe Car You Can't Buy," *The Nation 1865–1990: Selections from the Independent Magazine of Politics and Culture*, edited by Katrina vanden Heuvel (New York: Thunder's Mouth Press, 1990), p. 238.

29. Ralph Nader, *Unsafe at Any Speed* (New York: Grossman Publishers, 1965), p. 36.

30. Ibid., p. 26.

31. Ibid., p. 67.

32. Ibid., p. 5.

33. Ibid., p. 60.

34. Ibid., p. xi.

35. Ibid., pp. 65–66, 73.

36. Ibid., p. 40.

37. Ibid., p. 70.

38. U.S. Bureau of the Census, *Historical Statistics of the United States: Colonial Times to 1970* (Washington, D.C.: U.S. Government Printing Office, 1975), Part 2, pp. 719–720.

39. Nader himself refers to such policies as "saving an estimated 11,000 lives a year on the highways in 1981." Ralph Nader and Mark Green, "Passing on the Legacy of Shame," *The Nation*, April 2, 1990, p. 445.

40. Ibid., p. 718.

41. See *Congressional Record: Senate*, March 27, 1973, pp. 9748–9774.

42. Ralph de Toledano, *Hit and Run: The Rise—and Fall?—of Ralph Nader* (New Rochelle, N.Y.: Arlington House Publishers, 1975), p. 43.

43. Ralph Nader, *Unsafe at Any Speed*, Chapter 2.

44. Quoted in Ralph de Toledano, *Hit and Run*, p. 44.

45. Ibid.

46. Ibid., p. 45.

47. Ralph Nader, *Unsafe at Any Speed*, p. ix.

48. Ibid., p. viii.

49. Ralph Nader, "The Safe Car You Can't Buy," p. 238.

50. Ralph Nader, *Unsafe at Any Speed*, p. 25.

51. Ibid., p. 317.

52. Ibid., p. 42.

53. Charles McCarry, *Citizen Nader* (New York: Saturday Review Press, 1972), p. 13.

54. Rich Thomas, "Safe at This Speed?" *Newsweek*, August 22, 1994, p. 40.

55. It is not sufficient for the anointed to be able to set social goals. They must also be able to prescribe how those goals are to be met. Reducing air pollution, for example, can be accomplished in a number of ways, including allowing polluters to reduce pollution by prescribed amounts but in whatever ways they find most effective. Yet the anointed seldom find such policies acceptable, whatever their demonstrated efficacy, and prefer to micro-manage the process itself. One program, for example, allows companies to buy up old cars—a major source of air pollution— and destroy them, crediting the amount of pollution they reduce against the amount of pollution they are required to reduce from their own operations. Since it is often cheaper to do this than to make a corresponding reduction by installing cleaning devices on smokestacks, one oil company bought up thousands of old cars and destroyed them. Yet a Sierra Club spokesman opposed this program. It allowed no role for the anointed. See Sharon Begley and Mary Hagee, "Cold Cash for Old Clunkers," *Newsweek*, April 6, 1992, p. 61.

56. Quoted in Werner Meyer, "Snake Oil Salesmen," *Policy Review*, Summer 1986, pp. 74–76, passim.

57. "Can a Conservative Conserve Oil?" *New York Times*, November 14, 1980, p. A31.

58. Quoted in Werner Meyer, "Snake Oil Salesmen," p. 75.

59. Tom Wicker, "A Mere Beginning," *New York Times*, May 29, 1979, p. A23.

60. Ibid.

61. Werner Meyer, "Snake Oil Salesmen," p. 74.

62. American Petroleum Institute, *Basic Petroleum Data Book*, Vol. XIII, No. 3 (September 1993), Section VI, Table 3 (Washington, D.C.: American Petroleum Institute, 1993).

63. "Resolving the Energy Problem: Interview with James R. Schlesinger,

Secretary of Energy," *U.S. News and World Report,* July 10, 1978, p. 26; Dale Bumpers, "Ration Gasoline Now? Yes," *U.S. News and World Report,* July 9, 1979, p. 19; "What's Ahead for You at the Gas Pump: Interview with Charles W. Duncan, Jr., Secretary of Energy," *U.S. News and World Report,* February 25, 1980, p. 75.

64. American Petroleum Institute, *Basic Petroleum Data Book,* Vol. XIII, No. 3 (September 1993), Section IV, Table 1.

65. "Gas Is Cheap, But Taxes Are Rising," *Consumer Research,* August 1994, pp. 28–29.

66. "Transcript of Kennedy's Speech at Georgetown University on Campaign Issues," *New York Times,* January 29, 1980, p. A12.

67. Donella H. Meadows, et al., *The Limits to Growth: A Report for the Club of Rome's Project on the Predicament of Mankind* (New York: Universe Books, 1973), p. 124.

68. Ibid., p. 126.

69. Ibid., p. 44.

70. Ibid., p. 153.

71. Ibid., p. 162.

72. Ibid., pp. 181–182.

73. Ibid., pp. 196–197.

74. Ibid., p. 194.

75. Ibid., p. 195.

76. Ibid., p. 183.

77. Quoted in Edith Efron, *The Apocalyptics: Cancer and the Big Lie* (New York: Simon & Schuster, 1984).

78. Quoted in Robert L. Bartley, *The Seven Fat Years: And How to Do It Again* (New York: Free Press, 1992), p. 175.

79. U.S. Bureau of the Census, *Current Population Reports,* Series P-20, No. 468 (Washington, D.C.: U.S. Government Printing Office, 1992), p. vi.

80. Ibid., p. xii.

81. See ibid., p. 27.

82. Ibid., p. 37.

83. Henry A. Walker, "Black-White Differences in Marriage and Family Patterns," *Feminism, Children and New Families,* edited by Sanford M. Dornbusch and Myra H. Strober (New York: Guilford Press, 1988), p. 91.

84. See, for example, Thomas Sowell, *Ethnic America: A History* (New York: Basic Books, 1981), p. 198.

85. Ibid., p. 92.

86. Ibid., pp. 97–99.

87. Ibid., p. 98.

88. "Starved of tax revenues and confronted with a growing budget deficit," was Robert Reich's characterization of the federal government during the Reagan administration. Robert B. Reich, "Clintonomics 101," *New Republic,* August 31, 1992, p. 26.

89. See *Budget of the United States Government: Historical Tables* (Washington, D.C.: U.S. Government Printing Office, 1994), p. 14.

90. Quoted in Robert L. Bartley, *The Seven Fat Years*, p. 173.

91. Christopher Jencks, *The Homeless* (Cambridge, Mass.: Harvard University Press, 1994), pp. 96–98.

92. Quoted, with the last eight words italicized, in Gore Vidal, *United States: Essays 1952–1992* (New York: Random House, 1992), p. 1003.

93. Haynes Johnson, *Sleepwalking Through History* (New York: Anchor Books, 1992), p. 447.

94. Meg Greenfield, "Misplaying Gingrich," *Newsweek*, December 19, 1994, p. 78.

95. James Q. Wilson and Richard J. Herrnstein, *Crime and Human Nature* (New York: Simon & Schuster, 1985), pp. 430–433.

96. Ibid., p. 433.

97. Ibid., p. 428.

98. Ibid., pp. 426–428.

99. Some of the complexities of the death penalty debate are discussed in Thomas Sowell, *Knowledge and Decisions* (New York: Basic Books, 1980), pp. 283–288.

100. Anthony Lewis, "Life and Death," *New York Times*, April 23, 1992, p. A19.

101. *Planned Parenthood v. Casey*, 112 S. Ct. 2791 (1992) at 2844.

102. Ibid.

103. For an example of this kind of reasoning, see Jay Parini, "Academic Conservatives Who Decry 'Politicization' Show Staggering Naivete About Their Own Biases," *Chronicle of Higher Education*, December 7, 1988, p. B1.

104. Ronald Dworkin, *Taking Rights Seriously* (Cambridge, Mass.: Harvard University Press, 1980), p. 202.

105. Alexander M. Bickel, *The Least Dangerous Branch* (Indianapolis: Bobbs-Merrill, 1962), p. 36.

106. Edmund Burke, *Reflections on the Revolution in France* (New York: Everyman's Library, 1967), pp. 19–20.

107. Tom Wicker, "What Are the Real Issues?" *Current*, June 1969, p. 5.

108. Ibid.

109. Ibid., p. 6.

110. Ibid.

111. Frank Clifford and David Ferrell, "Los Angeles Strongly Condemns King Verdicts, Riots," *Los Angeles Times*, May 4, 1992, p. A4.

112. Ramsey Clark, *Crime in America: Observations on Its Nature, Causes, Prevention and Control* (New York: Simon & Schuster, 1970), pp. 37–38.

113. David Brion Davis, *The Problem of Slavery in Western Culture* (Ithaca, N.Y.: Cornell University Press, 1966), p. 27.

114. Anna Quindlen, *Thinking Out Loud: On the Personal, the Political, the Public and the Private* (New York: Random House, 1993), p. 252.

115. Ibid., p. 5.
116. "Text of Address by Clinton Accepting the Democratic Nomination," *New York Times*, July 17, 1992, p. A13.
117. Tom Wicker, "The Right to Income," *New York Times*, December 24, 1967, Section 4, p. E9.
118. See, for example, Ronald Dworkin, *Taking Rights Seriously*, p. xi.

CHAPTER 5: THE ANOINTED VERSUS THE BENIGHTED

1. Bertrand Russell, *Sceptical Essays* (New York: Norton, 1928), p. 28.
2. David L. Bazelon, *Questioning Authority: Justice and Criminal Law* (New York: Knopf, 1988), pp. 196–197.
3. Ibid., p. 295.
4. Adam Smith, *The Theory of Moral Sentiments* (Indianapolis: Liberty Classics, 1976), p. 170.
5. B. Bruce-Briggs, *The War Against the Automobile* (New York: E. P. Hutton, 1977), p. 125.
6. William Godwin, *Enquiry Concerning Political Justice and Its Influence on Morals and Happiness* (Toronto: University of Toronto Press, 1969), Vol. I, p. 276.
7. Ramsey Clark, *Crime in America: Observations on Its Nature, Causes, Prevention and Control* (New York: Simon & Schuster, 1970), p. 220.
8. William Godwin, *Enquiry Concerning Political Justice and Its Influence on Morals and Happiness* (Toronto: University of Toronto Press, 1946), Vol. II, pp. 144–145.
9. Neville Chamberlain, *In Search of Peace* (New York: G. P. Putnam's Sons, 1939), pp. 14, 34, 50, 52, 74, 97, 105, 106, 133, 210, 234, 252.
10. Ibid., pp. 34, 40, 120, 209, 210, 216, 230, 240, 242, 250, 271.
11. Ibid., p. 44.
12. Ibid., p. 37.
13. Ibid., p. 27.
14. Ibid., p. 163.
15. Ibid., p. 204.
16. Tom Wicker, "Plenty of Credit," *New York Times*, December 5, 1989, p. A35.
17. James Madison, Alexander Hamilton, and John Jay, *The Federalist Papers* (New York: New American Library, 1961), p. 46.
18. "Excerpts from Lyndon B. Johnson's Address to the Nation on Civil Disorders, July 27, 1967," *Report of the National Advisory Committee on Civil Disorders*, March 1, 1968, p. 297; "Transcript of Johnson's TV Address on the Riots," *New York Times*, July 28, 1968, p. A11.
19. "More Babies Are Dying," *New York Times*, August 9, 1990, p. A22.
20. Sidney E. Zion, "Attack on Court Heard by Warren," *New York Times*, September 10, 1965, pp. 1ff.

21. Karl Menninger, *Man and Society in an Age of Reconstruction* (London: Routledge and Kegan Paul, 1940), pp. 199–200.

22. Ibid., p. 201.

23. William Godwin, *Enquiry Concerning Political Justice and Its Influence on Morals and Happiness* (Toronto: University of Toronto Press, 1946), p. 123.

24. Edmund Burke, *The Correspondence of Edmund Burke*, edited by Albert Cobban and Robert A. Smith (Chicago: University of Chicago Press, 1967), Vol. VI, p. 392.

25. Adam Smith, *The Theory of Moral Sentiments* (Indianapolis: Liberty Classics, 1976), p. 380.

26. Will and Ariel Durant, *The Lessons of History* (New York: Simon & Schuster, 1968), p. 35.

27. Letter to Harold J. Laski, August 12, 1916, *Holmes-Laski Letters: The Correspondence of Mr. Justice Holmes and Harold J. Laski, 1916–1935*, edited by Mark DeWolfe Howe (Cambridge, Mass.: Harvard University Press, 1953), Vol. I, p. 12.

28. Oliver Wendell Holmes, "Speech at a Dinner Given to Chief Justice Holmes by the Bar Association of Boston on March 7, 1900," Oliver Wendell Holmes, *Collected Legal Papers* (New York: Peter Smith, 1952), p. 247. Holmes was chief justice of the Massachusetts Supreme Court at the time.

29. Mark DeWolfe Howe, ed., *Holmes-Laski Letters*, Vol. I, p. 42.

30. Ibid., p. 49.

31. Jean-François Revel, *The Flight from Truth: The Reign of Deceit in the Age of Information* (New York: Random House, 1991), p. 142.

32. John Stuart Mill, "Utilitarianism," *Collected Works of John Stuart Mill*, Vol. X: *Essays on Ethics, Religion and Society* (Toronto: University of Toronto Press, 1969), p. 215.

33. However, Mill's inconsistencies often had him contradicting his assertions with his provisos. See, for example, Thomas Sowell, *A Conflict of Visions* (New York: Morrow, 1987), pp. 111–112. For similar inconsistencies in Mill's discussions of technical economic issues, see Thomas Sowell, *Say's Law: An Historical Analysis* (Princeton, N.J.: Princeton University Press, 1972), Chapter 5.

34. John Stuart Mill, "Civilization," *Collected Works of John Stuart Mill*, Vol. XVIII: *Essays on Politics and Society* (Toronto: University of Toronto Press, 1977), p. 139.

35. John Stuart Mill, "De Tocqueville on Democracy in America [I]," ibid., p. 86.

36. John Stuart Mill, "Civilization," ibid., p. 128.

37. John Stuart Mill, "On Liberty," ibid., p. 269.

38. John Stuart Mill, "Civilization," ibid., p. 121.

39. John Stuart Mill, "De Tocqueville on Democracy in America," ibid., p. 86.

40. John Stuart Mill, "On Liberty," ibid., p. 222.

41. Letters to Alexander Bain, August 6, 1859, *Collected Works of John Stuart Mill*, Vol. XV: *The Later Letters of John Stuart Mill, 1849–1873*, edited by Francis E. Mineka and Dwight N. Lindsey (Toronto: University of Toronto Press, 1972), p. 631.

42. John Stuart Mill, "On Liberty," ibid., Vol. XVIII, p. 262.

43. Ibid., p. 263.

44. Ibid., p. 269.

45. Ibid.

46. Ibid., pp. 228, 240.

47. Ibid., p. 219.

48. Ibid., p. 272.

49. Ibid., p. 270.

50. Ronald Dworkin, *Taking Rights Seriously* (Cambridge, Mass.: Harvard University Press, 1980), p. 239.

51. See, for example, R. Bruce-Briggs, *The War Against the Automobile* (New York: E. P. Hutton, 1977), pp. 2–5, 24–29.

52. Alexander Hamilton, *Selected Speeches and Writings of Alexander Hamilton*, edited by Morton J. Frisch (Washington, D.C.: American Enterprise Institute, 1985), p. 210.

53. Oliver Wendell Holmes, Jr., *The Common Law* (Boston: Little, Brown, 1976), p. 2.

54. Edmund Burke, *Reflections on the Revolution in France* (London: J. M. Dent & Sons, Ltd., 1967), p. 93.

55. Ibid., p. 83.

56. Will and Ariel Durant, *The Lessons of History* (New York: Simon & Schuster, 1968), p. 101.

57. Edmund Burke, *Reflections on the Revolution in France* (London: J. M. Dent & Sons, Ltd., 1967), p. 84.

58. Keith Michael Baker, editor, *Condorcet: Selected Writings* (Indianapolis: Bobbs-Merrill, 1976), pp. 87, 157.

59. Quoted in Michael Stern, "Menninger Discounts Criminality in Nation," *New York Times*, December 30, 1968, p. 49.

60. Tom Wicker, "America, 1964," *The Johnson Years: The Difference He Made* (Austin: Lyndon B. Johnson School of Public Affairs, 1993), p. 10; Anna Quindlen, "Without Windows," *New York Times*, December 16, 1992, p. A17.

61. *U.S. News and World Report*, March 28, 1994, cover.

62. William L. Shirer, "The Hubris of a President," *The Nation, 1865–1990: Selections from the Independent Magazine of Politics and Culture*, edited by Katrina vanden Heuvel (New York: Thunder's Mouth Press, 1990), pp. 282, 284.

63. Vance Packard, *The Waste Makers* (New York: David McKay, 1960), p. 6.

64. "Transcript of President's Address to Country on Energy Problems," *New York Times*, July 16, 1979, p. A10.

65. "Address by Hillary Clinton," *Tikkun*, May–June 1993, p. 8.

66. "Transcript of President's Address to Country on Energy Problems," *New York Times*, July 16, 1979, p. A10.

67. Anna Quindlen, *Thinking Out Loud: On the Personal, the Political, the Public, and the Private* (New York: Random House, 1993), p. 252.

68. "Snoopy at the Smithsonian," *Wall Street Journal*, October 25, 1994, p. A18.

69. Ibid.

70. Ibid.

71. Jean-Jacques Rousseau, *The Social Contract* (New York: Penguin Books, 1968), p. 89.

72. Antoine-Nicolas de Condorcet, *Sketch for a Historical Picture of the Progress of the Human Mind* (Westport, Conn.: Hyperion Press, 1955), p. 114.

73. William Godwin, *Enquiry Concerning Political Justice*, Vol. I, p. 446.

74. Bernard Shaw, *The Intelligent Woman's Guide to Socialism and Capitalism* (New York: Brentano's Publishers, 1928) p. 456.

75. Edmund Wilson, *Letters on Literature and Politics: 1912–1972*, edited by Elena Wilson (New York: Farrar, Straus & Giroux, 1977), p. 36.

76. Ibid., pp. 217, 220. Decades later, upon seeing the poverty of Italy at the end of World War II, Wilson said, "that isn't the way white people ought to live." Ibid., p. 423.

77. William Godwin, *Enquiry Concerning Political Justice*, Vol. II, p. 122.

78. F. A. Hayek, *Studies in Philosophy, Politics and Economics* (New York: Simon & Schuster, 1969), pp. 96–105; F. A. Hayek, *Law, Legislation and Liberty*, Vol. I (Chicago: University of Chicago Press, 1973), pp. 35–54.

79. Adam Smith, *The Wealth of Nations* (New York: Modern Library, 1937), pp. 128, 249–250, 460, 537.

80. Ibid., p. 423.

81. Richard A. Lester, "Shortcomings of Marginal Analysis for Wage-Employment Problems," *American Economic Review*, March 1946, pp. 63–82.

82. George J. Stigler, "Professor Lester and the Marginalists," *American Economic Review*, March 1947, p. 157.

83. Thomas Hobbes, *Leviathan* (London: J. M. Dent & Sons, Ltd., 1970), p. 35.

84. Adam Smith, *The Wealth of Nations*, p. 16.

85. ". . . differences among individual men are probably smaller than those of some domesticated animals (especially dogs)." F. A. Hayek, *The Collected Works of F. A. Hayek*, Vol. I: *The Fatal Conceit: The Errors of Socialism*, edited by W. W. Bartley III (Chicago: University of Chicago Press, 1988), p. 79.

86. Oliver Wendell Holmes, *Collected Legal Papers* (New York: Peter Smith, 1952), p. 194.

87. F. A. Hayek, *The Constitution of Liberty* (Chicago: University of Chicago Press, 1960), p. 30.

88. See examples in Thomas Sowell, *Preferential Policies: An International Perspective* (New York: Morrow, 1993), pp. 22–24, 28–30, 32–35, 36, 51, 59, 64, 115, 142; Donald L. Horowitz, *Ethnic Groups in Conflict* (Berkeley: University of California Press, 1985), p. 662; Walter E. Williams, *South Africa's War Against Capitalism* (New York: Praeger, 1989), pp. 83–87.

89. See, for example, Walter E. Williams, *South Africa's War Against Capitalism* (New York: Praeger Publishers, 1989), pp. 81–82, 104–105, 112–113; Merle Lipton, *Capitalism and Apartheid: South Africa, 1910–1984* (Totowa, N.J.: Rowman and Allanheld, 1985), pp. 152, 153, 187, 208; Brian Lapping, *Apartheid: A History* (New York: George Braziller, 1986), pp. 164–165. Racial discrimination laws which existed before full-scale apartheid were likewise evaded. See W. H. Hutt, *The Economics of the Colour Bar: A Study of the Economic Origins and Consequences of Racial Segregation in South Africa* (London: Andre Deutsch, Ltd., 1964), pp. 83–84.

90. Walter E. Williams, *South Africa's War Against Capitalism*, pp. 112–113.

91. Professor Thomas Ferguson of the University of Massachusetts in Boston, quoted in *The Johnson Years: The Difference He Made*, edited by Robert L. Hardee (Austin, Tex.: Lyndon Baines Johnson Library, 1993), p. 117.

92. Neil Pedlar, *The Imported Pioneers: Westerners Who Helped Build Modern Japan* (New York: St. Martin's, 1990), pp. 22–23.

93. Herbert Stein, *Presidential Politics: The Making of Economic Policy from Roosevelt to Reagan and Beyond* (Washington, D.C.: American Enterprise Institute, 1988), p. 90.

94. "An Impact Analysis of Requiring Child Safety Seats in Air Transportation," *Child Restraint Systems on Aircraft*, Hearing Before the Subcommittee on Aviation of the Committee on Public Works and Transportation, House of Representatives, July 12, 1990, p. 215.

CHAPTER 6: CRUSADES OF THE ANOINTED

1. John Corry, *My Times: Adventures in the News Trade* (New York: G. P. Putnam's Sons, 1993), p. 131.

2. Elizabeth M. Whelan, *Toxic Terror* (Ottawa, Ill.: Jameson Books, 1985), p. 69.

3. Ibid., p. 76.

4. Peter W. Huber, *Liability: The Legal Revolution and Its Consequences* (New York: Basic Books, 1990), p. 104.

5. Quoted in Scott Minerbrook, "The Politics of Cartography," *U.S. News and World Report*, April 15, 1991, p. 60.

6. Ibid.

7. Ibid.

8. Quoted in John Dart, "'New' World Map Gets Church Council Support," *Los Angeles Times,* December 10, 1991, Section 1B, p. 11.

9. See, for example, *The Eyewitness Atlas of the World* (London: Dorling Kindersley, Ltd., 1994), p. 19.

10. *Style Manual for Authors, Editors and Printers,* fourth edition (Canberra: Australian Government Publishing Service, 1988), pp. 115, 116, 117, 120, 123.

11. Mary Munter, "Avoiding Sexism on the Job: A Test for Bias-Free Writing and Speaking," *Without Bias: A Guidebook for Nondiscrimination,* second edition (New York: Wiley, 1982), p. 88.

12. Senator Paul Simon said to Judge Souter: "What am I looking for? The two essentials I mentioned to you in your visit to my office: I want a champion of basic civil liberties, because the Supreme Court must be the bastion of liberty; and I want someone who will champion the cause of the less fortunate, the role assigned to the Court in our system." *Hearings Before the Committee on the Judiciary, United States Senate,* 101st Congress, 2nd Session (Washington, D.C.: U.S. Government Printing Office, 1991), p. 39.

13. William O. Douglas, *The Court Years, 1939–1975: The Autobiography of William O. Douglas* (New York: Random House, 1980), p. 160.

14. Linda Greenhouse, "A Capacity to Change as Well as to Challenge," *New York Times,* February 27, 1994, p. E4.

15. Harold Hongju Koh, "Justice Done," *New York Times,* April 8, 1994, p. A13.

16. *Richard F. Kreimer v. Bureau of Police for the Town of Morristown,* 958 F.2d 1242 (3rd Cir. 1992) at 1247.

17. David Ellis, "Star of His Own Sad Comedy," *Time,* March 9, 1992, p. 62.

18. *Richard F. Kreimer v. Bureau of Police for the Town of Morristown,* U.S. District Court 765 F. Supp. 181, at 183, 184.

19. David Ellis, "Star of His Own Sad Comedy," p. 63.

20. *Richard F. Kreimer vs. Bureau of Police for the Town of Morristown,* 765 F. Supp. 181 at 187.

21. Ibid., at 186.

22. Ibid., at 189.

23. Ibid., at 193.

24. Ibid., at 196.

25. Ibid., at 197.

26. *Kreimer v. Bureau of Police for Town of Morristown,* 865 F. Supp. 181 (D.N.J. 1991) at 183.

27. David Ellis, "Star of His Own Sad Comedy," p. 62.

28. Ibid., p. 63.

29. Jean-François Revel, *The Flight from Truth: The Reign of Deceit in the Age of Information* (New York: Random House, 1991), p. 262.

30. Richard W. White, Jr., *Rude Awakenings: What the Homeless Crisis Tells Us* (San Francisco: ICS Press, 1992), p. 13.

31. Ibid., p. 9.

32. Ibid., pp. 30–35.

33. Thomas Szasz, *The Myth of Mental Illness: Foundations of a Theory of Personal Conduct* (New York: Hoeber-Harper, 1961).

34. See, for example, Antoine-Nicolas de Condorcet, *Sketch for a Historical Picture of the Progress of the Human Mind* (Westport, Conn.: Hyperion Press, 1955), p. 193; William Godwin, *Enquiry Concerning Political Justice and Its Influence on Morals and Happiness* (Toronto: University of Toronto Press, 1969), Vol. II, pp. 323–324, 353–354, 462.

35. Joseph D. McNamara, "When in Trouble, Don't Call the Feds," *Wall Street Journal*, August 24, 1994, p. A10.

36. Ibid.

37. Ibid.

38. Fred Graham, *Happy Talk: Confessions of a TV Newsman* (New York: Norton, 1990), p. 134.

39. David L. Bazelon, *Questioning Authority: Justice and Criminal Law* (New York: Knopf, 1987), p. 44.

40. Ibid.

41. Ibid., p. 46.

42. Ibid., p. 67.

43. Phillip Hager, "U.S. Plans No Prosecution of Dan White," *Los Angeles Times*, November 22, 1983, p. 1.

44. Leon Dash, "Stealing Became a Way of Life for Rosa Lee," *Washington Post*, September 19, 1994, p. A8.

45. "Rosa Lee's Story," *Washington Post*, September 18, 1994, p. A1.

46. David L. Bazelon, *Questioning Authority*, p. 129.

47. Ibid., p. 14.

48. Ibid., p. 17.

49. Ibid., pp. 94–95.

50. "No judgment shall be set aside, or new trial granted, in any cause, on the ground of misdirection of the jury, or of the improper admission or rejection of evidence, or for any error as to any matter of pleading, or for any error as to any matter of procedure, unless, after an examination of the entire cause, including the evidence, the court shall be of the opinion that the error complained of has resulted in a miscarriage of justice." Constitution of the State of California, Section 13, adopted November 6, 1966.

51. *People v. Hamilton*, 46 Cal.3d, 123.

52. *People v. Frierson*, 39 Cal.3d, 803.

53. Tom Wicker, "A Naked Power Grab," *New York Times*, September 14, 1986, p. E25.

54. Tom Wicker, "Bradley and Bird," *New York Times*, January 17, 1986, p. A31.

55. Tom Wicker, "Bird and Rehnquist," *New York Times*, September 12, 1986, p. 27.

56. "Support for the Justices," *Los Angeles Times*, October 20, 1986, Section II, p. 6.

57. "Systemic Failure, and Support," *New York Times*, November 8, 1986, p. 30.

58. Anthony Lewis, "Chief Justice Bird: Calm at the Center," *New York Times*, October 23, 1986, p. A27.

59. "Rose Bird Results," *San Francisco Examiner*, November 5, 1986, p. A11.

60. "The 'Onion Field' Parole: Rose Bird's Parting Shot," *Newsweek*, January 12, 1987, p. 26.

61. *School Board of Nassau County, Florida, et al. v. Arline*, 480 U.S. 273, at 282.

62. Ibid., at 279.

63. Ibid., at 284.

64. Ibid., at 285.

65. Ibid.

66. Ibid., at 287.

67. Ibid., at 289.

68. Ibid., at 28, footnote 7.

69. Alan Sandres, "Fighting AIDS Discrimination," *Time*, September 5, 1988, p. 38.

70. Ronald Sullivan, "Ex-Inmate Wins Award in Bias Case," *New York Times*, August 6, 1992, p. B4.

71. Lynda Richardson, "Westchester Medical Faces Loss of Federal Funds," *New York Times*, October 1, 1992, p. B8.

72. Michael Wineship, "Groups Setting Up Own Blood Banks," *New York Times*, June 26, 1985, p. A26.

73. Michael Chapman, "How Safe Is the Blood Supply?" *Consumer's Research*, April 1994, p. 13.

74. Randy Shilts, "Rise in AIDS from Transfusions," *San Francisco Chronicle*, August 30, 1984, p. 4.

75. Geoffrey Cowley and Mary Hager, "How Safe Is the Blood Supply?" *Newsweek*, June 3, 1991, p. 58.

76. Michael Chapman, "How Safe Is the Blood Supply?" p. 10.

77. Howard Kurtz, "Heckler Discounts AIDS Disease Fear," *Washington Post*, June 15, 1983, p. A1.

78. Richard J. Newman et al., "Bad Blood," *U.S. News and World Report*, June 27, 1994, p. 69.

79. Mark Z. Barabak, "4 S.F. General Nurses Lose in Dispute over AIDS Masks," *San Francisco Chronicle*, September 10, 1985, p. 6.

80. Michael Specter, "CDC Report on AIDS Played Down," *Washington Post*, May 24, 1987, p. A11.

81. "AIDS Virus Infects 2 Workers," *San Francisco Chronicle,* September 27, 1985, p. 4.

82. "Doctors and AIDS," *Newsweek,* July 1, 1991, pp. 54–57.

83. Ibid., p. 48.

84. "The AIDS Secret Worth Keeping," *New York Times,* November 15, 1987, p. E26.

85. Randy Shilts, *And the Band Played On: Politics, People and the AIDS Epidemic* (New York: St. Martin's, 1987), p. 147.

86. Ibid., pp. 138, 196–197, 200, 208, 247, 251.

87. Ibid., p. 165. See also pp. 198, 200.

88. See, for example, "AIDS Virus Carrier Charged," *New York Times,* August 9, 1987, p. A24; "Deadly Weapon in AIDS Verdict Is Inmate's Teeth," *New York Times,* June 25, 1987, p. A18; "AIDS Virus Carrier Indicted," *New York Times,* April 12, 1987, p. 29; Kirk Johnson, "Woman Charged With Biting Officer," *New York Times,* June 10, 1987, p. A29; "Louisianian Convicted of Transmitting H.I.V.," *New York Times,* November 10, 1992, p. A19; "High Court to Hear AIDS Assault Case," *Los Angeles Times,* September 24, 1991.

89. "Paroling Prisoners with AIDS," *New York Times,* March 11, 1987, p. A30.

90. *Price v. Workman's Compensation Appeals Board,* 37 Cal.3d, 559.

91. *Ruth L. Hammond v. International Harvester,* 691 F.2d, 646 (1982) at 652.

92. *Ferebee v. Chevron Chemical Co.,* 736 F2d. 1529 at 1534.

93. Ibid., at 1542.

94. Ibid., at 1543.

95. Ibid., at 1539.

96. Peter W. Huber, *Liability: The Legal Revolution and Its Consequences* (New York: Basic Books, 1990), p. 76.

97. Ibid., pp. 56, 57, 59.

98. Ibid., pp. 81–82.

99. Ibid., p. 103.

100. Ibid., p. 110.

101. Ibid., p. 55.

102. "Asides," *Wall Street Journal,* August 27, 1994, p. A10.

103. Peter W. Huber, *Liability,* p. 111.

104. Ibid., p. 74.

105. Ibid., pp. 129–130.

106. Robert L. Maginnis, "The Myths of Domestic Violence," *Family Research Council,* p. 2U.

107. Christina Hoff Sommers, *Who Stole Feminism: How Women Have Betrayed Women* (New York: Simon & Schuster, 1994), pp. 199–200.

108. U.S. Department of Justice, *Criminal Victimization in the United States: 1973–1990 Trends: A National Crime Victimization Survey Report,*

December 1992, NCJ-139564 (Washington, D.C.: U.S. Department of Justice, 1992), pp. 40, 41.

109. Marilyn Gardner, "Sexual Harassment Is Never Acceptable," *Christian Science Monitor,* October 12, 1990, p. 13.

110. Multiplying 60 seconds in a minute by 60 minutes in an hour by 24 hours in a day and 365 days in a year, we get $60 \times 60 \times 24 \times 365 = 31,536,000$ seconds in a year. Divide that by the 5,000,000 women mentioned and the result is one every 6.3 seconds.

111. See Christina Hoff Sommers, *Who Stole Feminism?,* pp. 192–194.

112. Ibid., pp. 194–198.

113. Robert L. Maginnis, "The Myths of Domestic Violence," p. 4

114. Karl Marx and Friedrich Engels, *Collected Works* (New York: International Publishers), Vol. VI, p. 354.

115. See, for example, Hillary Rodham, "Children Under the Law," *Harvard Education Review,* Vol. 43, No. 4 (November 1973), pp. 487–514; "11-Year-Old Seeks Right to 'Divorce' Parents," *New York Times,* July 8, 1992, p. A10.

116. Emily Flynn, "Child Abuse: The Facts," *NZ Listener* (New Zealand), August 13, 1988, p. 17.

117. Stephen R. Redmond, M.D., and Michael E. Pichichero, M.D., "Hemophilus Influenzae Type b Disease: An Epidemiologic Study with Special Reference to Day Care Centers," *Journal of the American Medical Association,* Vol. 252, No. 18 (November 9, 1984), pp. 2581–2584.

118. Karl Zinsmeister, "Brave New World: How Day-Care Harms Children," *Policy Review,* Spring 1988, pp. 43–44.

119. Ibid., pp. 42–43.

120. Elena Neuman, "Child Welfare or Family Trauma?" *Insight,* May 8, 1994, p. 6.

121. Ibid.

122. Ibid., p. 10.

123. Ibid., p. 12.

124. *County of Allegheny, et al., v. American Civil Liberties Union, Greater Pittsburgh Chapter, et al.,* 492 U.S. 573 at 610.

125. Ibid.

126. Ibid., p. 611.

127. Ibid., p. 615.

128. Ibid., p. 615n.

129. Ibid., p. 615.

130. Ibid., p. 617.

131. Ibid., p. 620.

132. See, for example, Thomas Sowell, *Inside American Education* (New York: Free Press, 1992), Chapter 3.

133. *Mozert v. Hawkins County Public Schools,* 647 F. Supp. 1194 (E.D. Tenn., 1986), at 1195.

134. Stephen Bates, *Battleground: One Mother's Crusade, the Religious Right, and the Struggle for Control of Our Classrooms* (New York: Poseidon Press, 1993), p. 277.

135. *Board of Education of Kiryas Joel Village School District v. Louis Grumet et al.* in *Daily Appellate Report* (Supplement to the *Los Angeles Daily Journal*), p. 8926.

136. Ibid., p. 8927.

137. Ibid.

138. Ibid., p. 8921.

139. Ibid., p. 8922.

140. Ibid., p. 8939.

141. Ibid., p. 8926.

142. Ibid., p. 8925.

143. Ibid., p. 8934.

144. Ibid., p. 8924.

CHAPTER 7: THE VOCABULARY OF THE ANOINTED

1. James Fitzjames Stephen, *Liberty, Equality, Fraternity* (Indianapolis: Liberty Fund, 1993), pp. 121–122.

2. Vance Packard, *The Waste Makers* (New York: David McKay, 1960), p. 290.

3. Bob Herbert, "A Season of Service," *New York Times*, August 31, 1994, p. A13.

4. Richard D. McKenzie, "Decade of Greed? Far from It," *Wall Street Journal*, July 24, 1991, p. A10; Robert L. Bartley, *The Seven Fat Years: And How to Do It Again* (New York: Free Press, 1992), p. 5.

5. Jean Evangelauf, "Average Faculty Salary Reaches $41,650, up 6.1% in a Year, AAUP Survey Finds," *Chronicle of Higher Education*, April 18, 1990, p. A13.

6. Gary Putka, "Do Colleges Collude on Financial Aid?" *Wall Street Journal*, May 2, 1989, p. B1; Gary Putka, "Colleges Cancel Meetings Under Scrutiny," *Wall Street Journal*, March 12, 1991, p. B1.

7. "The Economic Role of Women," *The Economic Report of the President, 1973* (Washington, D.C.: U.S. Government Printing Office, 1973), p. 103.

8. Marcia I. LaGanga, "A Deck Stacked Against the Young," *Los Angeles Times*, December 29, 1994, p. A1.

9. David L. Bazelon, *Questioning Authority: Justice and Criminal Law* (New York: Knopf, 1987), p. 100.

10. Fred P. Graham, "Warren Says All Share Crime Onus," *New York Times*, August 2, 1968, p. 1.

11. Ramsey Clark, *Crime in America: Observations on Its Nature, Causes, Prevention and Control* (New York: Simon & Schuster, 1970), pp. 319–320.

12. *Miranda v. Arizona*, 384 U.S. 436 (1966), at 472.

13. Barbara J. Jordan and Elspeth D. Rostow, *The Great Society: A Twenty-Year Critique* (Austin, Tex.: Lyndon Baines Johnson Library, 1986), p. 71.

14. F. A. Hayek, *Law, Legislation and Liberty*, Vol. II: *The Mirage of Social Justice* (Chicago: University of Chicago Press, 1976), p. 64.

15. Ibid., p. 33.

16. Anna Quindlen, "No Bright Lines," *New York Times*, July 6, 1991, p. A21.

17. James Fitzjames Stephen, *Liberty, Equality, Fraternity* (Indianapolis: Liberty Fund, 1993), p. 212.

18. David L. Bazelon, *Questioning Authority*, p. 23.

19. Employee Benefit Research Institute, *Special Report and Issue Brief Number 133* (January 1993), p. 25.

20. Stanley Fish, "Reverse Racism or How the Pot Got to Call the Kettle Black," *Atlantic Monthly*, November 1993, p. 130.

21. Derek Bok, *Beyond the Ivory Tower* (Cambridge, Mass.: Harvard University Press, 1982), p. 103.

22. Stanley Fish, "Reverse Racism," p. 132.

23. During his career, Ted Williams hit home runs in 6.8 percent of his official times at bat—that is, not counting the times when he was walked—while the corresponding percentages were 5.4 percent for Roger Maris and 6.1 percent for Hank Aaron. *The Baseball Encyclopedia* (New York: Macmillan, 1990), pp. 617, 1180, 1601.

24. Ted Williams was walked 2,019 times during his career, compared to 1.402 times for Hank Aaron and 652 times for Roger Maris. Ibid.

25. J. M. Keynes, "Some Economic Consequences of a Declining Population," *Eugenics Review*, April 1937, p. 14.

26. "Excerpts from President Lyndon B. Johnson's Address to the Nation on Civil Disorders, July 27, 1967," *Report of the National Advisory Commission on Civil Disorders*, March 1, 1968, p. 297; "Transcript of Johnson's TV Address on the Riots," *New York Times*, July 28, 1967, p. A11.

27. Adam Smith, *The Wealth of Nations* (New York: Modern Library, 1937), pp. 3–21.

28. Edmund Burke, *Reflections on the Revolution in France* (New York: Everyman's Library, 1967), p. 42.

29. Oliver Wendell Holmes, *Collected Legal Papers* (New York: Peter Smith, 1952), pp. 47–48.

30. William J. Brennan, "Foreword," David L. Bazelon, *Questioning Authority*, p. xii.

31. John Dewey, "Traditional *vs.* Progressive Education," *Intelligence in the Modern World: John Dewey's Philosophy*, edited by Joseph Ratner (New York: Modern Library, 1939), p. 660.

32. Oliver Wendell Holmes, *Collected Legal Papers*, pp. 187, 301.

33. Ronald Dworkin, *A Matter of Principle* (Cambridge, Mass.: Harvard University Press, 1985), p. 144.

34. William O. Douglas, *The Court Years: 1939–1975* (New York: Random House, 1980), p. 174.

35. F. A. Hayek, "Why I Am Not a Conservative," *The Essence of Hayek*, edited by Chiaki Nishiyama and Kurt R. Leube (Stanford, Calif.: Hoover Institution Press, 1984), pp. 281–298.

36. Milton Friedman, *Capitalism and Freedom* (Chicago: University of Chicago Press, 1962), pp. 5–6.

37. Ronald Dworkin, *Taking Rights Seriously* (Cambridge, Mass.: Harvard University Press, 1980), p. xi.

38. John Rawls, *A Theory of Justice* (Cambridge, Mass.: Harvard University Press, 1976), p. 4.

39. Ibid., p. 43.

40. Ibid., p. 250.

41. Ibid., p. 301.

42. Ibid., p. 302.

43. Ronald Dworkin, "Will Clinton's Plan Be Fair?" *New York Review of Books*, January 13, 1994, p. 22.

44. See, for example, a review of *Race and Culture* in the *Wilson Quarterly*, October 4, 1994, p. 196.

45. *Durham v. United States* 214 F.2d. 862 at 871.

46. Ibid., p. 45.

47. Ibid., p. 46.

48. William J. Brennan, Jr., "Foreword," ibid., p. xi.

49. Ibid., p. xii.

50. Ibid., p. xxi.

51. David L. Bazelon, *Questioning Authority: Justice and Criminal Law* (New York: Knopf, 1987), p. 50.

52. Randy Shilts, *And the Band Played On: Politics, People, and the AIDS Epidemic* (New York: St. Martin's Press, 1987).

53. Paul Johnson, *Enemies of Society* (New York: Atheneum, 1977), p. 246.

54. Phil Gailey, "Jackson Condemns 'Economic Violence' as He Opens Headquarters in Iowa," *New York Times*, March 20, 1987, p. A14; Gerald F. Seib, "Jesse Jackson Enters Presidential Race Vowing an End to 'Economic Violence,'" *Wall Street Journal*, October 12, 1987, p. A44.

55. Quoted in David Sanford, *Me and Ralph: Is Nader Unsafe for America?* (Washington, D.C.: New Republic Book Co., 1976). p. 125.

56. Jonathan Kozol, *Savage Inequalities: Children in America's Schools* (New York: HarperCollins, 1991).

57. Kenneth B. Clark, "In Cities, Who Is the Real Mugger?" *New York Times*, January 14, 1985, p. 17.

58. Herbert Marcuse, *New York Times Magazine*, October 27, 1968. See also Paul Johnson, *Enemies of Society*, pp. 237, 245.

59. Hodding Carter III, "'Disarmament' Spells Defeat in War on Poverty," *Wall Street Journal*, August 11, 1983, p. 21.

60. Tom Wicker, "L.B.J.'s Great Society," *New York Times*, May 7, 1990, p. A15.

61. Philip Taylor, *The Distant Magnet: European Emigration to the U.S.A.* (New York: Harper & Row, 1971), pp. 86–88.

62. Compare U.S. Bureau of the Census, *Current Population Reports*, Series P-60, No. 167 (Washington, D.C.: U.S. Government Printing Office, 1990), pp. 9, 168.

63. See Thomas Sowell, *Civil Rights: Rhetoric or Reality?* (New York: Morrow, 1984), p. 49; Daniel P. Moynihan, "Employment, Income, and the Ordeal of the Negro Family," *Daedalus*, Fall 1965, p. 752.

CHAPTER 8: COURTING DISASTER

1. Bertrand de Jouvenel, *On Power: The Natural History of Its Growth* (Indianapolis: Liberty Fund, 1993), p. 351.

2. Quoted in Friedrich A. Hayek, *Law, Legislation and Liberty*, Vol. II: *The Mirage of Social Justice* (Chicago: University of Chicago Press, 1976), p. 86.

3. John Bartlett, *Bartlett's Familiar Quotations* (Boston: Little, Brown, 1968), p. 802.

4. David L. Bazelon, *Questioning Authority: Justice and Criminal Law* (New York: Knopf, 1988), pp. 152–153.

5. Ibid., p. 153.

6. Ibid., p. 151.

7. Noam Chomsky, "Equality," *The Noam Chomsky Reader*, edited by James Peck (New York: Pantheon, 1987), p. 185.

8. See, for example, Richard Epstein, *Takings: Private Property and the Power of Eminent Domain* (Cambridge, Mass.: Harvard University Press, 1985).

9. Justice Roy L. Herdon of the California Court of Appeal, quoted in Macklin Fleming, *The Price of Perfect Justice: The Adverse Consequences of Current Legal Doctrine on the American Courtroom* (New York: Basic Books, 1974), p. 17.

10. Judge J. Edward Lumbard quoted in ibid., p. 27.

11. Macklin Fleming, *The Price of Perfect Justice: The Adverse Consequences of Current Legal Doctrine on the American Courtroom* (New York: Basic Books, 1974).

12. Robert H. Bork, *Tradition and Morality in Constitutional Law* (Washington, D.C.: American Enterprise Institute, 1984), p. 7.

13. Richard Posner, *The Federal Courts: Crisis and Reform* (Cambridge, Mass.: Harvard University Press, 1985), p. 221.

14. Oliver Wendell Holmes, *Collected Legal Papers* (New York: Peter Smith, 1952), p. 307.

15. *Kuhn v. Fairmont Coal Co.*, 215 U.S. 349, at 372.

16. *Untermeyer v. Anderson*, 276 U.S. 440.

17. Ronald Dworkin, *A Matter of Principle* (Cambridge, Mass.: Harvard University Press, 1985), pp. 40, 43, 44.

18. Oliver Wendell Holmes, *Collected Legal Papers*, p. 204.

19. Ibid.

20. Ibid., p. 205.

21. Robert H. Bork, *The Tempting of America: The Political Seduction of the Law* (New York: Free Press, 1990), p. 144.

22. William J. Brennan, "The Constitution of the United States: Contemporary Ratification," speech at Georgetown University, October 12, 1985, p. 4.

23. Stephen Macedo, *The New Right v. the Constitution* (Washington, D.C.: Cato Institute, 1987), p. 10.

24. Jack Rakove, "Mr. Meese, Meet Mr. Madison," *Atlantic Monthly*, December 1986, p. 81.

25. Anthony Lewis, "The March Toward Equality," *Atlantic Monthly*, September 1964, p. 63.

26. Ronald Dworkin, *Taking Rights Seriously* (Cambridge, Mass.: Harvard University Press, 1980), p. 134.

27. William J. Brennan, "The Constitution of the United States: Contemporary Ratification," p. 8.

28. Chief Justice Earl Warren, *The Memoirs of Earl Warren* (Garden City, N.Y.: Doubleday, 1977), pp. 332–333.

29. The Supreme Court cases in question being, respectively *Roe v. Wade*, 410 U.S. 113 (1973); *Engel v. Vitale*, 370 U.S. 421 (1962); *Miranda v. Arizona*, 384 U.S. 436 (1966); *Brown v. Board of Education of Topeka, Kansas*, 347 U.S. 483 (1954); *Baker v. Carr*, 369 U.S. 186 (1962); *Furman v. Georgia*, 408 U.S. 238 (1972).

30. *United Steelworkers of America v. Brian F. Weber*, 443 U.S. 193 (1979) at 207, note 7.

31. Ibid., at 222.

32. William J. Brennan, "The Constitution of the United States: Contemporary Ratification," p. 4.

33. *United Steelworkers of America v. Brian F. Weber*, 443 U.S. 193 (1979) at 207, note 7.

34. U.S. Equal Employment Opportunity Commission, *Legislative History of Titles VII and XI of Civil Rights Act of 1964* (Washington, D.C.: U.S. Government Printing Office, no date), pp. 1007–1008, 1014, 3005, 3006, 3013, 3160, and *passim.*

35. Tom Wicker, "Justice or Hypocrisy?" *New York Times*, August 15, 1991, p. A23.

36. *Cheryl J. Hopwood, et al. vs. The State of Texas, U.S. District Court, Western District of Texas, Austin Division* (No. A 92 CA 563 SS), 1994, pp. 2–3.

37. *Planned Parenthood v. Casey*, 112 S. Ct, 2791 (1992).

38. *Thompson v. Oklahoma*, 487 U.S. 815 (1988).

39. Ibid., at 833.
40. Ibid., at 829.
41. *Planned Parenthood v. Casey*, 112 S. Ct. 2791 (1992), at 2813.
42. *Day-Brite Lighting, Inc. v. Missouri*, 342 U.S. 421 (1952), at 423.
43. *Olsen v. Nebraska*, 313 U.S. 246 (1941), at 247.
44. *Day-Brite Lighting, Inc. v. Missouri*, 342 U.S. 421 (1952), at 423.
45. *Williamson v. Lee Optical Co.*, 348 U.S. 483 (1955), at 488.
46. *Planned Parenthood v. Casey*, 112 S. Ct. 2797 (1992), at 2805.
47. Ibid., at 2806.
48. Ibid., at 2859–2860.
49. Ibid., at 2860.
50. Ibid., at 2879.
51. Ibid., at 2874.
52. Ibid., at 2861.
53. "Supreme—But Also Court," *New York Times*, June 30, 1991, p. E14.
54. "The Runaway Supreme Court," *New York Times*, February 2, 1992, p. E16.
55. Tom Wicker, "This Radical Court," *New York Times*, June 29, 1991, p. A23.
56. Linda Greenhouse, "The Conservative Majority Solidifies," *New York Times*, June 30, 1991, p. E1.
57. *Holder v. Hall* (1994), 114 S. Ct. 2581, at 2592.

CHAPTER 9: OPTIONAL REALITY

1. Jean-François Revel, *The Flight from Truth: The Reign of Deceit in the Age of Information* (New York: Random House, 1991), p. 228.
2. Barbara Ehrenreich, "Sorry, Sisters, This Is Not the Revolution," *Time*, Fall 1990, p. 15.
3. See, for example, Myron Magnet, *The Dream and the Nightmare: The Sixties' Legacy to the Underclass* (New York: Morrow, 1993), p. 155; James Fitzjames Stephen, *Liberty, Equality, Fraternity,* (Indianapolis; Liberty Ford, 1993), p. 169;
4. Charles E. Silberman, *Criminal Violence, Criminal Justice* (New York: Random House, 1978), p. 19.
5. John Bartlett, *Bartlett's Familiar Quotations* (Boston: Little, Brown, 1968), p. 851.
6. Jean-François Revel, *The Flight from Truth*, p. 142.
7. Leonard Read, "I, Pencil," *The Freeman*, December 1958, pp. 32–37.
8. See, for example, Thomas Sowell, *Marxism: Philosophy and Economics* (New York: Morrow, 1985), pp. 190–200.
9. Richard W. White, Jr., *Rude Awakenings: What the Homeless Crisis Tells Us* (San Francisco: ICS Press, 1992), Chapter 1.
10. Paul H. Weaver, "Selling the Story," *New York Times*, July 29, 1994, p. A13.

INDEX